THE DIPLOMA

to the uniformed personnel
of the United Nations Command
who fought such a worthwhile fight

and

to the diplomats and politicians
who managed to end the fighting

THE DIPLOMACY OF WAR

The Case of Korea

Graeme S. Mount

with Andre Laferriere

BLACK
ROSE
BOOKS

Montréal/New York/London

Black Rose Books No. GG323

National Library of Canada Cataloguing in Publication Data

Mount, Graeme S. (Graeme Stewart), 1939-

The diplomacy of war : the case of Korea / Graeme Mount, with Andre Laferriere

Includes bibliographical references and index.

Hardcover ISBN: 1-55164-239-5 (bound) Paperback ISBN: 1-55164-238-7 (pbk.)

1. Korean War, 1950-1953--Diplomatic history. 2. Korean War, 1950-1952--Peace.
3. United States--Foreign relations--1945-1953. 4. Canada--Foreign relations--1945-
I. Laferriere, Andre II. Title.

DS918.M68 2003   951.904'21   C2003-905800-X

We wish to thank the Harry S. Truman Library for permission to reproduce the National Park Service Photograph—Abbie Rowe, page x, #3.

Cover design: Associés libres

BLACK ROSE BOOKS

C.P. 1258	2250 Military Road	99 Wallis Road
Succ. Place du Parc	Tonawanda, NY	London, E9 5LN
Montréal, H2X 4A7	14150	England
Canada	USA	UK

To order books:

In Canada: (phone) 1-800-565-9523 (fax) 1-800-221-9985
email: utpbooks@utpress.utoronto.ca

In United States: (phone) 1-800-283-3572 (fax) 1-651-917-6406

In the UK & Europe: (phone) London 44 (0)20 8986-4854 (fax) 44 (0)20 8533-5821
email: order@centralbooks.com

Our Web Site address: http://www.web.net/blackrosebooks

A publication of the Institute of Policy Alternatives of Montréal (IPAM)

Printed in Canada

The Canada Council | Le Conseil des Arts
for the Arts | du Canada

Table of Contents

Acronyms

AA	Armistice Agreement
ANZUS	Australia-New Zealand-United States Military Alliance
CFI	Custodial Forces of India
CWIHP	*Cold War International History Project*
CIA	Central Intelligence Agency
CPV	Chinese People's Volunteers (Chinese soldiers in Korea)
CRO	Commonwealth Relations Office
DAFR	*Documents on Australian Foreign Relations*
DCER	*Documents on Canadian External Relations*
DDE	Dwight David Eisenhower Library, Abilene, Kansas
DEA	Department of External Affairs
DML	Demarcation Line
DMZ	Demilitarized Zone
DPBO	*Documents on British Policy Overseas*
DPRK	Democratic People's Republic of Korea (North Korea)
FRUS	*Foreign Relations of the United States*
HST	Harry S.Truman Library, Independence, Missouri
ICC	International Control Commission
KPA	Korean People's Army (The North Korean Army)
NAA	National Archives of Australia, Canberra
NAC	National Archives of Canada, Ottawa
NAFTA	North American Free Trade Agreement
NARA	National Archives and Records Administration, College Park, Maryland
NATO	North American Treaty Organization
NIE	National Intelligence Estimate
NNIT	Neutral Nations Intelligence Commission
NNRP	Neutral Nations Repatriation Commission
NNSC	Neutral Nations Supervisory Commission
POW	Prisoner(s)-of-War
PRO	Public Record Office, Kew Gardens, England
PSF	President's Secretary's Files
RAN	Royal Australian Navy
ROK	Republic of Korea (South Korea)
SE	Special Estimate
SMOF	Staff Members' Official Files
SWINK	State Department, War Department, Navy Department, Co-ordinating Committee
UN	United Nations
UNC	United Nations Command
UNCOK	United Nations Commission on Korea
UNCURK	United Nations Commission for the Unification and Rehabilitation of Korea
UNTCOK	United Nations Temporary Commission on Korea
USSR	Union of Soviet Socialist Republics

Acknowledgments

No author works alone, and the two of us acknowledge our indebtedness to many people: our wives, Joan and Darlene, who accompanied us on our travels to London and Canberra and encouraged us in this project; Laurentian University's indispensable secretary, Rose-May Démoré; colleagues and students at Laurentian University (Sudbury) and Australian National University (Canberra) who listened to a summary of the manuscript and offered comments; Professor Hank Nelson of Australian National University and secretary Oahn Collins, who proved marvelous hosts during our visit to the Australian capital; Peter Londey of the Australian War Memorial in Canberra, who could always send email information on the details of Australian military history; William R. Glover, Ph.D., who as president of the Canadian Nautical Research Society read the manuscript and offered encouragement; the personnel of the Desmarais Library at Laurentian University (especially Rick Hauta, Diane Tessier, and Ashley Thomson) and the Australian National Library in Canberra, as well as of the Public Record Office (London), the National Archives of Australia (Canberra), the National Archives and Records Administration (College Park, Maryland, especially John Taylor), the Harry S. Truman Presidential Library (Independence, Missouri, especially David Clark), and the Dwight David Eisenhower Library (Abilene, Kansas, especially Herbert Pankratz). Student Jay Hawrelluk accelerated the process through his skills at the photocopy machines in Independence and Abilene, and Judy Finn came to the rescue during a busy week at Laurentian University when a publisher's deadline loomed, putting her office photocopy machine and printer at our disposal. Special thanks go to Pictures Now of Sudbury, which printed the photographs, Roch Carrier, who helped prepare the index, and to Clint MacNeil, who prepared the map, as well as to Dieter Buse, Carolle Gagnon, Wendy Gerhard, Ian and Libby Keen, Melissa Keeping, and Edelgard Mahant. In particular, we would like to thank two former students of Laurentian University who subsequently moved to South Korea and arranged visits to important sites there, Donald Marleau and Earl Reid.

Graeme S. Mount
Andre Laferriere

Photographs

1. Monuments at Munsan's Unification Park north of Seoul honour heroes killed in conflict before, during, and since the actual Korean War.

2. Monument at Inchon commemorates the 1885 arrival in Korea of the first Protestant missionaries, who won many converts.

3. In December 1950, British Prime Minister Clement Attlee (seated, right) raced to Washington after President Harry S. Truman (seated left) appeared to threaten the use of nuclear weapons in the Korean War. Behind them stand Secretary of State Dean Acheson (left) and Secretary of State George Marshall (right).

4. The Government of Canada took so long to honour Canadian veterans of the Korean War that the veterans built a monument for themselves on land donated in Brampton, Ontario.

5. Canadian and South Korean veterans gathered at Brampton 27 July 2003, the 50th anniversary of the signing of the Armistice Accord concluded at Panmunjom.

6. The Australian National Korean War Memorial on Anzac Parade in Canberra was dedicated 18 April 2000. There were 304 Australian battle deaths before the end of the conflict 27 July 1953.

7. Canada's Korean War Memorial, unveiled 28 September 2003 beside Ottawa's Mackenzie King Bridge, shows a Canadian soldier assisting orphaned Korean children.

8. The Korean War Memorial on Washington's Mall recalls battlefield conditions.

9. Flags of the 16 nations of the United Nations Command which fought for the defence of South Korea fly over the United Nations Cemetery in Pusan. The remains of more than 2000 battle fatalities lie here.

10-11. Fifty years after the conclusion of the Panmunjom Armistice Agreement of 27 July 1953, some 37,000 soldiers of the United States Army remain in South Korea. Their base at Fort Bonifas—named for Captain Arthur Bonifas, a U.S. Army officer killed in a North Korean raid 18 August 1976—is located immediately south of the Demilitarized Zone.

12. A North Korean observation tower located metres from the Demarcation Line monitors developments in the South Korean portion of the Demilitarized Zone at Panmunjom. The South Korean army has a tower of its own, much more picturesque, for observing North Korea. Soldiers and visitors to Panmunjom receive strict instructions not to talk to nor in any way acknowledge the presence of North Korean soldiers.

13. The Bridge of No Return at Panmunjom has its name because so few people have made a return trip across the Imjin River, the Demarcation Line at this point.

14. Negotiators met in tents during the 1951-1953 truce talks at Panmunjom. Since then, buildings have replaced the tents. The one on the right and the large building behind the others belong to North Korea; the rest serve the United Nations Command (today, mainly South Korea and the United States).

15. A soldier of the the South Korean Army uses a building to shield his body from possible North Korean attack while protecting tourists at Panmunjom.

16. South Korean soldiers patrol their side of the Demarcation Line at Panmunjom, while a North Korean soldier stands guard at the entrance to the large building across the Demarcation Line.

1. Munsan Unification Park

2. Monument at Inchon

3. Washington, December 1950

4.	Brampton War Memorial

5.	Brampton, Ontario, 27 July 2003

6. Australian National Korean War Memorial

7. Canada's Korean War Memorial

8. Korean War Memorial, Washington's Mall

9. United Nations Cemetery, Pusan

10. U.S. Army base Fort Bonifas

11. Fort Bonifas, south of the Demilitarized Zone

12. North Korean observation tower, Demarcation Line

13. The Bridge of No Return, Panmunjom

14.   Site of the 1951-1953 truce talks, Panmunjom

15—16.   Demarcation Line, Panmunjom

Introduction

Canada, The Commonwealth Belligerents, And Korean War Diplomacy

I U.S. Unilateralism During the Presidency of George W. Bush

In March 2003, the administration led by President George W. Bush led the United States into war. Its goal was "régime change" in Iraq, and what people outside the United States thought really did not matter. The United Nations Security Council withheld approval, as did such powerful allies as France, Germany, and—given the importance of geography—the Turkish Parliament. Neighbours and NAFTA partners Canada and Mexico also disapproved, but the Bush administration persevered with its agenda nonetheless. It would lead a coalition of the willing, the bribed, and the intimidated. No other country or combination of countries could persuade it to change its agenda.

The second Bush administration was uncompromising in its unilateralism. On 6 May 2002, it announced that the United States would neither ratify nor respect the treaty creating an International Criminal Court, endorsed by some sixty other governments.[1] When the United Nations Security Council considered extension of peacekeeping operations in Bosnia, due to expire 30 June 2002, U.S. Ambassador John Negroponte vetoed the resolution. The fate of Bosnia was a lower priority than U.S. opposition to the International Criminal Court.[2]

Citizens of the United States itself have noted the unilateralism of George W. Bush and his advisers. On 30 July 2001, the *International Herald Tribune* reprinted an editorial from the *New York Times* entitled "America on the Sidelines." "Unless a treaty is fatally flawed," said the editorial, "Washington should not abruptly walk away from the agreement.

> The more responsible answer is to work with other countries to modify it...Mighty as it is, Washington cannot expect to lead the way to a less dangerous, more law-biding and environmentally sustainable world from the sidelines.

The administration's record in this regard is dismal. In January, even before Mr. Bush took office, his spokesmen declared that he would not seek Senate ratification of the treaty creating the International Criminal Court. In March, the White House announced that the United States was withdrawing from the Kyoto Protocol on global warming. In May, Mr. Bush made clear he was ready to set aside the constraints of the Anti-Ballistic Missile Treaty in order to test and build missile defences.

This month, American delegates insisted on diluting a United Nations agreement to reduce illegal trafficking in small arms. Last week, Washington pulled out of long-running efforts to negotiate enforcement provisions for the convention banning biological weapons. Meanwhile, the administration has indefinitely deferred seeking Senate ratification of the 1996 nuclear test ban treaty and the 1993 nuclear weapons reduction treaty with Russia negotiated by Mr. Bush's father.[3]

The *New York Times* did not even mention the 1997 Treaty of Ottawa, promoted by Canadian Foreign Minister Lloyd Axworthy and signed by 133 nations. The treaty committed signatories to outlaw the use of landmines by March 2001. Defence should be possible without such weapons, Axworthy had argued, and they killed and maimed innocent civilians long after conflicts ended. The Clinton administration had refused to sign the Treaty of Ottawa on the grounds that the United States needs landmines for the defence of South Korea. The well-fed, well-equipped, well-trained South Korean Army, assisted by 37,000 American service personnel and two coast-to-coast anti-tank walls between Seoul and the inter-Korean border, might prove insufficient for the task.

Despite support from a significant number of South Koreans, the second Bush administration is indifferent or hostile to the Treaty of Ottawa. The 43rd president adopted a much harder line on inter-Korean relations than did South Korean President Kim Dae Jung, at least before the violent clash of late June 2002 in the Yellow Sea near the inter-Korean border.[4] Indeed, when Kim visited the White House, Bush reprimanded him for naïveté and voiced displeasure over Kim's failure to support development of an anti-missile missile programme in violation of the 1972 U.S.-Soviet Anti-Ballistic Missile Treaty. Bush asked Kim Dae Jung, a Nobel Peace Prize winner, how—given the previous half-century of Korean history—he could side with the Russians against the United States. On his return to Seoul, Kim shuffled his cabinet, eliminating some of the people thought most offensive to official Washington.[5]

There is no indication that, despite support for the Treaty of Ottawa in South Korea, Kim bothered to ask the Canadian government for assistance in dealing with the second Bush administration. Nor, in all probability, would it have been worthwhile to do so. Christopher Sands, the Canadian specialist at the Center for Strategic and International Studies, a Washington think-tank, recently noted that Canada's influence in U.S. government circles is probably less than it has been since the Hoover administration. The Gross Domestic Product of many other countries has outstripped that of Canada. Successive Canadian governments have downsized the Canadian Armed Forces and slashed military spending. Moreover, as Americans have moved from the rust belt to the sun belt, dominant U.S. politicians tend to be people who have had little contact with Canada or Canadians.[6] Another factor, of course, is the development of technology. Long-range aircraft, inter-continental missiles, and communications satellites have stripped Canada of its role as a way station between the United States and Europe or Asia. Lamented London-based journalist John Lloyd, "This is not the Republican Party of Dwight Eisenhower…" (Lloyd meant that Eisenhower, unlike Bush, was willing to listen to the opinions of other governments and even adapt his policies to take account of their opinions.) Lloyd then referred to a recent article by the Republicans' elder statesman, Henry Kissinger, who in a recent article had written that Americans must be prepared to proceed, when necessary, "entirely on our own." Kissinger, Lloyd was suggesting, had become a unilateralist.[7]

II   Truman, Eisenhower, and Korea

There is good reason to argue that the Eisenhower administration, like its predecessor—the Truman administration—was much more internationalist in its outlook than the early George W. Bush team. Unlike Bush, Truman and Eisenhower were veterans of foreign wars. Eisenhower, in fact, had been the Supreme Allied Commander of both Allied forces in World War II and NATO forces in the early Cold War. The track record of both administrations demonstrates concern for the outside world. The Truman administration launched the Marshall Plan for the economic recovery of Europe. It signed the original North Atlantic Treaty, which created NATO. The Truman administration led a coalition of fifteen other member countries of the United Nations in the defence of South Korea. Eisenhower's advisers listened to America's allies as they negotiated an end to that war in 1953.

Canada was one of America's allies in both NATO and Korea. During the Truman and Eisenhower administrations, before the recovery of Western Europe and Japan from the destruction of World War II, Canada had one of the world's strongest es. Given the limited range of contemporary aircraft, Canada's air space appeared vital to the American military as it planned to defend North America from possible Soviet attack.

There is evidence that as the Truman and Eisenhower administrations worked with governments of other countries, they also heeded Canadian interests—at least to a point. Dean Acheson, Secretary of State from 1949 to 1953, had been a personal friend of Lester Pearson's[8] and had frequently vacationed in Canada.[9] Dwight David Eisenhower, President of the United States from 1953 to 1961, had commanded Canadian forces during World War II. However, one should not exaggerate Canada's influence in Washington even during the Truman and Eisenhower years. From London, U.S. Ambassador Julius Cecil Holmes wrote late in 1950 that despite their global commitments and troops commitments, many British authorities thought that the U.S. Government paid as little attention to their opinions as to the opinions of leaders of Denmark and Luxembourg.[10]

An earlier book, *Invisible and Inaudible in Washington*, is the inspiration for this one. *Invisible and Inaudible* dealt with U.S. policies toward Canada during the Cold War.[11] Research for that book indicated that invariably whenever there was a difference of opinion between the U.S. government and the Canadian government, the U.S. government had its way. Washington's will prevailed. Ottawa's counted for comparatively little. This was also the opinion of Tom Keating, who had written about Canada's role in many multinational organizations. Keating noted that Canadian officials who arranged Canadian membership in NATO hoped that Canada might have more influence in an organization with members on both sides of the Atlantic than in any bilateral relationship with the United States alone. However, that proved a vain hope.[12] Writing about Canada's role during the late 1990s (the post-Cold War period) in the former Yugoslavia, Nicholas Gammer says that Jean Chrétien's government did manage to soften a NATO ultimatum to the Serbs.[13] That happened when Canada had a significant number of combat forces in the line of fire and when a Democrat, Bill Clinton, was President of the United States. It does not appear to have happened very often.

III   The Perennial Challenge Faced by Canadian Diplomats

The litany of examples of Canadian ineffectiveness or irrelevance begins in 1949, when nations of the North Atlantic community were creating the North Atlantic Treaty Organization. U.S. Secretary of State Dean Acheson wanted an anti-Soviet military alliance, nothing more. Canada's Secretary of State for External Affairs,

Lester Bowles Pearson, thought that Canada should stand for something, not simply against something. An article on economic and social co-operation, thought Pearson, might make NATO more attractive to the hitherto isolationist voters of Quebec than could a charter which dealt exclusively with military matters. He then lobbied the British, French, Dutch and Belgian governments with some degree of success. In order to placate the Canadian government, NATO agreed to Article II:

> The parties will contribute toward the further development of peaceful and friendly international relations by strengthening their free institutions, by bringing about a better understanding of the principles upon which these institutions are founded, and by promoting conditions of stability and well-being. They will seek to eliminate conflict in their international economic policies and will encourage economic collaboration between any or all of them.[14]

However, Article II had considerably less input than Pearson would have wished.[15]

There were incessant differences of opinion over what to do in Asia. From 1950 to 1953, American officers led the United Nations Command (UNC) in the Korean War. Canadian soldiers, sailors, and air crews participated as part of the UNC. Before, during, and subsequent to the Korean conflict, the St. Laurent government in Ottawa disagreed with certain policies of the Truman administration (1945-1953) and the Eisenhower administration (1953-1961) in Washington. These will be the subject of this book.

Asia continued to plague relations between Canada and the United States. Throughout the 1950s, the Eisenhower administration appeared more willing than Canadian authorities thought appropriate to assist Chiang Kai Shek's Taiwan-based government to retain control over the Kinmen (then called Quemoy) and Matsu Islands off China's Fujiang province. President Dwight David Eisenhower and Secretary of State John Foster Dulles gave no indication of modifying their position.[16] The administration of Lyndon Baines Johnson (1963-1969) had nothing but contempt for Lester Pearson, Prime Minister of Canada from 1963 until 1968, and his Secretary of State for External Affairs, Paul Martin (Senior); the principal cause of that contempt was their lack of enthusiastic support for the U.S. war effort in Vietnam. Pearson and Martin could not persuade Johnson and his associates to change course, and they suffered ostracism from the Johnson White House, where their influence came to count for next to nothing.[17] Even when Prime Minister Pierre Elliott Trudeau (1968-1979, 1980-1984) did what the current U.S. administration—that of Richard Milhous Nixon—was planning to do with regard to ending the isolation of China, he found himself in trouble. Nixon had wanted to lead the way and resented the fact that a mere Canadian had pre-empted him. On at least one later occasion, Nixon referred to the Canadian Prime Minister as an "asshole."[18] The Nixon tapes indicate that Nixon frequently called Trudeau a "son of a bitch."[19]

John Diefenbaker parted company from the Eisenhower and Kennedy administrations on two Cold War issues, and paid the price. Diefenbaker favoured a business-almost-as-usual approach toward Castro's Cuba, but Eisenhower and Kennedy insisted on treating the Cuban revolutionaries as Soviet surrogates, if not outlaws. Disagreement over Cuba led to negative feelings, even bitterness, but Washington persevered in what it believed to be right. Differences of opinion over Cuba led to the marginalization of the Diefenbaker government as the Kennedy administration plotted its global strategies.[20] Moreover, in 1958, Diefenbaker agreed to accept nuclear weapons for the Canadian Armed Forces both in Canada and in Europe,[21] then, under pressure of public opinion had sober second thoughts. The Kennedy White House did not let him renege. In 1963, National Security Adviser McGeorge Bundy issued a press statement which undercut Diefenbaker's credibility. Within days, the Diefenbaker government lost a vote of confidence in the House of Commons, and it lost the ensuing national election as well. Lester Pearson became Prime Minister of Canada, and his government implemented the weapons programmes which Diefenbaker and his ministers had negotiated.

Ronald Reagan assumed the presidency in 1981 as a Cold Warrior, ready to challenge the Soviets' "Evil Empire." Trudeau did not share all Reagan's assumptions and feared that his rhetoric, if not his actions, might spark a nuclear war. Trudeau responded with a "peace offensive," during which he flew to as many world capitals as possible urging restraint. The Reagan White House was unimpressed. In 1983, the armed forces of the U.S. and most nations of the Commonwealth Caribbean invaded Grenada, whose government was friendly to Cuba, North Korea, East Germany, and Libya. Washington did not notify Ottawa in advance, let alone solicit advice. Not since 1812 had the armed forces of the United States invaded territory whose head of state was the British monarch, and Canada was the senior member of the Commonwealth west of the Atlantic, but Trudeau's opinions did not matter. As for the peace offensive, one would be hard pressed to find any historian who thinks that it contributed to the end of the Cold War.

Throughout the Cold War, Canada had a smaller population, a smaller economy, and considerably smaller armed forces than did the United States. It is understandable that in a bilateral context, the stronger country could ignore or overwhelm the lesser one. Historian Coral Bell drew similar conclusions regarding Australia's foreign relations during the same period.[22] However, Canada belonged to several multinational organizations, including the Commonwealth, NATO, and the United Nations. If bilateral talks were doomed to failure, perhaps it might have been possible to join forces with other countries and make a more forceful impression. Jeffrey Simpson—the leading political columnist of Canada's national newspaper—the *Globe and Mail*—has written:

> A mantra of Canadian foreign policy has been that, as a middle power, Canada tries to engage the U.S. multilaterally whenever possible. Canada likes to get the U.S. inside multilateral tents, where, with other like-minded countries, it can influence U.S. thinking before U.S. policy becomes carved in stone.[23]

Yet, even this assumption is dubious. Perhaps the instance of NATO's Article II, cited above, indicates some measure of "success." At the very least, with the help of four other prospective members, Pearson did manage to make Article II part of the Charter. However, as already indicated, such "success" proved minimal.

In 1987, Ryerson University in Toronto hosted a gathering of retired political leaders, retired civil servants, and academics to discuss the origins of NATO. Three former Secretaries of State for External Affairs attended: the elder Paul Martin (1963-1968); Mitchell Sharp (1968-1974); Mark MacGuigan (1980-1982). In private conversation, Paul Martin (Senior) claimed that Canada had had a number of successes in lobbying others to modify Washington's position. When pushed to provide examples of such successes, Martin responded that in 1964, when Cyprus erupted and threatened to provoke a war between two NATO allies, Greece and Turkey, he had persuaded the Johnson Administration to work through the United Nations rather than NATO. Six years later, in Austin, Texas, at the Lyndon Baines Johnson Archives to research *Invisible and Inaudible in Washington* (whose title had not yet been chosen), the present author discovered that President Johnson had always intended to pacify Cyprus through the United Nations rather than through NATO. He did not need any persuasion from Paul Martin! Forced through circumstances to deal with the Nixon administration, Mitchell Sharp made no such claim. Mark MacGuigan, whose tenure of office coincided with the end of the Carter administration and the first year of the Reagan presidency, confessed: "The only issue resolved during my watch was ownership of the Falkland Islands, and Canada had nothing to do with that outcome." British military superiority plus support from the Reagan administration for the British cause, not anything that happened in Ottawa, determined the British victory over Argentina in the Falklands War of 1982.

Perhaps this is too pessimistic a point of view. Perhaps Canada was more effective than the foregoing would indicate. Canadian diplomat John Holmes wrote that during his fifteen years at the United Nations:

> When the U.S. did get a resolution through [the Security] Council or [the General] Assembly it was nearly always a resolution that had been considerably altered to get the support of others. The most notable defiance of the United States was led by Canada in 1955 when Paul Martin took over the leadership of a lesser-power revolt to promote the package deal that brought into the UN all the outstanding applicants hitherto blocked by East and West. We persisted in spite of the fury of [Secretary of State] John Foster Dulles and the empty threats of [US Ambassador to the UN] Henry Cabot Lodge. Our action was about as consequential as anything ever done to shape the UN.[24]

IV The Commonwealth Belligerents and the Korean War

If ever there was an international event where Ottawa's opinions might have mattered to official Washington, the Korean War should have been it. For technological reasons (the short distances which aircraft could fly), Canada's air space remained important to the United States Air Force. Canada still had one of the world's most powerful economies. Canadian units were fighting alongside American ones as part of the United Nations Command, and although not nearly as numerous as the troops from the United States, they were part of a British Commonwealth contingent. Together the United Kingdom, Canada, Australia, New Zealand, and South Africa had more service personnel fighting for the defence of South Korea than anyone other than South Korea itself and the United States. Also, the Korean War took place at a time when the Commonwealth meant more to Canadians and was more cohesive than it would become in the aftermath of the Suez Crisis; the entry of dozens of new states from Africa, Asia, and the Caribbean; and the United Kingdom's entry into what is now the European Union. Conferences of Commonwealth leaders were discussion groups among a small number of gentlemen, who shared similar values. The Commonwealth was indeed a forum where Canada could look for allies in its dealings with Washington. Between the Commonwealth and the United Nations, Canada should have had opportunities to lobby diplomats and politicians who might collectively change the mind of official Washington. John Holmes has indicated that Canadian governments have long recognized the potential which multinational organizations offered for dealing with Great Powers,[25] but he also said:

> We had rejected any suggestion of a united Commonwealth policy, using
> often as an argument that we did not want to encourage American suspi-
> cions of the Commonwealth as a ganging-up.[26]

However, there are a time and a place for almost everything, including a change of
heart or a swallowing of one's principles, especially when matters of life and death are
at stake. Would 1950 be the time and Korea the place?

Korea provides a case study where a multilateral strategy might have had some
impact. Korean-related Ottawa-Washington differences involved other members of
the Commonwealth, who consulted with each other as they struggled to gain attention from the White House and the State Department. The five Korean War
belligerents from the British Commonwealth of Nations, identified in diplomatic correspondence as "the Old Commonwealth" to distinguish them from Commonwealth
members India, Pakistan, and Ceylon (now Sri Lanka), also had unparalleled access
to the Truman and Eisenhower administrations. Habits dating from World War II as
well as the size of the collective contribution gave members of the Old Commonwealth access to high places unavailable to other governments which had sent troops
to the United Nations Command.[27] Also, the Truman and Eisenhower administrations both hoped that after an armistice, Allied countries might leave their troops in
Korea for a reasonable period of time in order to deal with any Communist violations. In Eisenhower's words, Greek forces in Korea "would relieve American boys
and could be maintained cheaper."[28] Hence, U.S. self-interest dictated respect for
Allies' opinions. The purpose of this book is to determine the value of that Old Commonwealth access to the Truman and Eisenhower administrations and, by extension, the potential value to Canadians of lobbying official Washington in a
multinational forum.

Before the Korean War, the United Nations appointed Canada, as well as Australia, to its United Nations Temporary Commission on Korea (UNTCOK). Prime
Minister Mackenzie King did not want to accept the honour, but pressure from President Truman and members of his own cabinet persuaded him to acquiesce. Ottawa
and Washington then proceeded to disagree whether UNTCOK should organize
elections in South Korea even if the Soviet Union forbade them in its zone of occupation. Did the Canadian government co-ordinate strategy with the Australian, and if
so, with what effect?

Once the war started, the United States sought allies. A military coalition normally leads to differences of opinions among the partners, and such arose. How large
should the contributions of the Commonwealth countries be? Once it had the North

Koreans on the run, how far north should the United Nations Command proceed? Once the People's Republic of China intervened, what should be the collective response of the countries constituting the United Nations Command? There were differences of opinion over cease-fire terms, the Truman and Eisenhower administrations making demands on North Korea and the People's Republic of China which Commonwealth allies thought excessive and unnecessary.

Finally, one of the terms of the Armistice Agreement (AA) of 27 July 1953 was creation of a Neutral Nations Supervisory Commission (NNSC). It would be responsible for enforcement of the AA, but when the Eisenhower administration sought to violate Article 13(d), it wanted to restrict the NNSC to the Demilitarized Zone (DMZ). As a member of the parallel International Control Commission (ICC) in Vietnam, Canada objected. It feared that any restriction on the NNSC might serve as a dangerous precedent for the ICC, which was responsible for overseeing the enforcement of the cease-fire accord on Vietnam arranged at the Geneva Conference of 1954.

V   A Survey of Existing Literature

This book fills a gap. Written with the help of Soviet and Chinese sources which became accessible after the Cold War, it examines efforts to persuade two U.S. administrations—Truman's and Eisenhower's—to alter their course. It also benefits from records of Australian cabinet meetings, declassified shortly before the author's visit to Canberra, and from files regarding the Menzies government's attitude toward Korea in the immediate aftermath of the Cold War. These last were declassified at the request of the author, specifically for preparing this book. Also useful were National Intelligence Estimates (NIEs) and Special Estimates (SEs) from the Central Intelligence Agency (CIA) released only in 1993-1994.

As early as 1958, Alvin J. Cottrell and James E. Dougherty suggested that U.S. allies, especially the United Kingdom, had influenced the Truman administration's Korean War policies, but in their opinion, Allied influence had been negative. While it was arguably wise not to have used nuclear weapons in Korea, they say, a public statement of renunciation—issued when British Prime Minister Clement Attlee visited Washington in December 1950—"forfeit[ed] the psychological and political value inherent in the possession of the atomic bomb." Also, continued Allied trade with the People's Republic of China (PRC) minimized the economic consequences of Chinese intervention into the war. Cottrell and Dougherty think that the Truman administration was correct in seeing an economic embargo against the PRC and that the Allies were strong to argue, successfully, otherwise. Cottrell and Dougherty wrote without access to Allied or enemy documents.[29]

There has been some excellent literature on the diplomacy of the Korean War, especially in the 1980s and early 1990s—by which time relevant U.S., British, Canadian, and Australian documents had become available. (Six critical works which pre-dated such declassification are *Child of Conflict: The Korean-American Relationship, 1943-1945* by Bruce Cumings;[30] *Ernest Bevin, Foreign Secretary, 1945-1951* by Alan Bullock;[31] Stewart Lone, *Korea Since 1850*;[32] Gavan McCormack, *Cold War History: An Australian Perspective on the Korean War*;[33] Rosemary Foot, *The Wrong War: American Policy and the Dimensions of the Korean War*;[34] Steven Hugh Lee, *Outposts of Empire: Korea, Vietnam, and the Origin of the Cold War in Asia, 1949-1954*[35]). Lee has written extensively on British and Canadian efforts to influence U.S. policy during the Korean War, but he did not have access to any Soviet or Chinese documents, nor did he visit the Australian Archives. Lee argues that the British and Canadians realized that they often had little choice because they required U.S. support on other fronts, particularly in Europe. If the U.S. had to defend South Korea without allies, Americans might "favour preparing in isolation for the larger conflict ahead and writing...the allies off."[36] Lee says that it would be wrong to exaggerate the impact of the British and Canadian allies on the U.S., "particularly in the first year of the war."[37] Nor should those differences be exaggerated, writes Lee. During the winter of 1950-1951

> Canada and Great Britain consistently backed American diplomatic initiatives, and the United States was prepared to make concessions to its allies, though these were not major compromises. The United States altered the tone of some of its UN proposals, not simply as a result of allied pressure but because it acknowledged that a united front was crucial for its own objectives as well as for those of its allies.[38]

On such major points, notes Lee, as the priority of Europe over mainland Asia, the Americans, British, and Canadians agreed.[39]

Another Canadian author who agrees with Lee that there was a limit beyond which the St. Laurent government dared not attempt to restrain or otherwise influence the Truman administration is Robert S. Prince. Looking exclusively at the bilateral Ottawa-Washington relationship, and for only the first seven months of the Korean War, Prince says that good relations with the United States were so important that the Canadian cabinet dared not jeopardize them over Korea. Prince suggests that while Denis Stairs's *Diplomacy of Constraint* has merit, it may go too far.[40]

Anthony Farrar-Hockley, himself a POW from 1951-1953, visited archives and examined primary sources in the U.S., United Kingdom, Australia, and Canada while writing his mammoth two-volume *The British Part in the Korean War*.[41] However, he appears not to have examined Record Group 25—the Department of External Affairs file—when he went to the National Archives of Canada in Ottawa. Farrar-Hockley's work focuses on the Korean War itself—particularly the role of British soldiers in military operations but also on the activities of Commonwealth soldiers—and on Anglo-American diplomacy. It does not dwell on the use of the Old Commonwealth to promote policy changes in Washington. The index to the earlier volume, which deals with events from 1943 to 1950, includes no references to such key players as Canadian Prime Minister Louis St. Laurent or Australians Sir Percy Spender and Richard Casey, only one to Lester B. Pearson and two to Sir Robert Menzies. Under "Holland," the name of New Zealand's Prime Minister during the Korean War, it says "See Netherlands." There is next to nothing on South Africa. Casey and Spender do merit a single mention in the second volume, covering 1951 to 1953, but there remains much room for elaboration. By the time Farrar-Hockley wrote his second volume (published in 1995), he was aware of the findings of Kathryn Weathersby, an American scholar, in the Soviet archives with regard to the Korean War. By 1995, Farrar-Hockley too had access to other Soviet and Chinese sources. For his part, Eisenhower's biographer—Stephen Ambrose—makes no mention of Old Commonwealth leaders as playing any role at all in meaningful Korean War-related diplomacy prior to the cease-fire of 27 July 1953.[42] Stanley Weintraub, himself a Korean War veteran, deals at some length with the British, Canadian, Australian and New Zealand (but not South African) military contributions during the period which he covered–until President Truman dismissed General Douglas MacArthur in April 1951). However, apart from Attlee's Washington visit in December 1950 and a few scattered references to K.M. Panikkar, India's ambassador in Beijing, Weintraub ignores Commonwealth diplomacy.[43] Rosemary Foot's *A Substitute for Victory: The Politics of Peacemaking at the Korean Armistice Talks*, appeared in 1990, before the collapse of the Soviet Union and the availability of Soviet documents. An excellent book, it has a briefer time span than this manuscript. Foot limits herself to the truce talks which took place over a two year period (mid-1951 to mid-1953) at Kaesong and Panmunjom.[44] This manuscript deals with events across a decade (1947-1956).

More recently, Patrick C. Roe—an intelligence officer with the U.S. Marines during the Korean War—has written about U.S. intelligence preceding Chinese intervention and during the first few months of the conflict. Roe discusses the role of the British as intelligence partners of the United States, and he speculates that the Chinese might have benefited from intelligence supplied by such strategically placed British traitors as Kim Philby, Guy Burgess, and Donald MacLean. However, Roe says nothing about Canada and Australia, let alone New Zealand and South Africa.[45]

Similarly, a British writer who used Soviet and Chinese sources, Jennifer Milliken, noted the importance of "investigating the policies of Western states other than the United States." To that end, Millikin used British sources. However, she made only two passing references to Canada and failed altogether to mention Australia, New Zealand, or South Africa.[46] Meanwhile, the index to a recent history of the Korean War written by South Koreans does not even include such entries as "Australia" or "Canada."[47] In 2003, Margaret MacMillan and Francine Mackenzie released a collection of essays on Canadian-Australian relations, but they devoted only a few pages to the Korean War.[48]

The most thorough coverage of Korean-related diplomacy from the end of World War II until the Armistice Agreement of 1953 is undoubtedly William Stueck's *The Korean War: An International History*, published in 1995. Stueck says that his goal is "to explain the course of the war from the perspectives of the great powers most prominently involved—the United States, the Soviet Union, and China."[49] Stueck succeeds and displays a commanding knowledge of U.S., Soviet, and Chinese archival sources, memoirs, and secondary literature. In preparing for his work, Stueck visited the United Kingdom, Canada, and Australia, where he developed a formidable knowledge of those countries' sources and positions. Stueck discusses bilateral Anglo-American diplomacy, as well as British diplomacy at the United Nations, often in co-operation with India, Canada, Australia, or a combination thereof. He elaborates upon the positions of the other thirteen countries of the United Nations Command, including New Zealand and South Africa: why they sent forces to Korea, why they developed the positions that they did. Stueck's judgment is balanced and fair. However, there remains more to be said about the co-ordinated behind-the-scenes maneuvers of the Old Commonwealth governments. What did they have in common, and what were their differences? Why did they do what they did, and with what results? Dealing with these questions had not been part of Stueck's mandate. Unlike Stueck's book, this one will not deal with bilateral Anglo-Indian or Canadian-Indian diplomacy during the Korean War because India, unlike the Old Commonwealth countries, was not a belligerent. Nor will it discuss Anglo-American differences over the proposed government for a liberated North Korea, as North Korea remained "liberated" for only a few weeks in the autumn of 1952.[50] Rather, it will deal with issues which affected multiple countries of the Old Commonwealth and that had long-term implications, and it will deal with them at length. (The index of Stueck's recent book, *Rethinking the Korean War*, does not mention any Commonwealth country other than the United Kingdom.)[51]

Most Commonwealth historians have been more interested in their own country's bilateral relationship with the United States than with multilateral approaches.[52] Peter Lowe, from the University of Manchester, is among the most prolific. Lowe thinks that the impact of the diplomacy of the fifteen allies who assisted the United States as part of the United Nations Command was "marginal,"[53] and that British Prime Ministers Clement Attlee and Winston Churchill "were minor figures in the context of the Korean War."[54] Churchill's bilateral diplomacy with Moscow in 1952-1953, says Lowe, "annoyed [President] Eisenhower."[55] Lowe credits Indian Prime Minister Jawaharlal Nehru, Canada's Minister of External Affairs Lester Pearson, and British Foreign Secretary Anthony Eden with a diplomatic initiative which eventually provided a basis for the 1953 Armistice Agreement, but Lowe noted that Secretary of State Dean Acheson rejected it until Soviet Foreign Minister Andrei Vyshinsky also rejected it. If Vyshinsky would play "bad cop," Acheson could play "good cop." Vyshinsky, not Nehru, Pearson, or Eden, was the one who influenced Acheson, according to Lowe.[56] Nor did the Commonwealth offer a united front at that point. Australia sided with Acheson.[57] With the exception of this one incident, Peter Lowe ignores intra-Commonwealth diplomacy in connection with the Korean War. Another British writer, Max Hastings, wrote a military history of the Korean War but without benefit of Canadian or Australian archival sources, and he did so before Soviet and Chinese archival sources were available.[58] Similarly, most of the writers in *The Korean War in History*, edited by James Cotton and Ian Neary and published in 1989 by the University of Manchester Press, use only British archival sources. Now that Soviet, Soviet-bloc, and Chinese documents are accessible, it is possible as never before to judge the merits of the Commonwealth/British/Canadian ideas. Some of them really were good. According to military historian Brian Catchpole, Commonwealth forces fought well in Korea too.[59] Another military historian, also an American, Bevin Alexander, agrees.[60] With good ideas and good soldiers, the Commonwealth had the right to be taken seriously.

This book, then, is a study of Canadian diplomacy, some of it meritorious, which took place when it should have had maximum impact. Canada was as important to the United States as it ever was, and it had important allies in the Commonwealth. What was the impact? How possible was it to affect U.S. policies and goals? What had to be done to influence the outcome? The answers to these questions may deliver some insight into Canada's potential influence in the world in the twenty-first century.

VI   Terminology

Since the years described here, many Asian places have come to be known by names different from the ones used at the time. In the 1950s, the capital of the People's Republic of China appeared in English as Peking. Now it is Beijing. The island still controlled by Chinese Nationalists was Formosa, now Taiwan. The Commonwealth nation due south of India was Ceylon, now Sri Lanka. The island off the coast of the People's Republic of China, Quemoy, is now Kinmen. What is now Myanmar was Burma. The practice in these pages is to use the most recent transliteration of any place (or anyone) in the People's Republic of China since their real names at the time were Mandarin, not English. However, as Ceylon did not become Sri Lanka nor Burma Myanmar until later, it would be anachronistic to refer to those countries by any names other than the ones used at the time of the events described. Chiang Kai Shek remains more familiar under that name than as Jiang Jieshi, and he was never part of the People's Republic of China.

Notes
1. CBC News, 6 May 2002.

2. *New York Times*, 4 July 2002.

3. *The Korea Herald* (Seoul), 4 March 2001.

4. On 4 July 2002, the *New York Times* reported that in the aftermath of the Yellow Sea violence of 29 June, South Korea had suspended talks with North Korea about creating a mobile phone system in Pyongyang.

5. *The Korea Herald* (Seoul), successive issues, March 2001.

6. Christopher Sands, "How Canada Policy is Made in the United States," in Maureen Appel Molot and Fen Osler Hampson, *Vanishing Borders* (Don Mills: Oxford University Press, 2000), pp. 47-72.

7. *Globe and Mail*, 30 July 2001.

8. Lester B. Pearson, *Mike: The Memoirs of the Rt. Hon. Lester B. Pearson* (Toronto: University of Toronto Press, 1973), vol. II, p. 56. Confirming that they were no longer friendly during the Korean War is Andrew Cohen, *While Canada Slept: How We Lost our Place in the World*. Toronto: McClelland and Stewart, 2003, pp. 157-160.

9. Dean Acheson, *Present at the Creation: My Years in the State Department* (New York: W.W. Norton, 1969), pp. 122, 190, 192, 238-239.

10. Holmes, London, to the Secretary of State, Washington, 3 Dec. 1950, in "Briefing Book Prepared for President Truman before the Truman-Attlee Talks of 4-7 December 1950," President's Secretary's File: Subject File, 1945-1953: Conf Data, Harry S. Truman Presidential Archive, Independence, Missouri. Cited hereafter as HST.

11. Edelgard E. Mahant and Graeme S. Mount, *Invisible and Inaudible in Washington* (Vancouver: UBC Press, 1999).

12. Tom Keating, *Canada and World Order: The Multilateralist Tradition in Canadian Foreign Policy* (Toronto: McClelland and Stewart, 1993), pp. 94-95.

13. Nicholas Gammer, *From Peacekeeping to Peacemaking: Canada's Response to the Yugoslav Crisis* (Montreal and Kingston: McGill-Queen's University Press, 2001), p. 176.

14. Pearson, pp. 55-63. The quotation comes from p. 57.

15. John English, *The Worldly Years: The Life of Lester Pearson, 1949-1972* (Toronto: Knopf Canada, 1992), pp. 22-23.

16. Robert Redford, *Canada and Three Crises* (Toronto: Canadian Institute of International Affairs, 1968), pp. 9-72.

17. Mahant and Mount, pp. 49-60.

18. Robert Bothwell and J.L. Granatstein, *Pirouette: Pierre Trudeau and Canadian Foreign Policy* (Toronto: University of Toronto Press, 1990), pp. 50-51, 183-187 (the quotation comes from p. 50); Pierre Elliott Trudeau, *Memoirs* (Toronto: McClelland and Stewart, 1993), p. 211.

19. Lawrence Martin, "Thank you, Mr. Nixon: It was a good time for Canada's soul," *Globe and Mail*, 19 March 2002, A 15.

20. Jocelyn Maynard Ghent, "Canada, the United States, and the Cuban Missile Crisis," *Pacific Historical Review*, XLVIII, 2 (May 1979), pp. 159-194. For confirmation of Canada's near irrelevance in the eyes of the Kennedy administration during the Cuban Missile Crisis, see Ernest R. May and Philip D. Zelikow (editor), *The Kennedy Tapes: Inside the White House during the Cuban Missile Crisis* (Cambridge, Mass.: Harvard University Press, 1997).

21. Jon B. McLin, *Canada's Changing Defense Policy, 1957-1963: The Problems of a Middle Power in Alliance* (Baltimore: Johns Hopkins University Press, 1967).

22. Coral Bell, *Dependent Ally: A Study in Australian Foreign Policy* (St. Leonards, New South Wales: Allen and Unwin, 1984.

23. *Globe and Mail*, 6 April 2002.

24. John Holmes, *Life with Uncle: The Canadian-American Relationship* (Toronto: University of Toronto Press, 1981), p. 37.

25. Holmes, p. 7.

26. Holmes, p. 23.

27. For an assessment of their collective contribution, see in particular Jeffrey Grey, *The Commonwealth Armies and the Korean War: An Alliance Study* (Manchester: Manchester University Press, 1988).

28. Webb, Acting Secretary of State, Washington, to Secretary of State Dean Acheson, Rome, 26 Nov. 1951, PSF, Subject File, 1945-1953, Truman-Attlee Talks, Box 141, HST. Also, Minutes of the 148th meeting of the National Security Council (NSC), 4 June 1953, Dwight David Eisenhower Papers as President, 1953-1961, (Anne Whitman File, NSC Series), Box 4, Dwight David Eisenhower Presidential Archive, Abilene, Kansas. Cited hereafter as DDE.

29. Alvin J. Cottrell and James E. Dougherty, "The Lessons of Korea: War and the Power of Man," Orbis, II (Spring, 1958), pp. 39-65; reprinted in Sidney Fine (ed.), *Recent America: Conflicting Interpretations of the Great Issues* (New York: Macmillan, n.d.). The quotation is from p. 424.

30. Bruce Cumings (ed.), *Child of Conflict: The Korean-American Relationship, 1945-1953* (Seattle and London: University of Washington Press, 1983). For comments on U.S. diplomacy with Commonwealth countries, see in particular William Stueck, "The March to the Yalu: The Perspective from Washington," pp. 196-237; and Barton J. Bernstein, "The Struggle over the Korean Armistice: Prisoners of Reparation?," pp. 261-307.

31. Alan Bullock, *Ernest Bevin, Foreign Secretary, 1945-1951* (New York and London: W.W.Norton, 1983).

32. Stewart Lone, *Korea Since 1850* (Melbourne: Longman Cheshire, 1993).

33. Gavan McCormack, *Cold War History: An Australian Perspective on the Korean War* (Sydney: Hale and Ironmonger, 1982).

34. Rosemary Foot, *The Wrong War: American Policy and the Dimensions of the Korean War* (Ithaca: Cornell University Press, 1985).

35. Steven Hugh Lee, *Outposts of Empire: Korea, Vietnam, and the Origins of the Cold War in Asia, 1949-1954* (Montreal: McGill-Queen's University Press, 1995).

36. Lee, p. 87.

37. Lee, p. 75.

38. Lee, p. 76.

39. Lee, p. 101. See also Lee pp. 20-222, 29-30, 37-39, 75, 108-110.

40. Robert S. Prince, "The Limits of Constraint: Canadian-American Relations and the Korean War, 1950-1955," *Journal of Canadian Studies*, XXVII, 4 (Winter 1992-1993), pp. 129-152. Denis Stairs, *The Diplomacy of Constraint: Canada, the Korean War, and the United States* (Toronto: University of Toronto Press, 1974).

41. Anthony Farrar-Hockley, *A Distant Obligation* (London: HMSO), 1990; *An Honourable Discharge* (London: HMSO, 1995). The reference to his being a POW appears in *An Honourable Discharge*, p. ix.

42. Stephen Ambrose, *Eisenhower: The President* (New York: Simon and Schuster, 1984).

43. Stanley Weintraub, *MacArthur's War: Korea and the Undoing of an American Hero* (New York: Simon and Schuster, 2000).

44. Rosemary Foot, *A Substitute for Victory: The Politics of Peacemaking at the Korean Armistice Talks* (Ithaca: Cornell University Press, 1990).

45. Patrick C. Roe, *The Dragon Strikes–China and the Korean War: June-December 1950* (Novato, CA: Presidio Press, 2000). See especially pp. 104, 407-409.

46. Jennifer Milliken, *The Social Construction of the Korean War: Conflict and Its Possibilities* (Manchester: University of Manchester Press, 2001). The quotation appears on p. 3, the references to Canada on pp. 157 and 201.

47. Korean Institute of Military History, *The Korean War* (Lincoln and London: University of Nebraska Press, 2001). The Korean Institute of Military History published the initial edition in Seoul that same year.

48. Margaret MacMillan and Francine Mackenzie (editors), *Parties Long Estranged: Canada and Australia in the Twentieth Century* (Vancouver: UBC Press, 2003), pp. 212, 214-216.

49. William Stueck, *The Korean War: An International History* (Princeton: Princeton University Press, 1995), p. 7.

50. For Stueck's insights on this point, see p. 92.

51. William Stueck, *Rethinking the Korean War: A New Diplomatic and Strategic History* (Princeton: Princeton University Press, 2002).

52. Excellent works of this nature include David J. Bercuson, *Blood on the Hills: The Canadian Army in the Korean War* (Toronto: University of Toronto Press, 1999); and Robert O'Neill, *Australia in the Korean War: Strategy and Diplomacy* (Canberra: The Australian War Memorial and the Australian Government Publishing Service, 1981). This is the first of two volumes written by O'Neill on Australia's role in the Korean War. Peter Lowe, a British writer, has written a number of books and articles about the United Kingdom and the Korean War; *The Korean War* (New York: St. Martin's Press, 2000) is the most recent.

53. Lowe, p. 2.

54. Lowe, p. 4.

55. Lowe, p. 5.

56. Lowe, pp. 83-84.

57. Lowe, p. 85.

58. Max Hastings, *The Korean War* (New York: Simon and Schuster, 1988 [1987].

59. Brian Catchpole, *The Korean War* (New York: Carroll and Graf, 2001), pp. Xiii, 16, 101, 129-134, 271-287.

60. Bevin Alexander, *Korea: The First War We Lost* (New York: Hippercrene, 1993), especially pp. 191, 252.

Chapter One

Should There Be Elections *Only* In South Korea?[1]

I   Western Interests in Korea to 1945

Until 1947, few Canadians had given Korea much thought. Among those whose who had were Christians and Christian missionaries, who served as part of a larger contingent. A monument, erected in 1995 to American missionaries the Rev. and Mrs. Henry G. Appenzeller and the Rev. Horace G. Underwood, stands at Inchon, Seoul's port on the Yellow Sea. A sign indicates that they arrived Easter Sunday 5 April 1885 "to bring the great light of truth the Gospel of Christ." Roman Catholics had been there since the sixteenth century,[2] but Protestants—mainly Presbyterians and Methodists from the United States—had great success. Australian Presbyterians joined them in 1889, Canadian Presbyterians in 1898. Presbyterians from the northern states and from Canada focussed on what would become North Korea, the Americans on Pyongyang itself. By 1937, the United Church of Canada—which in 1925 had inherited the Korean responsibilities of the Presbyterian Church in Canada—had stations in Wonsan, Hamhung, and three other centres in North Korea. After the partition of 1945, many Christians migrated from the Soviet-occupied north to Seoul and other places in the U.S.-occupied zone, south of the 38th parallel.[3] The Australian Presbyterians worked in the Korean southeast, including the city of Pusan. One of the missionaries during the period before World War II was a woman who would be aunt to Sir Robert Menzies, Prime Minister of Australia during the Korean War.[4]

The missionaries did their work well, and Korea quickly became one of their most successful mission fields in Asia. Roman Catholic missionaries from Spain and France had laboured successfully in the Philippines and Vietnam, but the Philippines had been a Spanish possession for almost four centuries, Vietnam a French one for more than nine decades. Protestants established viable communities in India and Hong Kong, both British possessions. Korea, by contrast, was an independent kingdom until occupied by Japan during the Russo-Japanese War of 1904-1905 and annexed by Japan in 1910. Yet the proportion of Koreans who became Christians was without parallel in continental Asia, now roughly half the total population of South Korea.[5] In absolute numbers, India may have as many Christians as South Korea, but on the sub-continent they are a much smaller proportion of the total population. Only the Philippines would have more Christians in proportional terms, but most of those would be Roman Catholic. Korea would be the Asian country with the strongest Protestant tradition. According to historian Kenneth Scott Latourette, by 1914, almost 75% of Korea's Protestants were Presbyterian.[6] Another historian, Stanley Sandler, wrote in 1999 that South Korea had become "the third most committed Christian nation in the world, after the Vatican and the United States."[7] There is strong evidence that Christians relocated in droves from North Korea to South Korea while it was still possible to do so.[8]

Japan's enemies agreed that Japanese rule over Korea would terminate with Japan's defeat. President Franklin D. Roosevelt and British Prime Minister Winston Churchill had agreed on this when they met in Cairo in 1943. U.S., British and Soviet officials confirmed this decision at Potsdam in 1945. Stalin accepted this point when the Soviets declared war on Japan 8 August 1945. As World War II was ending, U.S. and Soviet officials agreed that Japanese forces in Korea would surrender to Soviet forces north of the 38th parallel, U.S. forces to the south.[9] There is no evidence that the location of Christian communities was a consideration in determining the location of the inter-Korean border. Dean Rusk, who would serve as Secretary of State throughout the Kennedy and Johnson administrations, was involved in the process and included an account in his memoirs. Rusk—then a colonel in the United States Army—explained that the State Department, War Department, and Navy Departments of the United States had a Co-ordinating Committee, which used the acronym SWINK. Among its many tasks was one to arrange the surrender of Japanese forces.

According to Rusk, the State Department wanted SWINK to arrange the surrender of Japanese forces in China as far to the north as possible, hopefully within Manchuria itself. However, the U.S. Army, with an eye to its future responsibilities as an occupation force, wanted to avoid the mainland altogether. A compromise resulted. Some U.S. forces would go to one section of Asia's mainland, "a sort of toehold on the Korean peninsula for symbolic purposes." Late in the evening of 14 August 1945, the day of Japan's surrender, Rusk and another army officer, Colonel Charles Bonesteel, studied a map of Korea to determine where the border between the Soviet-occupied and U.S.-occupied zones should be.

Rusk explained:

Neither Tic [Colonel Bonesteel] nor I was a Korea expert, but it seemed to us that Seoul, the capital, should be in the American sector. We also knew that the U.S. Army opposed an extensive area of occupation. Using a *National Geographic* map, we looked just north of Seoul for a convenient dividing line but could not find a natural geographic line. [GSM: There was none.] We saw instead the thirty-eighth parallel and decided to recommend that.[10]

SWINK, and to Rusk's surprise, the Soviets, accepted that recommendation. Given the location of the Soviet and U.S. armies at the time, Rusk thought that the Soviets might have demanded a more southerly location. (The Soviet army was already inside Korea, the American no closer than Okinawa.) Rusk later admitted that this entire "episode had greater significance than we realized at the time."[11] This is understandable. As in Europe, perceived Soviet interests diverged from perceived U.S. interests, and it proved as impossible for the occupying powers to agree on plans for a civilian government for Korea as it was for Germany.

Neither was the missionary presence a matter of much importance to the government of Canada. A memo prepared by the Department of External Affairs for the Canadian delegation of the United Nations in 1947 reviewed missionary accomplishments as it listed "Canadian interests in Korea." The statement did note that since World War II some Canadian missionaries had returned to Korea, but it noted that

so far they have been prevented from visiting their properties in the Soviet zone, where most were located. Unification of Korea would enable these Canadians to return to their pre-war mission stations.[12]

One Presbyterian minister from Korea, the Rev. K.S. Kim, visited Ottawa and met Louis St. Laurent, Canada's Minister of External Affairs, in the summer of 1947, and United Church officials thought that Kim had left a good impression. One found St. Laurent a "charming gentleman [who] gave Dr. Kim his undivided attention, asking many questions about Korea, all sympathetic in nature."[13] Whether memories of Dr. Kim had any impact on St. Laurent in his year-end confrontation with Prime Minister William Lyon Mackenzie King and on St. Laurent's later decision as Prime Minister to send Canadian combat forces into the Korean War is difficult to determine. However, historian Robert Bothwell reflects Conventional Wisdom:

What should be underlined here is that Canada did not participate in the UN expedition to Korea because of any intrinsic concern for Korea and

Koreans, but because of an interest in the UN, first, and in relations with the United States, second. The possibility that Korea was a prelude to a general Communist attack elsewhere on the vast periphery of the Soviet Union was...sufficient to bring the Canadian government to the contemplation of war. But it was the prospect of war in Europe that moved them, and not war on the continent of Asia.[14]

In all probability, Bothwell is right.

Research in Russian archives by Cold War historian Kathryn Weathersby indicates that Stalin sought control of North Korea, not *all* Korea) for economic and security reasons. He wanted access to North Korea's mineral wealth, especially monazite, a commodity useful for making nuclear weapons, and to that end, he stopped the flow of goods across the 38th parallel before he stopped the flow of people. Moreover, he wanted to keep a resurgent Japan or any other conceivable hostile power some distance from Soviet borders. To this end, he needed a friendly régime in North Korea but initially thought he could achieve this "through some sort of joint administration" with the U.S. Weathersby emphasizes that Korea was not Poland, where Stalin sought from the start to monopolize power. When co-operation proved impossible, Stalin quietly began to create a Communist régime for North Korea.[15]

II   The Formation of the United Nations Temporary Commission on Korea

Prodded by the United States, on 14 November 1947 the United Nations General Assembly established a multinational committee, the United Nations Temporary Commission on Korea (UNTCOK), whose task would be to terminate military rule throughout Korea, north and south of the 38th parallel, and establish a civilian authority. Australia and Canada were members of UNTCOK, as were Chiang Kai Shek's Republic of China (which still controlled most of the Chinese mainland), El Salvador, France, newly- independent India, the Philippines, Syria, and the Ukrainian Soviet Socialist Republic. (The Ukrainian Soviet Socialist Republic actually refused to serve on UNTCOK.) In giving formal notice of this development to St. Laurent, his superior, Under-Secretary of State for External Affairs Lester B. Pearson commented, "You will note from the line-up of countries represented on the Commission that Canada and Australia are likely to be expected to play a fairly important part of the work of the Commission..."[16]

In the absence of Prime Minister King—who was attending the wedding of then-Princess Elizabeth (now Queen Elizabeth II) and the Duke of Edinburgh in London—St. Laurent accepted the responsibility. On his return, King strongly disagreed. King, who had served as both Prime Minister and Minister of External Affairs throughout most of the inter-war period, sought to avoid international commitments for fear that they would involve Canada in some distant war. Over the Christmas holiday season, President Harry S. Truman intervened personally.[17] Canada *must* have some talented person who could work with UNTCOK, said a lengthy personal appeal from the State Department to the prime minister, and Canada had historic ties to Asia. The world would regard a Canadian refusal to participate in UNTCOK as a serious vote of non-confidence in the United States.[18]

Writing from notes taken at the time, Pearson noted in his memoirs that the American appeal was, if anything, counterproductive. King was furious.

> He said that if he had had any doubts before about the rightness of the case against Canadian participation in the work of this Commission, those doubts were removed by this communication. It merely confirmed his view that the Commission itself was completely useless, could do nothing to bring about a solution of the Korean problem and...could very definitely cause trouble between the USA and the USSR. He felt that the United States had proposed the establishment of this Commission for the purpose of relieving it of its responsibilities in Korea, and he was determined that Canada should not be a party to any such tactics. He was particularly incensed over the conclusion of...countries like El Salvador and the Philippines. He was convinced that Canada would be expected to take the lead in the work of the Commission and thereby get into most of the trouble.[19]

According to Pearson, King threatened to resign if the Canadian cabinet insisted on UNTCOK participation. Shocked that the Liberal government might disintegrate on such a matter, St. Laurent suggested that Pearson might explain personally to President Truman and Secretary of State George Marshall in Washington, and United Nations Secretary General Trygve Lie in New York, that without Soviet co-operation, UNTCOK was likely to be useless. Pearson went to Washington and met President Truman, but did not persuade him to change his mind. (He did not tell President Truman that the Canadian government might collapse over participation in UNTCOK.) Back in Ottawa, King remained so adamant that St. Laurent threatened that he would resign if Canada withdrew from UNTCOK. After all, he was the one who had initially agreed to Canadian participation. In short order, the two of them arranged a compromise. Canada would remain an UNTCOK member, but the Canadian member would leave the Commission if the Soviets refused to co-operate. Under no circumstances would Canada participate in elections restricted exclusively to the U.S. zone of Korea.

The King-St. Laurent compromise was stillborn, despite St. Laurent's instructions of 8 January 1948 to Dr. George Patterson, Canada's representative on UNTCOK.

> The General Assembly resolution setting up this committee gives the Commission the task to facilitate and expedite the holding of democratic elections in Korea and the establishment of a national government. We interpret this to mean that the elections are to be held for the whole of Korea and the government to be established for the whole of Korea. This necessitates, of course, that the Commission should operate in North Korea as well as South Korea and will require the co-operation of the USSR authorities in the northern zone...Unless some other member does so, you should bring this question up at the first meeting of the Commission which you attend. If the Soviet authorities co-operate, then the Commission can proceed with its work. If the Soviet authorities refuse to co-operate, then you are instructed to support any move on the part of the Commission to return its mandate to the United Nations in view of the impossibility of carrying out that mandate in the whole of Korea. If the Commission refuses to accept this policy, please report to us at once by cable, as you will be instructed, in such circumstances, to withdraw from the Commission and resume your duties in Tokyo.[20]

From his position as an insider, Pearson noted that Soviet co-operation did not materialize. The Canadian government wanted to withdraw Patterson and terminate UNTCOK. It did not do so, but had it done so, U.S. authorities might have been pleased. By mid-February 1948, the U.S. political advisor in Korea was complaining to Washington that Canada, Australia, India, and Syria constituted an "anti-American bloc" on UNTCOK. Both he and Ray Atherton, the U.S. Ambassador in Canada, attributed Canada's position to British influence and the Canadian government's desire to demonstrate to the Canadian electorate that Canada was no lapdog of the United States.[21] From Seoul, Lieutenant-General John R. Hodge, the Military Commander in the U.S. Zone, complained to Secretary of State Marshall that the Canadian and Australian positions were hopelessly naïve. The Canadian-Australian argument that "civil

liberties and freedom in South Korea are not on a par with stable Canada and Australia, therefore it is impossible to hold any elections," failed to take into account Cold
War hostilities, said Hodge.[22] Although Patterson had spent many years in Asia as a
missionary, YMCA official, and diplomat, Hodge labelled him "the number one out-
spoken apologist for Soviet Russia and for communism that I have encountered for
many months."[23] U.S. officials accused Patterson of trying to "sabotage the election in
South Korea."[24] Days later, according to Pearson,

> On 28 February, while Dr Patterson was absent in Japan, UNTCOK de-
> cided that elections should be held in the American zone before 10 May.
> This decision was taken in spite of the fact that Dr Patterson had left his
> telephone number in Japan with the principal secretary of the commission
> and asked that he be called, should any important matter arise.[25]

Why did the Canadian government ignore the King-St. Laurent compromise? Why
did it not order Patterson back to Canada? Pearson explained that the Liberal government allowed Patterson to observe the elections with the understanding that the
sponsor of the elections was the United States, not the United Nations. Nevertheless,
after the fact, UNTCOK voted unanimously that the elections had been "a valid ex-
pression of the free will of the electorate in those parts of Korea which were accessible
to the commission."[26] On the surface, it would appear that the United States had prevailed, and that Canadian opinions, rightly or wrongly, had not mattered at all.

III   UNTCOK's Dilemma

UNTCOK's minutes do not indicate which countries voted which ways on which
resolutions,[27] but enough resolutions passed to indicate that (a) a majority of
UNTCOK members thought elections in South Korea alone were contrary to their
instructions from the United Nations; and (b) conditions in South Korea were hardly
conducive to fair and free voting. Australian documents reveal that Australian authorities *did* co-ordinate their efforts on UNTCOK with those of Canada.[28]

Based in Seoul, site of all its meetings, UNTCOK began its work early in 1948.
At its 2nd meeting, 13 January 1948, delegates voted "that every opportunity be
taken to make it clear *that the sphere of this Commission is the whole of Korea and not
merely a section of Korea.*" [Emphasis: the author's.] At the 4th meeting, 16 January,
the Syrian delegate [*sic*] complained that South Korean authorities were interfering
with journalists. Police had seized issues of three newspapers from newsstands in Seoul and jailed a prominent editor. "It is our job," said the Syrian delegate,

to see to it that a free atmosphere of elections exists before the actual elections are carried out. If we cannot insure this atmosphere, our mission is necessarily a failure.[29]

At UNTCOK's 5th meeting the following day, delegates voted to establish a sub-committee (Sub-Committee I) "to consider ways and means of insuring a free atmosphere of elections in Korea." This was one of three sub-committees created at the 5th and 6th meetings. Australia was a member of Sub-Committee 2, and its envoy, Samuel Henry Jackson, became its chair. The task of Sub-Committee 2 was "To consider ways and means of ensuring a free atmosphere for elections in Korea..."[30] Canada, with France, the Philippines, and Syria, belonged to Sub-Committee 3, which was supposed to examine the compatibility of election laws in North and South Korea with recommendations of the UN General Assembly and "their consistency with democratic practices generally accepted in elections held in territories of Members of the United Nations."[31] Sub-Committee 3 elected Melecio Arranz of the Philippines as its chair, Patterson of Canada as "Rapporteur." (Later El Salvador replaced France, and the Republic of China joined Sub-Committee 3.) As Australia and Canada belonged to different sub-committees, their envoys, Jackson and Patterson respectively, could hardly co-ordinate their strategies.

It was clear from the start that the Soviet Union would not co-operate with UNTCOK. On 16 January, at the 4th meeting, Krishna Menon of India—UNTCOK's acting chair—presented letters which he had written to General Hodge in Seoul and his Soviet counterpart, Major General G.I Shanin, Chief of Staff at Soviet headquarters in Pyongyang. Menon asked both Hodge and Shanin when he might meet them face-to-face. On 28 January, UNTCOK received formal notification from Secretary General Trigve Lie that the Soviet Union would not co-operate. Andrei Gromyko, the Soviet ambassador to the United Nations, had forwarded to Lie a letter from his superiors in Moscow. "We find it necessary," said the letter,

> to remind you of the negative attitude taken by the Soviet Government towards the establishment of the UN Commission on Korea as already stated by the Soviet delegation during the second session of the General Assembly of the United Nations.[32]

That same day, UNTCOK also received formal notification that three days earlier, the Ukrainian ambassador to the United Nations had notified Lie that the Ukrainian Soviet Socialist Republic would not accept membership in UNTCOK, to which the General Assembly had elected it. On 31 January, at its 7th meeting, UNTCOK heard from Brigadier General John Weckerling of the U.S. Army that Shanin and the Soviet High Command in Pyongyang had refused to accept Menon's letter. Shanin told a Major Costello, the U.S. Liaison Officer in Pyongyang, that although the unification of Korea remained a possibility, UNTCOK was irrelevant to the process. Instead, U.S. Secretary of State George Marshall and Soviet Foreign Minister Vyacheslav Molotov should settle the issue on a bilateral basis. The preamble to a resolution adopted at UNTCOK's 11th meeting, 6 February 1948, noted "THAT the negative attitude of the Soviet authorities with regard to the work of the Commission has made it clear that it will not be possible for the Commission to exercise, for the time being, the functions conferred upon it by the General Assembly under the Resolution of 14 January 1947 in the part of Korea occupied by the armed forces of the USSR..."

Meanwhile, South Korean police continued to act in a manner unacceptable to UNTCOK. On 27 February, they arrested Chung Wo Ik, who was distributing leaflets near Seoul's Duk Soo Palace, UNTCOK's headquarters. UNTCOK protested to Hodge, who replied:

> Chung Wo Ik was detained at Duk Soo Palace because of the possession of some 1500 hand bills deemed by the police to be subversive. He was released the same day after examination of hand bills by responsible authority. After release, he was later arrested by police from another precinct who had been hunting him for subversive offenses since January. He was tried and sentenced to 30 days confinement for the January offense. Although investigation indicates that the entire action of the police was *bona fide* and in good faith, I have directed that Chung Wo Ik be released under suspended sentence.[33]

Hodge added that in accord with UNTCOK's wishes, he had taken action to prevent further arrests of peaceful protesters near Duk Soo Palace. Yet, Hodge noted, "it is becoming more difficult in the face of increasing attacks on police boxes and mounting toll of police deaths at the hands of Communist inspired mobs to convince police patrolmen that the Communist agitators have [a] legal right to stir up trouble..."[34]

Soon, Hodge and UNTCOK would express total disagreement over what might constitute acceptable conditions for fair and free elections. On 17 March, at its 26th meeting, UNTCOK noted that South Korean authorities had refused to provide Sub-Committee 2 with a list of political prisoners, despite a request from Sub-Committee 2. UNTCOK as a whole (not simply Sub-Committee 2) then voted:

> 21. It is the opinion of the Commission that participating in illegal meetings, [and] distributing handbills, unless accompanied by criminal act or

incitement to criminal acts, are to be considered as political [rather than criminal] offenses...

23. The Commisson recommends to the authorities that those who were imprisoned for political offenses...should be released without any reservation...[35]

Hodge responded angrily to Jean-Louis Paul-Boncour, the French diplomat who by then had replaced Menon as UNTCOK's chair:

I note with regret that the United Nations Temporary Commission on Korea...has chosen completely to ignore any recognition of or make recommendations pertaining to the most dangerous element to the holding of free elections in South Korea. This element is the Kremlin directed Communist effort to force the UN Commission out of Korea and to destroy all chance of holding elections or maintaining any other democratic processes in South Korea.[36]

While the Soviets wanted UNTCOK to cease its work and disband, U.S. authorities wanted it to add respectability to the U.S. agenda for Korea. UNTCOK as a whole went along with this.

Whether it should have done so was a matter of considerable debate. At UNTCOK's 8th meeting, 4 February 1948, Paul-Boncour wondered whether, given the Soviet refusal to co-operate, UNTCOK should disband.[37] The following day at the 9th meeting, Patterson thought that the Soviet refusal was so unequivocal that UNTCOK had no alternative but to seek new instructions from the United Nations. As far as he was concerned, UNTCOK's existing mandate—to arrange elections throughout Korea—was impossible. Jackson said that as Chair of Sub-Committee 2, he had not wanted to say what Patterson had just said, but that he had been waiting for somebody else to say exactly that. (While it is not altogether clear, the text appears to indicate that Jackson prodded Patterson through a series of questions into saying what he said, and that the two men had not co-ordinated strategy before the meeting.) Jackson then explained why he thought that elections organized by the United Nations and limited to South Korea would be counter-productive. Such elections would lead to the permanent division of Korea, and they would be taking place in an environment where the police had too much authority. They would remain a law unto themselves after any elections.

Still, if the General Assembly or its Interim Committee desired, Jackson was willing to consider ideas forwarded by the delegates of the Philippines and Nationalist

China. UNTCOK might say that it was organizing elections for all Korea but, for the moment could organize them exclusively in the south. Given that two-thirds of the population lived in the south, one-third of the positions in the Korean Congress would remain vacant, but South Koreans could vote for the other-two thirds. Paul-Boncour praised this idea. Patterson did not.

Divisions with UNTCOK bore no relationship to Commonwealth membership. Valle of El Salvador and Luna of the Philippines thought that Jackson's ideas had merit, although Liu from the Republic of China had some reservations. Liu had even stronger reservations about what he called the Canadian government's "passive attitude," a point on which he sparred at some length with Patterson. Finally Menon, as Chair expressed total disagreement with Patterson. If free and fair elections really were possible, Menon said,

> I would support the idea of having elections in South Korea alone...
>
> The Chairman of Sub-Committee 2 [Jackson] may say that this is against the view expressed by the majority of the people who appeared before him, but I feel that many of these people...would probably agree to elections in South Korea alone, if they could be assured that there was a possibility of a free election for the purpose of consultation...I believe that when the results of this election are known, the leaders who have come out of this election will make an attempt to get into touch with the leaders of the North. In other words, it may facilitate a rapprochement between the leaders who come out on top as a result of the elections in South Korea and the men in North Korea...[38]

One Australian historian attributes Menon's views to his "passionate attachment to a Korean woman poet."[39]

Patterson was by no means alone. Despite his bitter words at the 12th meeting of UNTCOK on 11 February 1948 that "my opinion is not worth much, nor, if I may so, is the opinion of the Commission as a whole," there were people who agreed with him, some of them within the Commonwealth. Patterson said that he found himself "in complete agreement" with the stated position of Luna of the Philippines, and Jackson declared that his position was "similar to that of the representative of Canada..." Menon said that he could understand Patterson's concern about Soviet-American differences:

> I can well understand his [Patterson's] point of view because there is this talk of what is going on between the USA and the USSR, and even if the

USA takes the attitude of "Go to Hell" toward the USSR, it is for other countries like Canada to try and do nothing which will increase the tension...[40]

For his part, Patterson managed to find some common ground with Dr. Liu, and Syria's Dr. Djabi expressed partial agreement. His position was "that the elections should be national ones for the whole of Korea" until and unless the Interim Committee decided otherwise. Menon, Patterson, and Jackson—all of whom were fluent in English—played a major role in selecting the words of the resolution which they would send to Lake Placid, temporary headquarters of the United Nations while construction continued on the site in New York.[41]

When the Interim Committee did indicate that elections in South Korea alone were preferable to no elections at all, both Jackson and Patterson expressed displeasure. Those instructions, said Jackson, "came as a surprise." Canberra thought that co-operation with the Soviet Union was not totally impossible. Under the circumstances, "Nothing should be done to widen the breech between North and South while further efforts were being made to secure USSR co-operation...

Australia's views have not changed and I must therefore vote against any proposal by this Commission to observe elections in South Korea alone...

Patterson agreed with the Interim Committee that South Korea needed a government, but he thought that if the elections were to take place exclusively in the U.S. zone of occupation, the U.S. could organize those elections. The United Nations should remain available for the day when the Soviet position might change, but it should not jeopardize the future by participating in elections limited to the south. Patterson wanted to build upon what the Australian envoy at Lake Placid had said:

The delegate from Australia to the Interim Committee suggested that it might be announced immediately that when conditions permit, an election for limited purposes of consultation might be held...I wonder if that could be broadened to an announcement that the Commission [UNTCOK] will stand by and be prepared to carry out the complete programme if conditions permit.

The third alternative would be as suggested by the representative of Australia to the Interim Committee to remain in order to seize every opportunity of fulfilling its task...

The Canadian Government would hope that the Commission would make a further effort to explore these possibilities before taking a decision to proceed with the implementation of the programme in South Korea alone.[42]

On 13 March, 1948, UNTCOK voted by the narrowest of margins to proceed with elections inside South Korea alone. In the absence of the Ukrainian Soviet Socialist Republic, the vote was four in favour (India, Chiang's China, El Salvador, and the Philippines), two abstentions (France and Syria), two opposed (Australia and Canada).[43] Menon and three states heavily influenced by the U.S. carried the day. In a subsequent vote on 4 May, Jackson voted with the four, and UNTCOK determined to proceed by majority vote. An official at Australia's Department of External Affairs back in Canberra referred to Jackson's vote as "a little surprising,"[44] and within weeks, the Chifley government recalled Jackson and replaced him with A.B. Jamieson. One of Canberra's first messages to Jamieson was, "You should keep in close touch with Canadian representative."[45]

Clearly, divisions within UNTCOK did not fall along Commonwealth versus non-Commonwealth lines. Within UNTCOK there was a consensus that its mandate was to arrange and supervise elections throughout Korea. Menon of India thought that, in the absence of Soviet co-operation, UNTCOK should supervise elections exclusively in South Korea. In that, his position was closer to that of the United States than were those of Australia and Canada. Australian and Canadian officials thought that it would be a mistake for the United Nations to sponsor elections exclusively in the south, but like most other members of UNTCOK, the Australians would defer to the wisdom of the Interim Committee at Lake Placid. The Canadian government and its representative, George Patterson, had even stronger doubts. Commonwealth delegates to UNTCOK—Menon, Jackson, and Patterson—unable to agree among themselves, were hardly in a position to influence other members of UNTCOK to pursue one particular course of action.

IV   A Review of U.S.-Australian Relations

For its part, Australia had a Labour government, led by Joseph Benedict Chifley. His Minister of External Affairs was Herbert Vere Evatt. During the Chifley/Evatt years, Australia's foreign policies were more antithetical toward those of the United States than at any time since the Japanese air force attacked Pearl Harbor—except, perhaps, for the brief period when another Labour Prime Minister, Gough Whitlam, was Australia's head of government (1972-1975). Evatt was a proud Australian who envisioned an alliance of two equally important partners, Australia and the United States. The Truman administration saw Australia as, at best, a very junior partner.

Chifley had become prime minister in 1945 when his predecessor, another Labour Prime Minister, John Curtin (1941-1945), died in office. Evatt had also served as Minister of External Affairs under Curtin, whose doubts about the United States extended back to 1942. At that time, Evatt and Curtin discovered to their horror that the United States was planning to give the war against Germany priority over the war against Japan. From Washington's perspective, it made sense to defeat Germany quickly, before Hitler's scientists developed nuclear weapons, then worry about Japan. To Curtin and Evatt, who knew nothing about nuclear weapons, Japan—the country which had attacked the United States and then sent its armed forces towards the shores of Australia—was a more immediate threat to their homeland than was Germany.

Other problems developed, even while World War II was in full fury. Frank Knox, U.S. Secretary of the Navy, suggested that when the war ended, the U.S. might want to acquire islands currently part of the British Commonwealth or former German islands of the Pacific mandated to Japan by the League of Nations after World War I. Evatt persuaded the government of New Zealand to issue a joint statement that the Australian and New Zealand governments both should have the right to veto any changes of sovereignty south of the equator in any of the former colonial possessions. For various reasons, including a rather difficult personality, U.S. officialdom tended to blame Evatt rather than New Zealanders for extraterritorial ambitions.

After the war, Evatt promoted the idea of a U.S.-Australian military alliance before the Truman administration was ready for one. The U.S. Navy was considering a naval base at Manus, an island in the Australian-mandated Admiralty Group, but Evatt imposed a condition. As a symbol of Australia's "equality," the Royal Australian Navy must have reciprocal facilities in U.S. ports. The U.S. government then killed the idea of the Manus base. Evatt wanted the peace treaty between the U.S. and Thailand to include a clause which forbade Thailand from establishing a formal commercial arrangement with any other country unless Australia had the right to participate. He told John R. Minter, chargé d'affaires at the U.S. legation in Canberra, that he considered U.S. involvement in Thailand as an unfriendly act. This was very strong language, comparable to that used by President James Monroe in 1823 as he warned the Holy Alliance not to establish new colonies in Latin America. The Truman administration rejected the Australian warnings, concluded its peace treaty with Thailand, and heeded the warnings of Dean Acheson, then Assistant-Secretary of State but the one who would serve as Secretary of State during Truman's second term (1949-1953), not to establish a bilateral U.S.-Australian military alliance.

Evatt and the Truman administration disagreed on the reconstruction of Japan. To official Washington, Japan was a potential Cold War ally. To official Canberra, Japan was the greatest potential security threat facing Australia. As *de facto* head of government in post-war Japan, General Douglas MacArthur permitted Japanese whalers to go to the Antarctic in 1946-1947. Evatt complained that MacArthur had allowed this without consulting Australia, an interested party, a charge various U.S. authorities denied. Secretary of State George Marshall (1956-1949) wanted the Japanese economy to recover and serve the interests of the Free World. Evatt was happy to see Japan remain, if not destitute, then close to it, without the capacity to wage war.

There were other problems. The CIA, established in 1947, regarded Evatt as "soft on Communism." In 1946, Australia and the United States upgraded their legations to embassy levels. (Canada had upgraded its legation in Washington to embassy level in 1944.) Australia appointed a veteran diplomat, Norman J. Makin, as its ambassador in Washington, but the U.S. appointed a businessman inexperienced in diplomacy, Robert Butler, to Canberra. The successor to the unpopular (among Australians) Butler was Myron M. Cowen, another businessman, who insulted Australians by asking for a transfer from Canberra to Manila (to head the U.S. embassy in the Philippines) before his term in Australia had expired. When he became Secretary of State in 1949, Dean Acheson strongly rejected Evatt's suggestion that Australia had an automatic right to attend international meetings on Pacific matters.[46]

On 18 August 1948, *after* UNTCOK had completed its work and South Korea's elections had taken place, a State Department official (or multiple State Department officials) prepared a Policy Statement on U.S.-Australian relations. The Statement noted Australia's "very independent line in UN affairs" and found the Australian delegation "sometimes troublesome in debate." Regarding External Affairs Minister Evatt, the Statement said:

> He vigorously opposes the veto; plays a self-appointed role as spokesman of
> the small and middle powers; and has sought to strengthen the General
> Assembly as against the Security Council.

Over the past months, the Statement noted, Evatt had been less inclined to support U.S. and British positions, more inclined to play "the more neutral role of mediator." A list of examples followed:

Evidence of this may be seen in a number of cases during the last General Assembly during which he refused to cooperate with us in rejecting the Soviet "war-mongering" resolution, was hostile to the establishment and work of the Temporary Commission on Korea [UNTCOK], and lukewarm towards the establishment of the Interim Committee [on Korea] of the Assembly. Australian members on UNSCOB [United Nations Special Commission on the Balkans] also displayed an obstructionist attitude. To the extent that this tendency on the part of Australia serves to weaken the democratic front, it has and will prove [sic] embarrassing to us.[47]

V   Canada and Australia as Members of UNTCOK

Canadian Prime Minister King then was too isolationist for the Truman administration, Australian External Affairs Minister Evatt too nationalistic, or, in the language of the aforementioned State Department Statement, consumed with his own "egotism."[48] Ironically, Evatt might have been somewhat responsible for the appointment of both Canada and Australia to UNTCOK. A memo of 20 December 1947 prepared for the Canadian cabinet explains why both Canada and Australia became UNTCOK members. On 17 September 1947, Secretary of State George Marshall had indicated that the Truman administration would ask for the assistance of the United Nations General Assembly in restoring civilian government to Korea. Shortly thereafter, the State Department delivered a document entitled "Achievement of Korean Independence" to the Canadian delegation at the United Nations. The document reminded those who read it of Canadian missionary, commercial, and strategic interests in Korea. The Australian delegation proposed that all member countries of the Far East Commission, an advisory body consisting of those countries which had helped to defeat Japan, should become members of UNTCOK. The Truman administration did not want to link the future of Korea with developments in Japan and suggested a compromise between the Australian proposal and its own preference based largely on geographical considerations. Either way, Canada appeared as a possible member. It had fought Japan, and it had a presence on the North Pacific. Moreover, the Canadian delegation had persuaded the Americans not to nominate Canada to the UN's Balkan Commission, and it had refused categorically to serve on the Palestine Commission. If Canada wished to maintain good relations with the United States, it could not continue with unlimited refusals, especially in an area of vital concern like the North Pacific. Despite Canadian attempts to stay off the list, the U.S. delegate to the United Nations, John Foster Dulles (who would serve as

Secretary of State for most of Eisenhower's presidency) made a public announcement that Canada would participate in UNTCOK. A refusal at that point would have been difficult and embarrassing. Arguably, said the writers of the 20 December memo, there might be advantages to UNTCOK membership. The work would not be onerous; it would be temporary; and it would not involve many Canadians. The United Nations would pay the bills—an important consideration as long as Mackenzie King remained prime minister. Moreover, the Canadian members of UNTCOK might be in a position to assist Canadian interests. The United Church of Canada had asked for Ottawa's help in arranging visits by two missionaries currently in South Korea to properties which it had owned north of the 38th parallel until Pearl Harbor. There might be commercial opportunities for Canada in Korea. "The work of this Commission is the least onerous of any of the three which were established at the last session of the General Assembly."[49]

In contrast to Canada, Australia joined UNTCOK willingly. One commentator has written:

> Australia had several motives for joining the Commission: External Affairs Minister Evatt was pursuing a policy of the fullest support for the United Nations in world affairs; Australia was concerned to promote American involvement in the Pacific and East Asia; and events in Korea had potential to influence the Japanese peace settlement in which Australia was acutely interested.[50]

Once UNTCOK had done its work and disbanded, Australia—unlike Canada—served on the two successor commissions, the United Nations Commission on Korea (UNCOK, 1948-1950) and the United Nations Commission for the Unification and Rehabilitation of Korea (UNCURK, from 1950). UNCOK's membership was that of UNTCOK, minus Canada, India and the Ukrainian Soviet Socialist Republic;[51] UNCURK included Australia, Chile, the Netherlands, Pakistan, the Philippines, Thailand, and Turkey.[52]

For both Canadian and Australian authorities, the experience on UNTCOK was not a happy one. Rather, it was one prolonged battle with representatives of the United States.[53] The Australians too had reservations about restricting their work to South Korea. An internal memo of the Australian Department of External Affairs dated 17 December 1947 warned:

> There is a *danger* [emphasis the author's] that, in the event of Soviet refusal to co-operate, the Commission will attempt to put the [General] Assembly's proposals into effect in the Southern Zone only, thereby perpetuating

the division of Korea...It is suggested that, if the Commission [UNTCOK] finds it impossible to work on a national basis, it should report to the [United Nations] Interim Committee before proceeding with action in the Southern Zone, which might prejudice the attainment of eventual unity. The Australian representative might be instructed to this effect.[54]

Yet, despite their common concern about elections limited to South Korea, Canada and Australia did not form an bilateral Commonwealth alliance within UNTCOK. On at least one occasion, they were at odds with each other. On 24 February 1948, Pearson was attending a meeting of the United Nations Interim Committee in connection with UNTCOK. He indicated his intention to oppose pending resolutions from both the United States and Australia, "even if he is a minority of one." If the Australian proposal went forward as an amendment to the U.S. proposal, he would support it "on the ground that it is less objectionable than the original United States proposal," then, even if the amendment carried, vote against the motion as a whole.[55] Pearson complained that eight of the ten speakers had agreed with the United States that elections in South Korea alone were better than none at all. The Australian delegate—the only one other than himself to disagree—thought that Canada went too far in its "all or nothing" approach. If it was impossible to work with the Soviets and to arrange elections in North Korea, said the Australian, South Koreans should choose an "Assembly of Korean representatives...who would consult with the Commission [UNTCOK] in regard to future developments. Delegates from Argentina, Bolivia, Brazil, Chiang Kai Shek's China, Ecuador, El Salvador, Greece, and Turkey agreed with the United States.[56] St. Laurent confirmed to Pearson that Prime Minister King thought that he should vote as he had thought he should—against both U.S. and Australian proposals, in favour of the Australian proposal if it went forward as an amendment, then against the U.S. resolution whether amended or not.[57]

In March, the Interim Committee voted by a margin of 31:2 (Australia and Canada) with 11 abstentions to support the U.S. contention that elections in South Korea alone were compatible with the UN General Assembly resolution of 14 November 1947. Historian William Stueck says that the U.S. had lobbied successfully and that the Communist takeover of Czechoslovakia early in 1948 had had a frightening impact.[58] In the aftermath of that defeat, the Australian delegation said that it would nevertheless accept the will of the majority and called upon Canada to do likewise.[59] Commonwealth foreign ministers met in Paris 29 September 1948 to discuss Korea, as did the prime ministers in London the following month,[60] but by then UNTCOK had done its work and disbanded.

According to historian Anthony Farrar-Hockley, the governments of Canada and Australia reflected British policy, while other UNTCOK members agreed with the U.S. position—the one which prevailed.[61] Surely Farrar-Hockley erred. Canadian and Australian sources do not support his contention, and given the nationalism of such personalities as St. Laurent and Evatt, British influence is highly doubtful. Moreover, on 25 February 1948, the Australian delegation to the United Nations informed Canberra that the United Kingdom definitely would support the U.S. position in favour of elections limited to South Korea, as in all probability would New Zealand.[62]

VI The Aftermath of UNTCOK-Sponsored Elections in South Korea

Historians cannot with confidence declare what would have happened under different circumstances. One cannot say for certain that if UNTCOK and the United Nations Interim Committee had listened to Ottawa and Canberra, there would have been no Korean War. If military government had lasted beyond Stalin's death in 1953, would Stalin's successors have agreed to an arrangement like that which they accepted for Austria in 1955? Would a government (like Austria's) without commitments to either Cold War bloc have proven acceptable to Stalin's successors? No one can say for certain. Korea, unlike Austria, shared a common border with the Soviet Union. Korea, unlike Austria, had a substantial Soviet-trained group of ambitious people.[63] The USSR *did* tolerate a neutral, non-Communist Finland on its borders.

Nevertheless, with benefit of hindsight and access to Soviet archives, it is clear that elections limited to South Korea alone did set the stage for the Korean War. UNTCOK-sponsored elections south of latitude 38 led to the assumption of office by Syngman Rhee as President of the Republic of Korea (ROK), the official name for South Korea. (Korean surnames precede given names. Syngman Rhee is unusual in this respect because he had lived many years in the United States.) By one estimate, 323 South Koreans died and another 10,000 were arrested during the elections of 10 May 1948.[64] Another scholar estimates 589 deaths.[65] The ROK capital would be Seoul, capital of the Kingdom of Korea extinguished earlier in the century.

Later in 1948, within months of Rhee's inauguration, the Soviets countered with the proclamation in Pyongyang of the Democratic People's Republic of Korea (DPRK), led by Kim Il Sung, a Pyongyang-born Soviet-trained Communist. In March 1949, Kim travelled by train to Moscow and had talks with Stalin. Kim requested economic aid for North Korea and described North Korea's economic needs. He also discussed North Korea's ability to defend itself against an attack launched from South Korea. Kim told Stalin that North Korean subversives were infiltrating South Korea's army but had not yet revealed themselves. Stalin agreed that it would be premature to do so. Both assumed that South Korean subversives were likewise infiltrating the North Korean army. The U.S. and the Soviets withdrew their forces from their respective zones. Opportunities to restrain their respective allies diminished with their withdrawal.

According to Farrar-Hockley, a second difference of opinion over Korea arose at this point. The Truman administration agreed with Syngman Rhee's claim to be president of all Korea, head of Korea's only legitimate government. The British Foreign Office feared that such an assertion on the part of Rhee would lead Kim Il Sung to make a similar counter-claim.[66] Indeed, that is exactly what did happen. Whether Kim would have shown greater restraint without Rhee's provocation is unclear. North Korean archives, other than those captured during the United Nations occupation of Pyongyang in the autumn of 1950, remain closed. However, it was a fear worthy of consideration, one supported by the governments of Australia, Canada, New Zealand, South Africa, and India. In view of this stand from the Commonwealth, the Truman administration softened a proposal which it was planning to submit to the General Assembly of the United Nations:

> The Government of the Republic of Korea which has come into existence at Seoul is entitled to be regarded as the Government of Korea envisaged in the [General Assembly] Resolution of November 14, 1947; and...it functions as such with respect to those parts of Korea where the Commission [UNTCOK] was in a position to observe elections.[67]

The Attlee government would have preferred no such proposal at all but was willing to support this amended version,[68] which the General Assembly endorsed 12 December 1948 by a margin of 48:6:1. All five Soviet-bloc delegations voted in the negative, as did Yugoslavia, while Sweden abstained.[69] At the same time, the General Assembly buried UNTCOK and created a successor to oversee Korean-related issues, the United Nations Commission on Korea (UNCOK).[70]

Stalin and Kim discussed clashes along the inter-Korean border. "Is it true," asked Stalin, "that several points have fallen to the southerners and have been seized, and then these points were taken back?" Kim confirmed that South Koreans had managed to capture a small part of Kangwon province, whose police "were not sufficiently armed at the time" and to hold it until the arrival of "regular units" of the North Korean army. Stalin asked whether the southerners then left voluntarily, and Kim replied in the negative. The North Korean army had fought a battle and ejected them.[71] Cold War historians Vladislav Zubok and Constantine Pleshakov say that Stalin agreed at once to strengthen Kim's armed forces and poured military equipment into North Korea.[72]

On 3 September the same year, Mun Il—Kim Il Sung's personal secretary—went to the Soviet Embassy in Pyongyang, North Korea's capital, and told Soviet Ambassador Terenty Shtykov of intelligence which Kim's government had received. According to Mun Il, South Koreans were planning to seize the North Korean part of the Ongjin Peninsula—a tongue of land which extends southward from the North Korean mainland across the 38th parallel. That part of the peninsula south of the parallel was South Korean territory, without land connections to the rest of South Korea. Mun Il added that the South Koreans also planned "to bombard the cement plant in the city of Kaisiu." Under the circumstances, Kim wanted Soviet permission to seize the South Korean portion of the Ongjin Peninsula and adjacent territory as far as Kaesong, "so as to shorten the line of defense." Shtykov warned Mun Il that this was a very serious matter which required some thought. To Soviet Foreign Minister Andrei Vyshinsky, Shtykov forwarded Mun Il's evidence. Shtykov believed that North Koreans really did

> seize an order to the [South Korean] commander of troops on the Ongjin peninsula to begin artillery fire on the cement plant in Kaisiu on September 2 at 8:00 and to destroy it. From the order it is clear that the southerners consider this plant to be military.[73]

Shtykov noted, however, that the time for the attack had passed and that nothing had happened. North Koreans, continued Shytov, had made the necessary preparations to defend the cement factory if the South Koreans should attack. Reports of the alleged South Korean plans to "seize" the North Korean portion of the Ongjin Peninsula came from South Korean deserters, said Shtykov, with the implication that these were unreliable. The area along the border had been quiet since 15 August.[74]

There is little reason to doubt Shtykov. That border raids were taking place is clear. In 1999, the present author passed through Munsan in South Korea, just south of the Demilitarized Zone. There were monuments in Munsan to South Korean patriots who had died fighting the Communists in 1948 and 1949. On 22 February 1949, the Rev. D.H. Gallagher of the United Church of Canada received a letter from one of the Church's missionaries in Seoul. "There are small across-the-border raids all the time," said the letter writer, "but not yet enough to cause the missionaries from Kaesong to move south, and that town is just a couple of miles from the border."[75] Shtykov was certainly not going out of his way to invent a pretext for war.

Andrei Gromyko, then first deputy minister of foreign affairs of the USSR, replied more than a week later with a list of questions. How strong was South Korea's army? What would be the reaction if North Koreans launched an attack? Did U.S. forces remain in South Korea, and what would Americans do? What was the capacity of the North Korean army?[76] Soviet officials obviously were not in a hurry to take action. An official at the Soviet embassy in Pyongyang, not Shtykov himself—as one would expect in a critical situation—advised that there would not be much assistance from China if the North Koreans launched a pre-emptive strike. Mao Zedong's People's Liberation Army had not yet destroyed Chiang Kai Shek and the Republic of China, and Mao had warned that he had higher priorities than a war to help foreign Communists in Korea. Tunkin, the Soviet official, said that Kim realized that a prolonged civil war would not be to his advantage and that a "rapid victory" was far from guaranteed. Hence, Tunkin continued, Kim did not want to launch a civil war

> but only to secure the Ongjin peninsula and a portion of the territory of
> South Korea to the east of this peninsula...[77]

In the event of a civil war, said Tunkin, Kim expected the U.S. to send Chinese and Japanese soldiers to assist the South Koreans, to commit the U.S. Air Force and the U.S. Navy to the defence of South Korea, and to send military instructors to the South Korean army.

Even Kim realized, concluded Tunkin, that a pre-emptive strike on and around the Ongjin Peninsula could lead to civil war. "We [at the Soviet Embassy in Pyongyang] propose that this is not advisable." Tunkin said categorically that the North Korean army was incapable of a swift, decisive victory. The U.S. might use a protracted war "for purposes of agitation against the Soviet Union and for further inflaming war hysteria." Even if Kim's army managed to capture the territory which it wanted, the world would accuse North Korea of risking "a fratricidal war," and the U.S. would have a pretext to become more deeply involved in South Korea. Tunkin concluded: "We [at the Soviet Embassy in Pyongyang] propose that...to begin the partial operation conceived by Kim Il Sung is inadvisable."[78]

The Politburo in Moscow accepted Tunkin's advice. Ten days later, it agreed that an attack on South Korea would be premature.

> As concerns a partial operation to seize Ongjin peninsula and the region of
> Kaesong, as a result of which the borders of North Korea would be moved
> almost to Seoul itself, it is impossible to view this operation other than as
> the beginning of a war between North and south Korea, for which North
> Korea is not prepared either militarily or politically...[79]

One week later, on 1 October 1949, the world changed when a triumphant Mao Zedong stood in Tiananmen Square in the centre of Beijing and proclaimed the People's Republic of China. Mao had conquered the mainland, although not Taiwan and other islands off China's south and east coasts. Early in 1950, Shtykov attended a farewell party for North Korean diplomat Yi Chu Yon, who was departing for Beijing as North Korea's ambassador. The drinks flowed freely, and so did conversation. Since much of it was in Chinese or Korean, Shtykov was not able to follow all of it, but he believed that he understood the essence of the conversations, and when Chinese and North Korean officials wanted him to understand, they spoke Russian. Evidently Mao's triumph had been an inspiration.

Shtykov wrote to Vyshinsky, "After the luncheon Kim Il Sung was in a mood of some intoxication." In that condition, he said what Shtykov thought he had long been wanting to say. He wanted to attack South Korea, and Stalin had stopped him from doing so. If Syngman Rhee would attack the North, Stalin would support Kim in a counter-offensive. Unfortunately, Rhee was "still not instigating an attack." The reunification of Korea and the "liberation" of the south would have to wait, and that was not right. Mao, said Kim, had promised military assistance as soon as the unification of China was complete. Under the circumstances, he would like to see Stalin once more. Turning to Shtykov, Kim asked why the Soviet ambassador did not let him attack the Ongjin Peninsula. The North Korean army, said Kim, "could take [the peninsula] in three days, and with a general attack could be in Seoul in several days." Shtykov tried to dampen Kim's enthusiasm.[80]

Six days later, Stalin himself wrote to Shtykov. Stalin had his doubts, but he was willing to talk to Kim once again:

> I understand the dissatisfaction of Comrade Kim Il Sung, but he must understand that such a large matter in regard to South Korea such as he wants to undertake needs large preparation. The matter must be organized so that there would not be too great a risk. If he wants to discuss the matter with me, then I will always be ready to receive him and discuss with him. Transmit all this to Kim Il Sung and tell him that I am ready to help him in this matter.[81]

Stalin evidently felt that this time he was in a position to give Kim more than a categorical refusal. The crisis of the Berlin Blockade had ended, and the USSR had successfully tested a nuclear weapon. Even more important, Mao had triumphed on the Chinese mainland.

Historian Shen Zhihua has made an extensive study of Soviet documents relevant to the outbreak of the Korean War, and he says that Stalin was not altogether happy about this last development. As long as Chiang Kai Shek's government controlled China, the Soviet Union benefited from a bilateral Sino-Soviet treaty which the governments of Stalin and Chiang had concluded in 1945. That treaty allowed Soviet forces to occupy part of Manchuria, most notably its ice-free port of Lushun. It also allowed Soviet control of the Chinese Eastern Railroad, which linked Lushun with the USSR. The Soviet Union had no ice free ports of its own on the Pacific. Mao's government insisted on a new Sino-Soviet treaty which would end these privileges. Once Mao and Stalin met face to face at a series of meetings during December 1949 and January 1950, Stalin became aware of the seriousness of Mao's demands. Late in January, he accepted them.

The loss of these privileges in Manchuria jeopardized Soviet interests in northeast Asia. Mao resented Soviet support for anti-Chinese Muslim nationalists in Xinjiang, and the two governments disagreed over China's right to own Outer Mongolia. Despite its commitment to leave Manchuria, the USSR had an imperialist record there. Stalin wanted ice-free ports which he could control, and Inchon and Pusan in South Korea appeared as alternatives to Lushun. Moreover, Kim Il Sung would be more dependent on Stalin than Mao was or was likely to be. Suddenly, a North Korean invasion of South Korea seemed a good idea, especially as Acheson had publicly declared that South Korea was outside the U.S. defence perimeter. Shtykov had come to see merit in a North Korean invasion of South Korea before Stalin or Tunkin did, and he certainly did not object. Stalin saw this as a win/win situation for himself, even if the United States and South Korea managed to defeat North Korea. In that eventuality, Mao would want Soviet forces to remain in Lushun, from which the new Sino-Soviet treaty of 1950 did not require their withdrawal before a peace treaty with Japan was in place.[82]

On 9 March, through Shtykov, Kim Il Sung sent to Moscow a shopping list of military equipment which he wanted. On 18 March, Stalin replied that he would "satisfy fully this request of yours."[83] In April, Kim made a second visit to Moscow. Records of that visit are unavailable,[84] but in its aftermath, North Korea and the USSR prepared for war. In the words of Ambassador Shtykov:

> The concentration of the People's Army [i.e., the North Korean Army] near the 38th parallel began on June 12 and was concluded on June 23, as was prescribed in the plan of the General Staff. The redeployment of troops took place in an orderly fashion, without incident...

The planning of the operation at the divisional level and the reconnaissance of the area was carried out with the participation of Soviet advisers.

All preparatory measures for the operation were completed by June 24th. On June 24th divisional commanders were given orders about "D" [day] and "H" [hour].

The political order of the Minister of Defense was read to the troops, which explained that the South Korean army had provoked a military attack by violating the 38th parallel and that the government of the DPRK [Democratic People's Republic of Korea; i.e., North Korea] had given an order to the Korean People's Army [the North Korean army] to go over to the counterattack.

The order to counter-attack was met with great enthusiasm by the soldiers and officers of the Korean People's Army.

The troops went to their starting positions by 24:00 hours on June 24th. Military operations began at 4 hours 40 minutes local time...[85]

North Korea's invasion of South Korea had taken place. The Korean War had begun. The Soviet Union supplied North Korea with military equipment. Seoul's War Museum proudly displays a Soviet tank captured during the Korean War. Before the war ended, almost one and one-half million people on both sides, soldiers and civilians, would die. An even larger number suffered injuries.[86] The Cold War in Europe would also intensify as Canadian soldiers returned to Europe for the first time since World War II and the countries which had fought Germany during that war arranged for the creation of a German army in the non-communist part of Germany and the admission of the Federal Republic of Germany into full NATO membership.

VII Reactions to North Korea's Invasion of South Korea

Any Western leader old enough to hold office in 1950 was old enough to remember the 1930s. In 1931, Imperial Japan marched into Manchuria, Chinese territory. The world voiced displeasure, and the United States failed to recognize the conquest, but did little more. The Japanese military machine continued to advance into China and then into China's neighbours, all the way to New Guinea north of Australia. Four years later, Mussolini's Italy invaded Ethiopia, a member of the League of Nations which other nations had military commitments to defend under Article X of the League of Nations Charter. They failed to do more than protest and impose tolerable sanctions, and Mussolini decided that he could invade such neighbours as France, Albania, and Greece. Early in 1938, Hitler annexed Austria, a German-speaking nation. Later that year he prepared to invade Czechoslovakia, ostensibly to liberate German-speaking people who lived in that part of Czechoslovakia called the Sudetenland. British Prime Minister Neville Chamberlain and French Prime Minister Edouard Daladier—the last despite French military commitments to Czechoslovakia—let him do so in order to preserve the peace. The Sudentenland, Hitler assured Chamberlain, would be his final territorial demand. Six months later, Hitler exploited the geographical advantage which control of the Sudetenland gave him and annexed the Czech part of Czechoslovakia, site of munitions factories. Output from those factories assisted Hitler's invasion of Poland in September 1939 and his campaign throughout World War II. At the same time, Austrians augmented Hitler's armed forces. In 1950, Western leaders thought they saw an analogous situation. South Korea was Stalin's Sudetenland. If Soviet surrogates, the North Koreans, managed to grab South Korea without serious opposition, might not Stalin think as Hitler did that he could take even more territory? That was certainly the opinion of U.S. President Harry S. Truman.[87] In Missouri when he learned of North Korea's invasion of South Korea, he headed back to Washington with heavy thoughts.

> In my generation, this was not the first occasion when the strong had attacked the weak. I recalled some earlier instances: Manchuria, Ethiopia, Austria. I remembered how each time that the democracies failed to act it had encouraged the aggressors to keep going ahead. Communism was acting in Korea just as Hitler, Mussolini, and the Japanese had acted ten, fifteen, and twenty years earlier.[88]

For its part, on 8 August 1950, the National Security Council (NSC) received a submission that clearly blamed "the Kremlin" for "causing the attack to be launched in Korea" and which warned that if the attack succeeded, the following countries might anticipate Soviet or Soviet-sponsored aggression: Iran, for its oil; Turkey, for its access routes between the Black Sea and the Mediterranean; Greece, for its strategic location; Yugoslavia, for its location as a possible springboard for an attack on Greece; Afghanistan and Pakistan, for their strategic locations; even Finland, although that appeared unlikely because Finnish neutrality would be less costly to the Soviet Union than would another war against Finland.[89]

Secretary of State Dean Acheson had similar thoughts. Acheson considered it "close to certain that the attack had been mounted, supplied, and instigated by the Soviet Union and that it would not be stopped by anything short of force."[90]

Sir Oliver Franks, British Ambassador to the United States, said that George Kennan, Counsellor at the State Department and Director of the Policy Planning Staff, shared similar thoughts. Kennan told Franks

> that if Korea went, Formosa [Taiwan] would be next on the list. The Philippines were of course sensitive to anything that might happen in Formosa and there was a chain reaction which, if it revealed weakness in the attitude of Western Powers, would cause discouragement which would most likely spread to Europe after doing its damage in Japan.[91]

British officials agreed. From Moscow, British Ambassador Sir David Kelly forwarded similar information. Kelly's guess was that North Korea launched its attack "with Soviet knowledge and almost certainly at Soviet instigation." Sir David feared that appeasement in Korea would mean trouble in Berlin, Yugoslavia, or Iran in the near future.[92] A Foreign Office Memorandum of 13 July 1950 cited Taiwan, Iran, and Berlin as the most probable sites of the next Soviet provocation.[93] Sir A. Gascoigne—head of the British Liaison Mission in Tokyo, where there would be no embassy until conclusion of a peace treaty in 1951—saw parallels between Soviet and Nazi techniques. "After South Korea would...come Formosa [Taiwan], then Indo-China [Vietnam, Laos, Cambodia], then Thailand, Malaya, etc." he wrote.[94] These were reasonable assumptions by men who had observed what they had observed.

Such thinking definitely made sense at the time. If surrogates of Stalin, the new Hitler, could conquer South Korea with impunity, might Stalin not next attempt to seize Greece, Turkey, Iran, even Norway?[95] It seemed wise to give Stalin the message that aggression did not pay before other acts of aggression against neighbours of the USSR or its client states could take place. However, Soviet documents released by Russian President Boris Yeltsin, first when he visited South Korea in June 1994, then others later, tell a different story.[96] Stalin was no Hitler, a gambler willing to take his chances. A dreadful man who authorized aggression against South Korea, Stalin nevertheless was cautious. The idea of the attack against South Korea was not his. For months he, like his ambassador in Pyongyang, had resisted the temptation as too risky. Finally he succumbed to Kim Il Sung's nagging and permitted a war against South Korea. Available documents do not hint that any other country might have been on the menu if the pickings in South Korea were good.

It would be unwise to insist that if advice from Ottawa and Canberra against elections exclusively in South Korea had prevailed, there would have been no Korean War, more than one million premature deaths would not have taken place, and

Europe would not have experienced a military build-up. Since Ottawa and Canberra did not carry the day, one can only speculate. However, what happened when Washington carried the day is clear. UNTCOK did organize elections in South Korea. Stalin responded by organizing Kim Il Sung's government. U.S. and Soviet troops withdrew from Korea. First Rhee, then Kim, claimed the right to govern all Korea. Given his new authority, Kim nagged Stalin and Shtykov until Shtykov arranged a second trip to Moscow and Stalin delivered what Kim wanted. Stalin interpreted the withdrawal of U.S. forces from South Korea both as indications that Rhee had received a free hand from Washington to attack North Korea[97] and that U.S. interest in Korea was not very strong. Admittedly, Mao would probably have wanted Stalin to surrender Soviet interests in Manchuria whether Korea north of the 38th parallel was in Kim's Democratic People's Republic of Korea or simply a Soviet zone of occupation. However, Stalin would have had greater control over a North Korea administered by the Soviet Army than over one led by Kim Il Sung. For his part, Kim would have been more concerned with gaining control over North Korea than with lobbying Stalin for permission to invade South Korea. Above all, to have ordered Soviet forces to attack South Korea, administered and occupied by the U.S. Army, even to the extent that the U.S. Army administered and occupied part of West Berlin, would definitely have been incompatible with Stalin's actions elsewhere. It is not unreasonable to suggest that South Korea under U.S. military government and North Korea under Soviet occupation might have co-existed at least until March 1953, when Stalin died and some seemingly insoluble problems became soluble.

Although Canadian and Australian policymakers did co-ordinate their strategies to a certain extent, they failed to prevent a war. Nor did their policies coincide with those of India.

Notes

1. One of the best books to date on this topic has been that by James Irving Matray, *The Reluctant Crusade: American Foreign Policy in Korea, 1941-1950* (Honolulu: University of Hawaii Press, 1985). However, Matray had to write on the basis of sources available in 1985, and he mistakenly identified Lester Pearson–then Canada's Under-Secretary of State for External Affairs–as "Foreign Minister" in the government of Prime Minister Mackenzie King.

2. Han Woo-Keun, *The History of Korea* (translated by Lee Kyung-shik, Seoul: Eul Yoo, 1987 [1940]), pp. 318-323, 345-350, 364, 348-349, 371.

3. One of the authors (Mount) has seen the Inchon monument for himself. For an overview of early Roman Catholic and Protestant activity in Korea, see Kenneth Scott Latourette, *A History of the Expansion of Christianity* (New York: Harper and Brothers, 1944), vol. VI, pp. 413-422. There is useful information about Presbyterians in the archives of the United Church of Canada in Toronto, cited hererafter as UCC. See in particular "COVERING LETTER EXPLAINING THE FOLLOWING RESOLUTION ADOPTED AT COUNCIL MEETING JULY 1937: History of Five Stations" located in the Board of Overseas Missions Section, sub-section 83.006C, box 4, file 108. The Rev. K.S. Kim's 1946 report, "The present situation of the Christian Church in Korea," in Box 5, file 141, notes the migration from north to south.

4. Robert O'Neill, *Australia in the Korean War, 1950-53* (Canberra: The Australian War Memorial and the Australian Government Publishing Service, 1981), vol. I, pp. 4-5.

5. *Time Almanac, 2001* divides South Korea's population: Christian, 48.2%; Buddhist, 48.8%; other, 3%; p. 802. Most sources agree that there is little religious activity of any description in North Korea.

6. Latourette, p. 422.

7. Stanley Sandler, *The Korean War: No Victors, No Vanquished* (Lexington: University Press of Kentucky, 1999), p. 19.

8. Kathryn Weathersby, "Soviet Aims in Korea and the Origins of the Korean War, 1945-1950: New Evidence from Russian Archives," *Cold War International History Project Working Paper #8* (Nov. 1993), p. 13. See also Charles K. Armstrong, *The North Korean Revolution, 1945-1950* (Ithaca: Cornell University Press, 2003), pp. 56, 116-119.

9. Dean Rusk, *As I Saw It* (New York: W.W. Norton, 1990), p. 124.

10. Rusk, p. 124.

11. Rusk, p. 123.

12. Extract from Memorandum for Delegation to the Second Session of the General Assembly of the United Nations, 24 October, 1947, *Documents on Canadian External Relations*, 1947, pp. 953-954. Cited hereafter as *DCER*.

13. Rev. E.J.O. Fraser, Board of Overseas Missions, San Francisco, to Rev. A.E. Armstrong, United Church headquarters, Toronto, 15 July 1947, Board of Overseas Missions 83.006C, Box 6, file 146, UCC. The quotation comes from a letter of Bev Owens, Ottawa, to "Wilf," n.p., 24 June 1947, Burbidge Family Fonds, Box 1, File 9, 1946-1949, UCC.

14. Robert Bothwell, "Eyes West: Canada and the Cold War in Asia," in Greg Donaghy (ed.), *Canada and the Early Cold War, 1943-1957* (Ottawa: Canadian Government Publishing, 2001), p. 67.

15. Weathersby, "Soviet Aims...," especially pp. 9-13, 16-17, 20, 22-23, 26-27. The quotation comes from p. 16.

16. Memorandum from Under-Secretary of State for External Affairs to Secretary of State for External Affairs, Ottawa, 10 November 1947, *DCER*, 1947, p. 970.

17. A copy of President Truman's letter of 27 Dec. 1947 to Prime Minister King appears in *DCER*, 1947, p. 997.

18. Acting Secretary of State (Robert Lovett), Washington, to the Canadian Prime Minister, Ottawa, telephoned via Ambassador Ray Atherton (US Ambassador in Ottawa), 30 Dec. 1947, *Foreign Relations of the United States*, 1947, VI, pp. 883-886. Cited hereafter as *FRUS*.

19. Lester B. Pearson, *Mike: The Memoirs of the Rt. Hon. Lester B. Pearson* (Toronto: University of Toronto Press, 1973), p. 136. What Pearson says there is thoroughly compatible with the documentation on the subject in *DCER*,1947, pp. 986-1007. That documentation includes extracts from the prime minister's diary. The quotation here is repeated in *DCER*, pp. 1002-1003.

20. St. Laurent, Ottawa, to Canadian Liaison Office, Tokyo, 8 Jan. 1948, *DCER*, 1948, p. 151.

21. Political Advisor in Korea (Jacobs), Seoul, to the Secretary of State, Washington, 12 Feb. 1948, *FRUS*, 1948, VI, p. 1107; Deputy Director of the Office of European Affairs (Reber), Washington, memorandum of telephone conversation, 30 Dec. 1947, *FRUS*, 1947, VI, p. 887.

22. Hodge, Seoul, to Marshall, Washington, 22 Feb. 1948, *FRUS*, 1948, VI, pp. 1126.

23. Hodge, Seoul, to Marshall, Washington, 26 Feb. 1948, *FRUS*, 1948, VI,p. 1133.

24. Jacobs, Seoul, to Marshall, Washington, 22 April 1948, *FRUS*, 1948, VI, p. 1180; Under-Secretary of the Army (Draper), Washington, to the Under-Secretary of State (Lovett), 3 May 1948, *FRUS*, 1948, VI, p. 1187.

25. Pearson, p. 144.

26. Pearson, p. 145.

27. Series S-0684-001, Boxes 1-3, UN Archives, New York. Cited hereafter as UN Archives.

28. E.g., Australian delegation, United Nations, to Department of External Affairs, Canberra, 20 Feb. 1948, *DAFR*, XVI, pp. 139-140; J.W. Burton (Secretary of External Affairs), Canberra, to S.H. Jackson, Seoul, 5 March 1948, *DAFR*, XVI, p. 142.

29. UN Archives, Box 1.

30. UNTCOK MINUTES, Fifth Meeting, 17 Jan. 1948, UN Archives, Box 1.

31. Sixth meeting, 19 Jan. 1948, UN Archives, Box 1.

32. Lie, United Nations, to Menon, Seoul, 28 Jan. 1948, UN Archives, Box 1.

33. Hodge, Seoul, to Menon, Seoul, 11 March 1948, UN Archives, Box 1.

34. *Ibid.*

35. UN Archives, Box 1.

36. Hodge, Seoul, to Paul-Boncour, Seoul, 24 March 1948, UN Archives, Box 1.

37. Summary Records of 8th meeting, 4 Feb. 1948, UN Archives, Box 3.

38. Summary Records, 9th Meeting, 5 Feb. 1948, UN Archives, Box 3. (The actual records date the 8th meeting as Wednesday, 4 Feb., and the 9th meeting as Thursday, 4 Feb., but in 1948, 4 Feb. fell on a Wednesday and 5 Feb. on a Thursday.)

39. Stewart, p. 102.

40. Summary Records, 12th Session, 11 Feb. 1948, UN Archives, Box 3. This source also applies to information in the next paragraph.

41. *Ibid.*

42. Summary Record, 19th meeting, 10 March 1948, UN Archives, Box 3.

43. Patrick Shaw (head of the Australian Mission in Japan), Tokyo, to Department of External Affairs, Canberra, 14 March 1948, *DAFR*, XVI, p. 145.

44. L.R. McIntyre, Canberra, to Keith Shann (Australian Ambassador to the United Nations), 7 March 1948, *DAFR*, XVI, p. 147.

45. Department of External Affairs, Canberra, to Jamieson, Seoul, *DAFR*, XVI, 16 July 1948, p. 151.

46. Joseph M. Siracusa and Yeong-Han Cheong, *America's Australia: Australia's America* (Claremont, California: Regina, 1997), especially pp. 17-26. Their observations are compatible with those of I.M. Cumpston, *History of Australian Foreign Policy, 1901-1991* (Canberra: I.M. Cumpston, 1991), Vol. I, pp. 159-161; Bell; and David Lowe, "Divining a Later Line: Conservative Constructions of Labor Foreign Policy, 1944-49," in David Lee and Christopher Waters (editors), *Evatt to Evans: The Labor Tradition in Australian Foreign Policy* (St. Leonards, New South Wales: Allen and Unwin, 1997), pp. 62-74.

47. Policy Statement of the Department of State, Washington, 18 Aug. 1948, *FRUS*, 1948, vol. VI, pp. 1-8. The quotations come from p. 2.

48. Policy Statement, 18 Aug. 1948, p. 8.

49. Memorandum for Cabinet "Canada and the United Nations Temporary Commission on Korea," Ottawa, 20 Dec. 1947, *DCER*, 1947, pp. 983-985.

50. O'Neill, p. 8.

51. O'Neill, p. 9.

52. O'Neill, p. 121.

53. *DCER*, 1948, pp. 136-201.

54. Internal memo (Shann to Burton), Department of External Affairs, Canberra, 17 Dec. 1947, *Documents on Australian Foreign Policy*, 1947, pp. 830-831. Cited hereafter as DAFP.

55. Memorandum from Head, United Nations Division, to Prime Minister, 25 Feb. 1948, *DCER*, 1948, p. 165.

56. Permanent Delegate to United Nations to St. Laurent, Ottawa, 24 Feb. 1948, *DCER*, 1948, p. 166.

57. St. Laurent, Ottawa, to Permanent Delegate to United Nations, 25 Feb. 1948, *DCER*, 1948, pp. 167-168.

58. Stueck, pp. 26-27.

59. St. Laurent, Ottawa, to Liaison Office, Tokyo, 6 March 1948, *DCER*, 1948, p. 174.

60. Farrar-Hockley, I, pp. 24-25.

61. Farrar-Hockley, I, p. 21.

62. Australian Delegation, United Nations, to Department of External Affairs, Canberra, 24 Feb. 1948, DFAR, XVI, pp. 141-142.

63. Among the many who make this point is Farrar-Hockley, I, p. 39.

64. McCormack, p. 44.

65. Stewart, p. 102.

66. Farrar-Hockley, I, pp. 22-23.

67. Farrar-Hockley, I, p. 23.

68. Farrar-Hockley, I, pp. 23-24.

69. Farrar-Hockley, I, p. 28, *United Nations Yearbook*, 1948-49, p. 289.

70. Farrar-Hockley, I, p. 29.

71. Document I: Stalin's Meeting with Kim Il Sung, Moscow, 5 March 1949, Woodrow Wilson International Center for Scholars, *Cold War International History Project*, Issue V (Spring 1995), pp. 4-6. Cited hereafter as *CWIHP*.

72. Vladislav Zubok and Constantine Pleshakov, *Inside the Kremlin's Cold War: From Stalin to Khrushchev* (Cambridge, Mass.: Harvard University Press, 1997 [1996]), p. 55.

73. Document II: Ciphered Telegram from Shtykov , Pyongyang, to Vyshinsky, Moscow, 3 Sept. 1949, *CWIHP*, V, p. 6.

74. *Ibid.*

75. E.J.D. Fraser, Seoul, to the Rev. D.H. Gallagher, Toronto, 22 Feb. 1949, Board of Overseas Missions, sub-section 83.006C, box 6, file 156, UCC.

76. Document III: Ciphered telegram from Gromykom Moscow, to Tunkin at the Soviet Embassy in Pyongyang, 11 Sept. 1949, *CWIHP*, V, p. 6.

77. Document IV: Ciphered telegram from Tunkin, Pyongyang, to Soviet Foreign Ministry, Moscow (in reply to telegram of 11 September), 14 Sept. 1949, *CWIHP*, V, pp. 6-7.

78. Ibid.

79. Document V, Politburo decision to confirm the following directive to the Soviet ambassador in Korea, 24 Sept. 1949, *CWIHP*, V, pp. 7-8. The quotation comes from p. 8.

80. Document VI, Ciphered Telegram from Shtykov, Pyongyang, to Vyshinsky, Moscow, 19 Jan. 1950, *CWIHP*, V, p. 8.

81. Ciphered telegram from Stalin, Moscow, to Shtykov, Pyongyang, 30 Jan. 1950, *CWIHP*, V, p. 9.

82. Shen Zhihua, "Sino-Soviet Relations and the Origins of the Korean War: Stalin's Strategic Goals in the Far East," *Journal of Cold War Studies*, II, 2 (Spring 2000), pp. 44-68. See also Kathryn Weathersby, "New Russian Documents on the Korean War," *CWIHP*, VI-VII (Winter 1995/1996), pp. 30-31.

83. Shtykov, Pyongyang, to Vyshinsky, Moscow, 9 March 1950; Stalin, Moscow, to Kim Il Sung (via Shtykov), Pyongyang, 18 March 1950; *CWIHP*, VI-VII, p. 37. For a brief summary of Soviet

involvement in the Korean War, see Brian Crozier, *The Rise and Fall of the Soviet Empire* (Roseville, California: Forum, 2000 [1999]), pp. 150-157.

84. Weatherby, p. 31.

85. Shtykov, Pyongyang, to Comrade Zakharov, Moscow, 26 June 1950, CWIHP, VI-VII, p. 39.

86. Andrew C. Nahm, *An Introduction to Korean History and Culture* (Seoul: Hollym, 1993), p. 255. Nahm tabulates the dead: South Korean military, 225,784; South Korean civilians, 244,663; U.S. dead, 33,625; other UN dead, 3,188; North Korean soldiers, 294, 151; North Korean civilians, 406,000; Chinese, 184,128. Nahm says that 43,572 South Korean soldiers were missing, 387,744 civilians. In North Korea, 91,206 military were missing, as were 680 civilians and 21,836 Chinese. Wounded were South Korean soldiers, 717,073; South Korean civilians, 229,000; Americans, 123,875; other UN, 10,812; North Korean soldiers, 229,848; North Korean civilians, 1,594,000; Chinese, 711,872.

87. Truman, pp. 331-333.

88. Harry S. Truman, *Years of Trial and Hope: Memoirs* (New York: Signet, 1956), pp. 378-379.

89. A report to the National Security Council by the Executive Secretary on THE POSITION AND ACTIONS OF THE UNITED STATES WITH RESPECT TO FURTHER POSSIBLE SOVIET MOVES IN THE LIGHT OF THE KOREAN SITUATION, 8 August 1950, Student Research File (B File), Korean War: Response to North Korea's Invasion, 43B, Box 2 of 2, HST.

90. Dean Acheson, *Present at the Creation: My Years in the State Department* (New York: W.W. Norton, 1969), p. 405.

91. Franks, Washington, to K.G. Younger (Minister of State, Acting Foreign Secretary during an illness of Foreign Secretary Ernest Bevin), London, 27 June 1950, Foreign and Commonwealth Office, *Documents on British Policy Overseas*, Series II, Vol. IV (Korea, 1950-1951) (London: Her Majesty's Stationery Office, 1991), p. 5. Cited hereafter as DBPO.

92. Kelly, Moscow, to Younger, London, 30 June 1950, DBPO, pp. 18-19.

93. Memorandum, 13 July 1950, DBPO, p. 54.

94. Gascoigne, Tokyo, to M.E. Denning, Assistant Under Secretary of State, Foreign Office, London, 5 July 1950, DBPO, pp. 31-34.

95. Sir Pierson Dixon of the Foreign Office indicated Norwegian concern for Norway's safety; FO 1023/76, quoted in DBPO, p. 20.

96. Kathryn Weathersby, "Korea, 1949-1950: To Attack or Not to Attack? Stalin, Kim Il Sung, and the Prelude to War," CWIHP, V, p. 1; Kathryn Weathersby, "New Russian Documents on the Korean War," CWIHP, VI-VII, p. 30. Also, Shen Zhihua, "Sino-Soviet Relations and the Origins of the Korean War: Stalin's Strategic Goals in the Far East," *Journal of Cold War Studies*, II, 2 (Spring 2000), pp. 44-68.

97. Shen Zhihua, p. 47.

Chapter Two

How Extensive Should The Commonwealth Commitment Be, And How Far North Should The United Nations Command Go?

I   Internationalizing the Conflict

Making the defence of South Korea an international matter would serve several purposes. It would reduce the number of U.S. casualties and thereby, presumably, make the war effort more acceptable to American voters. It would also give the military campaign an aura of legality or legitimacy which it might otherwise lack. As the Soviets were at that point boycotting the United Nations in order to protest that body's failure to seat delegates from the newly constituted People's Republic of China, a Soviet veto was not a problem. On 25 June 1950, the Security Council endorsed a resolution which called upon member countries to assist in ousting the North Korean invaders from South Korea. The Resolution confirmed the legitimacy of the South Korean government and called upon

> —the authorities of North Korea (a) to cease hostilities forthwith; and (b) to withdraw their armed forces to the 38th parallel...

> —all Members to render every assistance to the United Nations in the execution of this resolution and to refrain from giving assistance to the North Korean authorities.[1]

Two days later, the Security Council passed another resolution noting that the North Koreans had not withdrawn from South Korea despite the resolution of 25 June. The new resolution therefore specifically recommended

> that the Members of the United Nations furnish such assistance to the Republic of Korea as may be necessary to repel the armed attack and to restore international peace and security to the area.[2]

On 7 July 1950, the Security Council held its 476th meeting. There the ongoing absence of the Soviet delegation allowed a joint French-British resolution and supported by the Taiwan-based Republic of China, Cuba, and Norway, to pass. Resolution S/-1587 welcomed the "prompt and vigorous" support which UN members had given to the resolutions of 25 and 27 June, recommended that all UN members providing military forces under those resolutions "make such forces and other assistance available to a unified command under the United States," requested the U.S. to "designate the commander" of such force and "to provide the Security Council with reports as appropriate on the course of action taken under the unified command." Seven countries supported the resolution, and three (Egypt, India, Yugoslavia) abstained.[3] The Truman administration appointed General Douglas MacArthur, commander of the U.S. Army of Occupation in Japan, to lead the United Nations Command. For his part, MacArthur was not inclined to consult with his own government, let alone with the Security Council of the United Nations.[4]

Commonwealth Countries—the United Kingdom, Canada, Australia, New Zealand, and South Africa—agreed to contribute combat forces to the cause. Other United Nations contributors were Belgium, Colombia, Ethiopia, France, Luxembourg, Greece, the Netherlands, the Philippines, Thailand and Turkey. Nor were those contributions merely symbolic. The table of military personnel buried at the United Nations cemetery in Pusan records the following: Australia, 281; Canada, 378; France, 44; Netherlands, 117; United Kingdom, 885; Norway, 1 [medical, not combat]; South Africa, 11; South Korea, 36; Turkey, 462; USA, 36; Unknown Soldiers, 4; non-belligerents, 11; New Zealand, 34. Most of the many more numerous American and South Korean fatalities lie buried elsewhere, as do some others. Statistics at the Harry S. Truman Museum in Independence, Missouri, indicate the following numbers of service personnel and battle deaths of the United Nations Command during the Korean War:

	Total Uniformed Personnel	Battle Deaths
Australia	2,282	304
Belgium	900	99
Canada	6,146	309
Columbia	1,068	140
Ethiopia	1,271	121
France	1,119	288
Greece	1,263	196
Luxembourg	44	2
Netherlands	819	120

New Zealand	1,389	31
Phillippines	1,496	112
South Africa	826	20
South Korea	590,911	58,809
Thailand	1,294	129
Turkey	5,455	741
United Kingdom	14,198	722
United States	302,483	33,629

Documents in the Truman and Eisenhower presidential archives indicate that correspondence between the White House on the one hand and British authorities on the other was considerably more voluminous than that with any other Commonwealth country.

All five Old Commonwealth countries had governments strongly opposed to Soviet expansion. Until the election of 25 October 1951, Clement Attlee was Prime Minister of the United Kingdom, and Ernest Bevin was his Foreign Secretary. They had supported the Berlin Air Lift of 1948-1949 and the negotiation of the North Atlantic Treaty in 1948-1949. Sadly, during the period between the outbreak of the Korean War in June 1950 and Bevin's death in April 1951, Bevin was frequently ill and his responsibilities became those of Sir Kenneth Younger, Minister of State. Younger and Attlee may or may not have shared all Bevin's opinions,[5] but British policy on Korea remained consistent. North Korea was the enemy, the People's Republic of China a country with which good relations were desirable and perhaps possible.

Historian Steven Hugh Lee argues that Anthony Eden, who became British Foreign Secretary when the Conservatives, led by Winston Churchill, returned to office in October 1951, proved less supportive of U.S. policies than his Labour predecessors had been. Lee attributes Eden's stance to both the provocative nature of some of those U.S. policies and Eden's inherent sense of British nationalism.[6] Both Labour and Conservative governments wanted support from newly independent India (1947) in Southeast Asia. However, when forced to make a choice between India and the United States, both British governments sided with the U.S. Lee cites as evidence the United Nations Resolution of 1 February 1951 which condemned China, and British support for the U.S. position at the Panmunjom truce talks in May 1953.[7]

In Canada, Mackenzie King had retired, Louis St. Laurent had become prime minister, and Lester Pearson had left the civil service to take his chances as a cabinet minister, Minister of External Affairs. Both St. Laurent and Pearson had disagreed with King on UNTCOK and had a more international outlook than that of Mackenzie King.[8] Lee rightly notes that successive Canadian governments, Liberal or Conservative, showed their greatest support for the United Kingdom when its survival was at stake, as during the two world wars. The Korean War did not threaten British survival. Also, members of the St. Laurent government were well aware that World War II had weakened the United Kingdom, and that the United States was unquestionably the leader of the Western World. Official Ottawa focussed on Washington, a capital it dared not ignore.[9] Asia in general and Korea in particular ranked lower on the spectrum. At the outbreak of the Korean War, the Government of Canada did not even have its own ambassador in Seoul but relied on the British ambassador.[10]

With the defeat of the Labour Party in Australia's federal election of 1949, Sir Robert Menzies became prime minister of a right-wing coalition of the Liberal and Country parties. Menzies, who had been prime minister from 1939 to 1941, would remain in office until 1966, and when President Lyndon Johnson sought allies in the Vietnam War, Menzies would send Australian forces there. There is little evidence that Menzies' Presbyterian connections, described in the first chapter, influenced his actions with regard to the Korean War. Menzies' Minister of External Affairs at the outbreak of the Korean War was Sir Percy Spender. Spender in particular regarded a close relationship with the U.S. as vital to Australian security.

New Zealand also had a change of government in 1949. There the right-wing National Party led by Sidney Holland defeated the Labour Party, which had held office since 1935. Holland would remain New Zealand's Prime Minister until 1957. During the Korean War he had two ministers of external affairs: Frederick Doidge (until 1951) and Sir Clifton Webb.

In South Africa, where only citizens of European descent could vote, the prime minister was Daniel Malan, of the Nationalist Party. The Nationalists, who had won the election of 1948 and would remain in office until 1994 under a series of leaders, represented the most nationalist Afrikaners or Boers. They resented the British victory of the Boer War (1899-1902) over the two Boer republics, the Transvaal and the Orange Free State, and many in the party had not wanted to participate in the war against Hitler. Most South Africans of British extraction voted for the opposition United Party, and the Nationalist Party did little to include them or to protect their interests.

Nor were South African Nationalists deeply committed to Asia's defence. On 14 February 1952, Prime Minister Malan explained to the U.S. ambassador in Cape Town why South Africa's commitment to Korea was no larger than it was and why it was unlikely to increase. First, many South Africans, he said, had already died in Korea, and few were volunteering to replace them. "Military service had to be on a voluntary basis." Secondly, South Africa also had responsibilities in the Middle East. Thirdly, South Africa's primary concern had to be the African continent itself.[11] At the time, South Africa had a fighter squadron in Korea.

Demography, geography, and political determination meant that the United Kingdom, Canada, and Australia played a more vital role in the making of the Old Commonwealth's policies toward the Korean War than did New Zealand or South Africa. At the time, the British had a Commonwealth Relations Office (CRO), quite separate from the Foreign Office, to handle its relations with both the Old Commonwealth Countries and the new members.

If members of the United Nations were to help oust the North Korean aggressors from South Korea, the Truman administration had every reason to expect assistance from the United Kingdom. The UK had been America's most powerful and loyal ally through two world wars and the early years of the Cold War. However, the British had problems of their own—quite apart from economic recovery after World War II. Even Attlee's government, which had granted independence to India, Pakistan, Ceylon, and Burma (which left the Commonwealth), did not plan to dismantle the British Empire any faster than necessary. The British army had problems of its own dealing with Communist insurgents in Malaya. Moreover, there was no guarantee that Mao Zedong's army would not invade Hong Kong, which British authorities wanted to keep for a number of reasons, both economical and psychological. The greater the number of combat forces Attlee's government could persuade other Old Commonwealth governments to send to Korea, the less the pressure on the British army would be.

Farrar-Hockley makes a credible case for the importance of the Commonwealth's military effort. Attlee's government certainly spurred the other Old Commonwealth governments to action. Without London's active participation, there would have been less interest in Ottawa, Canberra, Wellington, and Pretoria. France's economy allowed only a limited effort, and France already had military commitments in Europe and Indo-China (Vietnam, Laos, Cambodia). No other possible ally had armed forces as powerful as those of the United Kingdom, and without Commonwealth participation, an even larger number of Americans would have had to go into battle and risk death or injury.[12] State Department documents confirm Farrar-Hockley's assertion that British participation was critical. Regarding a meeting of State Department officials with British Ambassador Sir Oliver Franks on 3 August 1950, Acheson wrote:

I told Sir Oliver that...we felt the action which the British government in-dicated it was willing to take...would set a good pattern for other European countries.[13]

There was no question that the British would be militarily supportive. On 27 June 1950, the cabinet met and agreed:

The United Kingdom Government should in principle support the action which the United States Government were [sic] proposing to take to halt Communist aggression in Asia.

Note that the statement mentioned "the United States Government," not "the United Nations." Similarly, the British representative on the Security Council" should support the U.S. motion which asked "the members of the United Nations to furnish such assistance to the Republic of Korea [South Korea] as may be necessary to repel the armed attack." However, the U.S. government should not include in the preamble any reference to "Communist encroachments in other parts of Asia which were not before the Security Council," and American authorities should drop the ref-erence to "centrally-directed Communist imperialism" from a planned forthcoming statement about South Korea.

The British were right, of course. As the previous chapter indicates, the attack on South Korea was a North Korean initiative, not a Soviet one, and relations with the USSR were sufficiently bad without what were then unverifiable and what are now seen to be false accusations. Attlee's cabinet agreed:

It had not been proven that, in carrying out this aggression on North Ko-rea, the North Koreans had been acting on instructions from Moscow; and it was suggested that there might have been an advantage in seeking to iso-late this incident and to deal with it as an act of aggression committed by the North Koreans on their own initiative. This would have enabled the Soviet Government to withdraw, without loss of prestige, any encouragement or support which they might have been giving to the North Koreans. The an-nouncement which the United States Government were [sic] proposing to make, by linking this up with Communist threats in other parts of Asia, would present a major challenge to the Soviet Government; it would bring into controversy other issues which had not yet been brought before the Se-curity Council; and its reference to Formosa (now Taiwan) might embarrass the United Kingdom Government in their [sic] relations with the Commu-nist Government of China and might even provoke that Government to at-tack Hong Kong or to foment disorders there.[14]

Attlee and his ministers did achieve a victory. The resolution approved by the Security Council later that same day made no mention of Taiwan or any other part of Asia. Nor, when President Truman issued his own statement a few hours later yet, did he use the words "centrally-directed Communist imperialism." He implied it. He said that "communism has passed beyond the use of subversion to conquer independent nations and will now use armed invasion and war," but he did not use the words which the British cabinet asked him not to use.[15] However, this victory may not have been entirely a British one. Historian Brian Catchpole says: "Acheson...recommended that the President should not publicly brand the Soviet Union as the evil genius behind the invasion but should try to contain the crisis as a 'local war' in the Far East."[16] It undoubtedly helped the British cause that the Secretary of State was leaning in the same direction.

The only real issue was the extent of the British commitment. The Chiefs of Staff met 27 June and agreed that an Australian squadron under U.S. (not UN) command was preferable to a British one. The Chiefs also agreed

> that it would be most desirable for as many Commonwealth countries as possible to participate in the military co-operation. This would further strengthen an impression of strength on the part of United Nations countries.[17]

British military insights proved as brilliant as the political ones exhibited by the cabinet. On 1 July, the Chiefs of Staff predicted that the Soviets would not "give active military support to the North Korean forces, or make this an excuse for launching a major war." They predicted that Mao's forces would postpone "indefinitely" their invasion of Taiwan.[18] On 28 August 1950, Air Vice Marshal Sir Cecil Arthur Bouchier at the British Embassy in Tokyo wrote with prescience to the Chiefs of Staff. At the time, South Korean and United Nations forces had retreated to a small perimeter around Pusan, but Bouchier foresaw that there would be a successful counter offensive. With total accuracy Bouchier forecast, "When the counter offensive does start the North Koreans will crumble very fast." For political reasons, thought Bouchier, the British forces should arrive before the successful counter-offensive. Otherwise, the British contribution would count for very little.[19]

Prior to a meeting with Commonwealth High Commissioners, Kenneth Younger—the Minister of State who was serving as acting Foreign Secretary because of the illness of Foreign Secretary Ernest Bevin—received a brief. R.H. Scott of the Foreign Office advised Younger that all Commonwealth governments had received telegrams advising that the Attlee government was sending to Korean waters one light fleet carrier, two cruisers, five destroyers and frigates. The telegram indicated "that we should welcome any support of the Security Council resolution that Commonwealth governments were able to make." The Australian and New Zealand governments, said Scott, had already indicated their willingness to place ships of their respective navies "under the control of the United States [sic! not United Nations] authorities," while Canada's two largest political parties "fully endorse[d] the Security Council resolution." Scott advised Younger of a two-tier structure within the Commonwealth, at least with regard to Korean matters, even before South Africa had decided to contribute to the cause:

> All telegrams sent to Commonwealth Governments by the C.R.O. [Commonwealth Relations Office] have been copied to their High Commissioners in London. In addition High Commissioners of the four "old" Commonwealth Governments but not those of the three "new" ones [India, Pakistan, Ceylon (now Sri Lanka)] have received copies of all the relevant Foreign Office telegrams. The "old" High Commissioners are always briefed not to reveal at meetings their privileged position under standing arrangements.[20]

As ships of the British, Australian, Canadian, and New Zealand fleets reached Korean waters, they formed a Commonwealth Squadron, under the command of General MacArthur.[21]

II   The British Role in the Summer of 1950

For his part, Secretary of State Dean Acheson found the British diplomatic contribution less than impressive. While grateful for the speedy British military contribution, he regarded as a nuisance the "unsolicited initiative" which the British proposed for finding a peaceful solution to the conflict. The British Foreign Office had long believed," he commented, "more than evidence seemed to warrant, that it understood the Russians and could negotiate with them compromise solutions of difficult situations."[22] Bevin suggested that the Soviets might be willing to pressure the North Koreans into withdrawing from South Korea in exchange for an agreement that the People's Republic of China be allowed to capture Taiwan. "We should avoid risking Western solidarity by playing down those parts of the President's statement of June 27 that did not bear directly on Korea," he said. Truman and Acheson categorically rejected that idea. They also rejected the British suggestion that the PRC take the Chinese seat in the Security Council, so firmly, in fact, that correspondence on that subject came to an abrupt end. Talks between British Air Marshal Lord Arthur

Tedder, head of the British Joint Services Mission in Washington, and General Omar Bradley, Chairman of the Joint Chiefs of Staff of the United States, also proved fruitless.[23] The British would participate in the Korean War on American terms.

Despite these disagreements, the British Chiefs of Staff moved quickly to muster their armed forces and those of the Old Commonwealth countries. By 1 July, they had already placed one carrier, two cruisers, two destroyers, and three frigates—all of which had been doing occupation duty in Japan—"at the disposal of the United States Commander-in-Chief," who was General Douglas MacArthur. Commanding officers of those ships had instructions to "operate in conjunction with the United States naval forces in giving cover support to the Korean Republic [South Korea]," but they were not to participate in the defence of Taiwan. Ships off Malaya and Hong Kong should stay where they were, thought the Chiefs of Staff. The Chiefs noted Canada's willingness to send three destroyers based in Esquimalt to Korean waters, where they should arrive in more or less three weeks. That offer, they said, "represents a fair contribution from the Canadians." The Chiefs also noted that Australia had placed one destroyer and one frigate currently off Japan "at the disposal of the United Nations through the United States authorities in support of the Republic of Korea." At the time, that seemed reasonable, and they were not going to ask the Australians to do more. New Zealand was prepared to offer three frigates and one cruiser, which could set sail from New Zealand for Korean waters within three to fourteen days. The Chiefs of Staff thought it unwise to denude Malaya and Hong Kong of Royal Air Force (RAF) protection for the sake of Korea but noted that Australia had offered a fighter squadron of Mustangs currently in Japan and thought that the Royal Australian Air Force (RAAF) might later transfer some of its aircraft from Malaya to Korea, if that proved necessary. Canada and New Zealand had not yet offered any military aircraft to the cause, but the Chiefs of Staff thought that they could both afford to do so.

Regarding soldiers, the British Chiefs of Staff were blunt:

As ships of the British, Australian, Canadian, and New Zealand fleets reached Korean waters, they formed a Commonwealth Squadron, under the command of General MacArthur. The Americans have expressed the view unofficially that a United Kingdom and Commonwealth contribution of land forces, however small, would have an excellent political effect in sealing even more firmly our complete unity on this issue. We agree.[24]

Realistically, it appeared unwise to save South Korea by exposing Malaya and Hong Kong, and British forces in those colonies should stay there. Perhaps the War Office might decide to relocate British soldiers from some other theatre. Happily, the outbreak of war in Korea had led the Australian government to cancel plans to withdraw an Australian infantry battalion on occupation duty in Japan. Perhaps, said the Chiefs of Staff, it "might be persuaded to place it at the disposal of the United States authorities for active operations."[25]

The urgency of the situation led to a swift change of mind. Sir Oliver Franks, British Ambassador in Washington from June 1948 to November 1952, warned his government that if it wished to maintain a special Anglo-American relationship, it must send ground troops. Unless it did, the White House would regard the United Kingdom as no more than one among many European countries.[26] Franks had, what one recent commentator calls an "exceptional working relationship" with Acheson and thus knew whereof he spoke.[27] British soldiers *did* arrive in Korea during the summer of 1950, and they made a formidable difference. Diplomacy triumphed over short-term British military interests. The Defence Committee of Attlee's cabinet met 6 July 1950 and reaffirmed the dangers of trying to do too much with too few soldiers. The more the Truman administration did in Taiwan, the greater they thought the danger of a Chinese attack on Hong Kong might be. Already the British army was fighting insurgents in Malaya, and there were important interests in the Middle East, source of the British oil supply. Indeed, the United Kingdom could use Australian troops in Malaya, a point which the Minister of Defence intended to raise when Australian Prime Minister Menzies reached London within the next few days.[28] However, the Minister of State, Kenneth Younger, advised some of his Foreign Office colleagues that the Truman administration was certain to complain if the United States had to resist North Korean aggression by itself.[29] Sir Oliver Franks warned that the United Kingdom had little choice but to send ground forces to Korea:

> The United States Administration believes it essential for the United Nations character of the Korean operations that they should not be carried out solely by United States forces. They foresee a long and difficult ground campaign...They know that many nations will follow the British on this matter...[T]here is a steady and unquestioning assumption that we are the only dependable ally and partner...The...American people are not happy if they feel alone...For these reasons I should expect the reaction of the United States to a negative decision by us to be deep and prolonged.[30]

On 29 August, British infantry forces became the first United Nations troops from a country other than the United States to reach Korea. The British Army's 1st Battalion of the Argyll and Sutherland Highlanders, the 1st Battalion of the Middlesex Regiment, and the headquarters of the 27th Infantry Brigade were all professional soldiers, not raw conscripts. They went to Taegu near the edge of the Pusan Perimeter, the small area of south Korea which the North Koreans had not overrun, where General Walton Walker—chief United States/United Nations commander in the area—had sensitive listening devices which could intercept North Korean messages. Unaware that U.S. intelligence had cracked their cipher, the North Koreans communicated at length by radio, and General Walker, aware of their every move, knew where to deploy his limited manpower. The British forces successfully defended Taegu and prevented any further North Korean advance.[31]

Fifty years later, a U.S. Marine who had served in Korea commented on the British Army's record generally. Speaking to the Society of Historians of American Foreign Relations, Retired General Bernard Trainor (currently employed at Harvard University) said that the British Army was "terrible" at offensive action but "impregnable" in defence. The British, said Trainor, had a long tradition of defending their territory, including their Empire, and it showed. The U.S. Army of occupation relocated from Japan had "gone to rot," but the Marines were fierce fighters. Once the U.S. Army managed to recover from its initial inadequacies, it excelled at offensive war, a skill developed during the Civil War. Trainor also had high praise for the Canadian and Australian soldiers who went to Korea, but they were not available in time to defend the Pusan Perimeter.[32]

III The Australian Role in the Summer of 1950

The next Old Commonwealth government to take action was that of Australia. Sir Robert Menzies was much more friendly to the United States than Herbert Evatt had been,[33] and he was also an anglophile. Menzies' Minister of External Affairs, Sir Percy Spender, was even more enthusiastic about the U.S. connection and less attached to the British than was Menzies.[34] From the perspectives of Menzies and Spender, an Australian military intervention in Korea served several useful purposes. It cemented the relationship with both the United States and the United Kingdom, helped with the "containment of Communism," allowed Australia some influence in connection with the forthcoming Japanese peace treaty, and continued Australia's policy of involvement with the United Nations.[35]

Like most democracies, Australia had disarmed after World War II, and in 1950 its armed forces were unprepared for combat. In March of that year, the Australian government had given notice of its intention to withdraw its forces from occupation duty in Japan, gradually, and in April the United States government had indicated acceptance of this decision.[36] That same month, Attlee's government notified Canberra that it really could appreciate Australian troops in Malaya to assist in the war against the Communist insurgents.[37] Two days after North Korea's invasion of South Korea, the Australian government sent Lincoln bombers to Malaya, convinced of the reality, as were many in Washington, of "centrally-directed Communist imperialism." Spender said as much in a speech of 26 June. If the Communists captured South Korea, they would try to grab other targets throughout Asia.[38] On 27 June, Menzies told the cabinet:

> It is quite clear that, although the invading forces are those of the North Korean Government, they represent Communist expansion. It therefore seems to the Cabinet that this attack is a Communist inspired and directed move...

> The Korea incident cannot be looked at in isolation, nor can we in Australia regard it as remote from our own interests and safety. There are other points of possible attack on or off the coast of China. There is also, at this very moment, a Communist led campaign in Indo-China. Much nearer home there are the operations of the Communist guerrillas in Malaya who are making it their business to render British control of Malaya difficult and who, if they succeed, will make it impossible. These operations may well be stimulated by events in Korea.

> The preservation of British authority in Malaya is vital to Australia's security. We cannot regard the task in that country as solely one for the United Kingdom; nor would the Australian people desire us to. It must be made clear to Communist movements everywhere that if they promote aggressive campaigns for the acquisition of new territory, they will find no division among the British countries of the world.[39]

As indicated by subsequently released Soviet documents and outlined in Chapter I, Menzies had misread the situation, but he remembered the 1930s and he did not have access to the Soviet or Chinese documents.

Menzies elaborated on Stalin's supposed guilt at a cabinet meeting of 25 August 1950. Stalin saw North Korea as a useful surrogate, said Menzies. Stalin had decided that South Korea was the place where the West was most vulnerable, where he could make the greatest gains at the least expense, without even using his own forces. At the very least, Stalin hoped to spark a round of inflation and thereby damage Western economies. With Germany and Japan now part of the West, Menzies continued, the West had 80 per cent of the world's industrial power. Surely Stalin did not want global war under such circumstances. Still, Australia should send "a small force very quickly...for its psychological effect in [the] USA."[40]

Australian historian David Lowe says that for Menzies, Korea in 1950 was analogous to Spain at the time of its Civil War (1936-1939), a place where the aggressors tested the will of the democracies to resist. Malaya and the Middle East were more vital Australian interests than Korea, as other places in the 1930s had been more important than Spain. Nevertheless, Korea was what Spain had been.[41] Later in 1950, the Menzies government also agreed to send troops to the Middle East.[42] Indeed, given Menzies' impression that Malaya and the Middle East might be more important than Korea, Menzies wanted to confine the Korean War to the Korean peninsula and to end it as quickly as possible.[43] However, given the circumstances, Menzies did not actually send soldiers to the Middle East; Malaya and Korea appeared as far more immediate demands.[44] By 1952-1953, the Middle East had definitely become a lower priority, although Australia sent two fighter squadrons to Malta in 1952, where they remained until 1954.[45]

Anxious as the prime minister was to contain international Communism, Sir Alan Stewart Watt—Secretary of the Department of External Affairs—responded to a formal U.S. request for combat forces that any commitment must await consultations with the British government. Watt made this reply after discussion with Spender. In less than half an hour later, the Department of External Affairs sent cables to Washington and London requesting further information.[46]

Within hours, the British government ordered its ships in Japanese waters to serve under General MacArthur and assist in the evacuation of U.S. citizens and British subjects from South Korea. On 28 June, the Australian government gave similar instructions to two ships of the Australian Navy, *Shoalhaven* and *Bataan*. Seoul fell to the North Korean enemy later that same day.

MacArthur, always one for direct action, then sent an uncoded radio message to Lieutenant General Sir Horace Clement Robertson, the highest ranking British officer in Japan, requesting the service of Royal Australian Air Force Squadron No. 77 for use south of the 38th parallel. MacArthur took no steps to prevent the message from reaching journalists, and Australian newspapers reported the request before the

Australian government had made a decision. Menzies and other members of the cabinet were not pleased. Before it did, Menzies ordered the *Shoalhaven* and the *Bataan* to avoid operations around Taiwan. Then on 30 June, the Australian government committed Squadron 77 to battle. At least one American soldier was grateful when it appeared overhead during the Battle of the Pusan Perimeter.[47]

On 14 July, as South Korean forces retreated toward the Pusan Perimeter, United Nations Secretary General Trygve Lie appealed for ground forces. By then Menzies had left on an around-the-world trip to capitals of friendly governments. Back in Canberra, Spender thought that the government should comply with this request. Even if it meant the transfer of the bomber squadron from Malaya, the despatch of RAN ships, or the creation of an additional brigade, the Australian government must do so. The good will of the United States was essential to Australia's long-term best interests, and failure to send the forces could have devastating consequences. Menzies regarded the Middle East as the place where Australia should send its troops in the event of a major war.[48] However, in London, Attlee informed Menzies that New Zealand's Prime Minister Sidney Holland might well send soldiers or a ground support squadron of the Royal New Zealand Air Force to Korea, perhaps to serve with the British brigade.[49] On 26 July, after his visit to London and immediately before a meeting with President Truman and an address to Congress, Menzies agreed, and the Australian government announced a commitment of ground forces to the Korean campaign.[50] (The first Australian soldiers, one battalion, arrived in Korea 28 September.[51]) Days later, Spender addressed a conference of the Liberal Party of New South Wales and complained of a lack of consultation with the British government. The United Kingdom, he said, should consult with its Commonwealth partners more regularly and more often.[52]

Actually, Menzies had little choice but to promise ground troops when he did. The British had decided to send soldiers of their own while Menzies was crossing the Atlantic. Back in Canberra, Spender persuaded Acting Prime Minister Sir Arthur Fadden to announce that Australia would also be sending combat forces.[53] Menzies could hardly repudiate that decision on the eve of his meeting with President Truman.

Menzies met President Truman, along with Dean Acheson, 28 July.[54] Three days later Menzies assured Secretary Acheson that his government intended to strengthen Australia's armed forces. With regard to Korea, reported Acheson, Menzies said that Australians "were very anxious to work closely with us on what they should do and what equipment they should provide."[55] In November, on the eve of the Chinese offensive, Acheson advised Defense Secretary George Marshall that

Australia's contribution to the cause, "considering Australian resources," had been "substantial."[56] (Marshall, who had been Secretary of State, was now Secretary of Defence.)

Yet, that is not to say that Menzies regarded North Korea's invasion of South Korea as a threat to Australia. On 15 August 1950, when United Nations forces were experiencing their nadir and in the aftermath of his trip to Washington, Menzies—in the presence of his military advisers—addressed his cabinet. Australia, said Menzies, had entered the war because the United States did. The United Nations Command was but a "pretence," and of the other Old Commonwealth countries, only the United Kingdom and New Zealand mattered in Korea.[57] On 15 February 1951, Menzies presented his strategic priorities to the cabinet: Netherlands New Guinea, Malaya, "maybe [French] Indo China," and the Middle East. He did not as much as mention Korea.[58]

IV   The New Zealand Role in the Summer of 1950

The National (conservative) government of New Zealand, elected to office in 1949 under the leadership of Prime Minister Sidney Holland and with Frederick Doidge as Minister of External Affairs, was also quick to perceive a threat to national security when North Korea invaded South Korea. On 27 June 1950, the United Nations Security Council called upon member states to assist in South Korea's defence. By then it was late afternoon 28 June in New Zealand. The following day, even before United Nations Secretary General Trygve Lie had issued a formal request, Holland told parliament that ships of the Royal New Zealand Navy would be available for Korean duty. Holland consulted British officials, although not other Old Commonwealth governments, then announced the despatch of two freighters, *Pukaki* and *Tutira*. They left Aukland for Hong Kong 3 July and reached Korean waters early in August.[59]

Both Holland and Doidge were anglophiles, often referring to "the British Empire" rather than "the British Commonwealth."[60] Until 1955, New Zealand lacked high-level diplomats of its own in Asia but trusted the British for advice and leadership. The Japanese capture of Singapore in 1942 demonstrated that the British connection, while still regarded as good, was less than perfect in itself. New Zealand must also find other allies. Moreover, even the Holland government had begun to dissociate itself from British leadership. The Asian members of the Commonwealth recognized the People's Republic of China as China's legitimate government: India, 31 December 1949; Pakistan, 5 January 1950; Ceylon, 6 January 1950. The United Kingdom did likewise 6 January, but the other Old Commonwealth countries did not.

New Zealand's government strongly disapproved of this particular British action. Some officials saw Mao and his associates as Soviet surrogates.

Until World War II, New Zealanders and Koreans had ignored each other, but during that conflict, New Zealand POWs reportedly found Korean guards in the service of Japan to be particularly cruel. After the war, successive New Zealand governments—that of Labour Prime Minister Peter Fraser and then Holland's National Government—assumed that in the event of a major war against the Soviet Union, South Korea appeared to be a lost cause. Nevertheless, Conventional Wisdom in Wellington was that life in U.S.-dominated South Korea had to be better than life in Soviet-dominated North Korea, that South Korea's flawed elections were nevertheless a better gauge of opinion than anything attempted in North Korea, and that the Soviet Union constituted a threat to both world peace and the independence of many countries, including New Zealand. To New Zealand authorities, Kim Il Sung appeared a Soviet puppet. On 20 June 1949, after the United Kingdom but before Australia and Canada, New Zealand's Minister (Head of Legation) in Washington, Carl Berendsen, informed South Korea's ambassador in the U.S. capital, John M. Chang (Chang Myun), that New Zealand recognized the Rhee government as the legitimate government of South Korea. At the same time, New Zealand authorities rejected South Korean initiatives to exchange diplomats or to recognize South Korean authority north of Latitude 38. New Zealand's business community appeared to share its government's lack of enthusiasm for all things Korean. Late in May 1950, fourteen south Koreans toured New Zealand in search of trading opportunities, but the New Zealanders failed to respond.

In mid-July 1950, the Holland government decided to send ground troops to Korea. Initially Defence Minister Thomas Macdonald objected. He feared that the despatch of soldiers to Korea would handicap any New Zealand military efforts in the Middle East. Doidge feared U.S. wrath if New Zealand did not send ground forces, but his influence in cabinet was limited. His cabinet colleagues sought to determine what the British, Canadian, and Australian governments planned to do, and Patrick Gordon-Walker, the Secretary of State for Commonwealth Relations, happened to be in Wellington. His impression was that the British army had higher priorities than Korea. On the other hand, Carl Berendsen, who doubled as New Zealand's Ambassador to the United Nations, reported pressure from the State Department and from the State Department and from UN Secretary-General Trygve Lie. Both Lie and Secretary of State Dean Acheson made clear that the U.S. wanted and needed troops from Australia and New Zealand. New Zealand's Chiefs of Staff advised that they could spare some soldiers for Korea without jeopardizing their responsibilities in the Middle East.

In the end, British action proved decisive. On 26 July, the British High Commissioner in Wellington, Sir Roy Price, told Holland that the Attlee government would announce its decision to send British soldiers at what would be 2 a.m. New Zealand time. Holland was angry that the Attlee government had not consulted him, or, as he correctly assumed, any other Commonwealth governments and decided to give the impression of a New Zealand initiative. Asia, after all, was closer to New Zealand than to the United Kingdom, and New Zealand national pride would find satisfaction in acting more quickly than Australia. Holland announced his government's decision that very evening, 26 July. The fact that British and Australian governments made similar announcements within hours gave the impression that there had been co-ordination among all three Old Commonwealth governments, but this was an illusion. Each responded unilaterally to U.S. pressure, and New Zealand triumphed at the game of one-up-man-ship.[61]

V   The Canadian Role in the Summer of 1950

Given its geographical location, Canada could be somewhat more complacent than Australia or New Zealand. Both Prime Minister St. Laurent and Defence Minister Brooke Claxton placed a higher priority on Western Europe than on Korea and initially anticipated no Canadian commitment of ground forces.[62] Three Royal Canadian Navy destroyers, the *Cayuga*, the *Sioux*, and the *Athabaska*, received orders 30 June to sail to Korea,[63] where they arrived late in July. The destroyers participated in convoys headed for Pusan, and on 15 August, the *Cayuga* and a British ship fired at the enemy-held port of Yosu. Canadian destroyers protected MacArthur's invasion flotilla as it approached Inchon.[64] However, despite a request from the U.S. Ambassador in Ottawa, Stanley Woodward,[65] Canada did not agree to commit ground forces until 7 August 1950, ironically as the cabinet held an emergency meeting aboard a train while returning from the funeral of Mackenzie King.[66] Three days earlier, even the South African government had said that it would despatch a fighter squadron.[67] Prince suggests that the British, Australian, and New Zealand commitments convinced the Canadian cabinet that if it wanted any influence in Washington, Canada must also send ground troops.[68] (Australian historian Jeffrey Grey has another explanation. According to Grey, New Zealand's government shamed the Canadian government into acting.[69]) Lester Pearson, who remained Minister of External Affairs throughout and well beyond the Korean War, said that he saw Korea as a case for

Collective Security. He and other members of St. Laurent's cabinet believed that if members of the League of Nations had collectively taken a firm stand when Mussolini invaded Ethiopia in 1935 or when Hitler initially defied the Treaty of Versailles and committed acts of aggression, it might have been possible to avoid World War II. Those who supported them, if not Hitler and Mussolini themselves, would have learned early in their careers that aggression did not pay. Joint action by the United Nations might send a similar message to Stalin. Unaware Stalin was responding to pressure from Kim Il Sung, Pearson thought it possible that a firm stand in Korea might avert a European war.[70]

Yet there were limits—sensible limits—as to how firm that stand should be. Like the British, Pearson thought that any reference to "Communist imperialism" in President Truman's public statement of 27 June 1950 was undesirable.[71] As Soviet-bloc documents now indicate, the invasion of South Korea was a North Korean, not a Soviet, initiative, and like Bevin, Pearson did not want to complicate a bad situation by laying false charges. Canada's Ambassador in Washington, Hume Wrong, had discussed the text with Sir Oliver Franks, his British counterpart in the American capital. Franks and Wrong knew that the State Department had discussed the forthcoming presidential statement with other NATO ambassadors as well. In the end, the words "Communist imperialism" did not appear in President Truman's public statement.

That, however, was but a minor victory. The statement still blamed "communism" as well as North Korea for the attack. The statement also contained the implication that "communism" had one centre of power and expanded according to one master plan. If "communism" would attack South Korea, it might also attack Taiwan.

> The attack upon Korea makes it plain beyond all doubt that communism
> has passed beyond the use of subversion to conquer independent nations
> and will now use armed invasion and war. It has defied the orders of the
> Security Council of the United Nations...In these circumstances the occu-
> pation of Formosa [Taiwan] by Communist forces would be a direct threat
> to the security of the Pacific area...[72]

Pearson thought that what came next made little sense, but nevertheless it appeared in the public statement. While President Truman recognized Chiang Kai Shek's government as the legitimate government of China, the statement called upon "the Chinese Government on Formosa to cease all air and sea operations against the mainland. The 7th Fleet will see that this is done."[73] The United States had every right to declare a *de facto* protectorate over Taiwan, thought Pearson, but Canada had the right to "bring our doubts to the notice of the U.S. Government."[74]

Pearson definitely had mixed feelings about Korea. Earlier in 1950, before the outbreak of hostilities, he had met General MacArthur in Tokyo, and MacArthur had told him that South Korea was expendable, not vital to U.S. interests. On the other hand, Pearson *did* like the idea of Collective Security, noted the creation of a United Nations Command ten days after approval of the 27 June Resolution at the United Nations, and hoped that Canada's contribution could be minimal: three destroyers from the Royal Canadian Navy, some equipment and supplies. Canadian authorities were not appeasers. Their concern was that the Western world's military might was finite. There was a limit to what was possible. The defence of Western Europe was more important than any action on the mainland of Asia.[75]

Late in July as the North Korean army overran most of South Korea, Pearson and Prime Minister St. Laurent approved the sending of ground forces.[76] The cabinet agreed, and recruitment of a special brigade for Korea began.[77] Canada became the fourth largest contributor of forces to the United Nations Command, after South Korea, the United States, and the United Kingdom. Collectively, the British, Canadians, Australians, New Zealanders, and South Africans would fight together in one British Commonwealth Division. This was a pragmatic move as the armed forces of all those countries used British-type equipment.[78] Ottawa was not enthusiastic, especially given the absence of any Asian members of the Commonwealth, but eventually it accepted the idea.[79]

Nevertheless, it does not appear as though negotiations with Old Commonwealth members were significant in July 1950. The correspondence published in *Documents on Canadian External Relations* for July 1950 indicates correspondence from Trygve Lie, the Secretary-General of the United Nations.[80] As already mentioned, Hume Wrong spoke to Oliver Franks, and on at least one occasion, Canada's Acting Permanent Delegate to the United Nations, John Holmes, spoke to the Australian representative.[81] On 1 August, Lie initiated a conversation with Holmes.[82] However, one searches in vain for evidence of correspondence between Ottawa on the one hand and London, Canberra, Wellington, or Pretoria on the other.

VI The Northward Thrust: British Diplomacy

For more than two months, the war went badly for the United Nations Command (UNC). Kim Il Sung's Korean People's Army (KPA) had the advantage of surprise. Several of its officers, including Kim Il Sung himself, had lived in the Soviet Union when the Japanese occupied Korea and had had combat experience with the Red Army. Others had fought in Mao Zedong's People's Liberation Army to establish the

People's Republic of China.[83] The most readily available U.S. forces came from the army of occupation in post-war Japan. Occupation is far less formidable than war itself, and the troops were far from battle-ready. The North Korean army captured Seoul within four days of invading South Korea and advanced to the south, occupying all the ROK except for a small perimeter around Pusan.

On 15 September, General Douglas MacArthur, commander of the U.S. army of occupation in Japan and commander of the United Nations forces in Korea, turned the tide. Most commanders would have taken advantage of the beachhead at Pusan, landed reinforcements there, and then fought, as in Normandy in 1944, to expand the perimeter. MacArthur did the totally unexpected. He orchestrated an amphibious attack at Inchon and caught the KPA completely off guard. Tides rise and fall quickly at Inchon, and success required split second precision. As though that were not enough, the UNC then had to cross the Han River, which is as wide near Seoul as the St. Lawrence near Montreal or the St. Mary's as it exits Lake Superior and passes Sault Ste. Marie. All went well for the UNC, which shattered the KPA and entered Seoul 25 September, three months since the outbreak of war.[84] Ships of the U.S., Australian, British, Canadian, New Zealand, Dutch and French navies protected the ships transporting the marines to Inchon.[85] British marines assisted U.S. marines in the ensuing landing.[86]

By the end of September, the UNC managed to regain control of all Korea south of the 38th parallel. Soldiers of the KPA were dead, prisoners-of-war, or in full flight to points farther north. The UNC might have declared victory and terminated the war, as the first President George Bush was to do in 1991 once Coalition forces had liberated Kuwait. Unfortunately, that did not happen.

For the Commonwealth belligerents, this was a missed opportunity. Had they insisted that the UN's role was to repel the aggressors from South Korea, not to liberate North Korea, they would have had some powerful allies in Washington. On 1 September 1950, the National Security Council received a report that the UN's mandate was to oust the North Koreans from South Korea, no more than that. The advisory continued:

> Military actions north of the 38th parallel which go beyond the accomplishment of this mission, for example, to accomplish the political objective of unifying Korea under the Republic of Korea, are not clearly authorized by existing Security Council resolutions. Accordingly, United Nations approval for such further military actions is a prerequisite to their initiation. Should such approval not be forthcoming, accomplishment of this political objective would not be feasible.[87]

Yet before the end of the month, Defense Secretary George Marshall drafted instructions which authorized General MacArthur to occupy North Korea as long as Chinese or Soviet forces appeared unlikely to intervene, and only South Korean ground forces occupy positions near the Soviet and Chinese borders.[88]

General MacArthur and policymakers in Washington had strong memories of World War II, when the Allies fought the Axis aggressors to unconditional surrender. Conventional wisdom was that aggressors should pay for their actions. They should not profit; they should not even return to the *status quo ante bellum*, as though there were little to risk by starting a war. President Truman sought the destruction of North Korean forces.[89] Dean Rusk, who in 1945 as a U.S. Army colonel had negotiated the 38th parallel as the zonal boundary and subsequently become Assistant-Secretary of State for Far Eastern Affairs, was to explain:

> Retreating North Korean forces were regrouping north of the parallel, and it made little sense for allied forces to mark time below the thirty-eighth parallel, with an army in the field getting ready to renew the attack. Additionally, to me, a divided Korea made little sense. We had not selected the thirty-eighty parallel as a permanent boundary; we had simply proposed it to facilitate the acceptance of the Japanese surrender. It was designed to serve a temporary military expediency. Division along the parallel made no sense economically or geographically as far as Korea itself was concerned.[90]

The UNC pursued the KPA into North Korea right to the Yalu River, which forms the border between North Korea and the People's Republic of China. President Truman, members of his administration, and Joint Chiefs of Staff had concerns lest General MacArthur provoke a war with the PRC, a war which might siphon America's limited military strength from Western Europe and invite Soviet aggression there. However, while they warned him to keep United States forces a respectable distance from the Yalu River, they did authorize MacArthur's North Korean offensive and must assume some responsibility for what happened.

The initial assumption of the British Ministry of Defence had been "that the American intention [was] to clear the [South Korean] territory up to the 38th parallel."[91] Professional diplomats agreed. A Foreign Office memorandum of 9 July 1950 pondered the then-hypothetical question of the northern limits of any counterthrust and decided that the disadvantages outweighed any advantages. Syngman Rhee's government was one of "black reaction, brutality and extreme incompetence." Crossing the parallel might provoke Soviet intervention.[92] As late as 20 September, five days after the Inchon landing, the Chiefs of Staff advised that the British government consider the Korean War a success and encourage the United Nations to declare a cease-fire once its forces had reached the 38th parallel. From Tokyo, Air Vice Marshal Bouchier had forwarded a reminder that the highest priority must remain the defence of Western Europe. The Chiefs of Staff noted that Western armies would abandon Korea for more strategic locations if a world war actually did break out. Their advice was "to get as many as possible of our troops out of Korea as early as possible, leaving behind the minimum commitment for the minimum time."[93]

As the situation in South Korea deteriorated, or, in the words of Dean Acheson, "while our troops were fighting against heavy odds to keep a toehold in Korea,"[94] Bevin found himself less than favourably impressed. He seemed to imply that the United States had brought this disaster upon itself. To a point, Bevin was entitled to his opinion. Historian Anthony Farrar-Hockley agrees that before the outbreak of hostilities, U.S. officials in Seoul "had neither instructions nor inclination to work closely with their British colleague." That unfortunate colleague, Captain Sir Vyvyan Holt, the highest ranking British diplomat in the South Korean capital, became a prisoner of the North Koreans when they occupied Seoul in June 1950, and he remained in their custody until 9 April 1953—after Stalin's death.[95] In mid-August 1950, he had suggested that Attlee should consider a trip to Washington to discuss the international situation with President Truman,[96] but Sir Oliver Franks, the British Ambassador in the American capital, threw cold water upon the idea. "There would...be a strong tendency to believe that the world situation must have got suddenly worse," warned Sir Oliver, nor would the United Kingdom be able to deliver as much assistance as the U.S. government would expect.[97] The Americans would have a free hand to direct the war their way.

A few days later, on 30 August, a frustrated Bevin wrote a lengthy memo for the cabinet. Since 1945, he said, the United States had given the United Kingdom a free hand in South and South-East Asia but regarded the Far East as its preserve. There, he said, the Americans "tended to be a law unto themselves...with results which have been far from happy." Internal U.S. politics were determining the agenda, he feared. Mao's triumph in China and the forthcoming Congressional elections in the United States encouraged partisan strife in Washington. The U.S. was ignoring Asian opinion. Unfortunately, there was little the British could do.

> No effort is likely to succeed which, just before elections, has the result that the United States Administration appears to have given way to United Kingdom pressure. We cannot expect the Administration to do things which will lead to its certain downfall.

Clearly, therefore, the United Kingdom should not be intrusive in its efforts to influence United States policy in the right direction, nor must the onus fall on us alone for bringing about a chance in American policy, if that can be effected.[98]

Nevertheless, Bevin saw reason for optimism. The Truman administration was consulting London "for the first time since the war [World War II]," and perhaps it might "modify" its policies if recommendations came not only from the United Kingdom but from the UK and a number of other United Nations members. To that end, he would consult "with Commonwealth countries, with France, and possibly some other European countries."[99]

MacArthur's "miracle at Inchon" brought a change of attitude on the part of Bevin, even if not among the Chiefs of Staff. When he produced his first post-Inchon memo for the cabinet, Bevin said that that success had eased domestic pressure on the Truman administration and allowed it to modify its policies along the lines which the British government desired. He had gone to the United States, held talks with U.S. officials, and was able to report, "There was no divergence of view between us and the United States Government on Korea." Nor did Bevin think that MacArthur should stop at the 38th parallel when his armies had pushed the North Koreans out of South Korea. He referred to the 38th parallel as "an obsession in people's minds" and noted that it had "never had any international recognition as a boundary." Bevin continued that while he was in the United States,

> It had become increasingly apparent that by constant mention of the 38th Parallel…we were creating a barrier for ourselves which it might be difficult to break down at a subsequent stage.

Bevin regretted that Indian Prime Minister Pandit Nehru took the 38th parallel much too seriously.

> To Pandit Nehru the 38th Parallel seemed to have assumed nightmare proportions, and it is by no means certain that this imaginary line will not in the end defeat our aims if we are not careful. I accordingly made every effort while I was in New York to discourage reference to the 38th Parallel.[100]

Certainly, the information which Bevin was receiving from his ambassadors in Moscow and Beijing indicated that there was likely to be minimal risk in crossing the parallel. From Moscow, Ambassador Sir David Kelly accurately predicted that if the alternative was war with the United States and the United Kingdom, Stalin would acquiesce in the liquidation of North Korea. Kelly's reasons included Stalin's cautious track record, the horrendous losses suffered by the Soviet people during World War II, as well as U.S. superiority in industrial output and military strength.[101] From Beijing, and despite warnings from the Burmese and Indian ambassadors to the People's Republic of China, Ambassador Sir J.C. Hutchison thought that Chinese intervention in Korea was unlikely, and he advised Bevin accordingly. On 30 September, roughly a week before the Chinese government decided to intervene (see below), Hutchison notified the Foreign Office:

> (a) There are at present in Peking [Beijing] (obviously for the 1st October parade [in commemoration of the first anniversary of the establishment of the People's Republic of China]) about 100 tanks...It seems to be improbable that if large scale intervention in Korea is intended the Chinese would keep as many tanks here, though no conclusive deduction can be made from this;

> (b) Rail travellers on the Peking-Tientsin railway have not (repeat not) observed any significant movements. On the other hand, there are large numbers of troops and material already in Manchuria, a considerable portion of which may be concentrated on the border...

> (c) In view of the avowed Chinese communist's [sic] military strategy not to attack unless success is assured, it seems improbable that the Chinese would choose as the time for large scale intervention (whether openly or in the form of 'volunteers') the moment when North Korean forces appear to be in process of being decisively defeated. Against this however can be set the psychological considerations which the Burmese Ambassador mentioned to me which suggested that they might take a decision to intervene more on political than on military grounds.[102]

Not surprisingly, the British cabinet agreed with the Foreign Secretary. Minutes of a 26 September meeting of the cabinet note that if the United States Command destroyed North Korean forces before they retreated across the parallel, North Korea faced one of two probable alternatives, neither conducive to stability in South Korea. Either the Soviets would occupy North Korea, or there would be chaos throughout North Korea. "There was general agreement that military operations could not be stopped at the 38th parallel," the cabinet decided. Also, "If the United Nations forces had to proceed beyond the 38th parallel, it would not be practicable to stipulate that United Kingdom forces should not go with them."[103]

The next day Sir Gladwyn Jebb, British Ambassador at the United Nations, wrote about the "clearly limited objectives of the United Nations. There is," said Sir Gladwyn, "no threat against China. On the other hand, if the United Nations are to have no access to North Korea, all the efforts of those who have fought the battle—and it has been a hard battle—will have been in vain."[104]

For their part, the Chiefs of Staff remained unconvinced. In their opinion, as of 5 October, there was "no immediate military need" to cross the parallel. They suggested an ultimatum to North Korea. Surrender within the next one to two weeks, or the United Nations Command would invade.[105] Despite this advice, the attack on North Korea began 7 October. At the time, General MacArthur was promising that UN forces would proceed only to the Nampo-Pyongyang-Wonsan line. Only South Koreans would advance to the Yalu and Tumen Rivers (the Chinese and Soviet borders).[106] The promise was not, in fact, kept. On 6 October, Bevin said, "We have no desire to take the very heavy responsibility of pressing the Americans to abandon any operations which may be contemplated north of the Parallel."[107] (See map, p.156.)

On 14 November, just before the tide of battle turned and the People's Republic of China launched its massive offensive, Bevin advised Franks that the United Nations Command should halt at a line from Hungnam to Chongju. After all, Korea was of "little strategic importance" and that line, 150 miles in length, was more defensible than North Korea's border with the USSR and China–400 miles long. The area north of the Hungnam-Chongju line should be demilitarized, said Bevin. This would not be "a unilateral concession on the part of the United Nations."[108] Unfortunately, in very short order, British authorities would be singing from a different hymn book, wondering whether the United Nations could retain a toehold in South Korea or might have to consider a Dunkirk-like withdrawal from the mainland of northeast Asia. (See Chapter 3.)

Bevin's suggestion of the Chongju-Hungnam line would not have prevented the horrors which followed. Chinese forces were already inside Korea; General William F. Dean had seen them as early as 13 October, ten days before Truman met MacArthur at Wake Island.[109] Planning for the 25 November offensive was well under way when Bevin suggested that line 14 November. Yet, unaware of what was to come, the Joint Chiefs of Staff (JCS) and members of the Truman administration seriously considered the Chongju-Hungnam line and other British ideas.

Patrick C. Roe, the intelligence historian mentioned in the Introduction, says:

concerned that bombing the Yalu bridges might spill over into Chinese territory in Manchuria, the JCS, after hurried consultation with the president, instructed MacArthur, late on 5 November, to postpone all bombing of targets within five miles of the Manchurian border...Of serious concern was the U.S. commitment not to take action affecting Manchuria without consultation with the British...[110]

MacArthur replied with such ferocity that the Joint Chiefs of Staff rescinded the order. As far as MacArthur was concerned, any British plan to leave Communists in charge of any part of Korea was reminiscent of British cowardice at Munich in 1938, when Prime Minister Neville Chamberlain allowed Hitler to occupy parts of Czechoslovakia. The State Department saw merit in the British proposal, but any discussion was academic. As far as Beijing was concerned, the Chongju-Hungnam line was too far north. Even if MacArthur had accepted it, the Chinese offensive of 25 November would have proceeded.

Roe does agree, however, that U.S. allies (not necessarily members of the Commonwealth) might have had some impact in the debate whether to bomb Manchurian bases from which the Chinese were launching attacks on United Nations forces inside Korea. MacArthur wanted to bomb them, and the Joint Chiefs of Staff were sympathetic. Both Secretary of State Acheson and General Omar Bradley, Chairman of the Joint Chiefs of Staff, agreed that UN consent was necessary before the United Nations Command could bomb targets inside Manchuria.[111] The Central Intelligence Agency minimized the risks of such an escalation, and Acheson discussed the idea informally at the United Nations with diplomats from allied countries. Opposition to carrying the war into Manchuria was overwhelming. According to Roe,

> There was the genuine possibility that other UN members might dissociate themselves with [sic] any action across the Manchurian frontier, destroying the UN solidarity so necessary to the action. The French, knowing of MacArthur's reputation for independence, were particularly concerned—and especially concerned about what MacArthur would do.[112]

U.S. authorities accepted the arguments of their allies. The Korean War would be fought exclusively inside Korea.

VII The Northward Thrust: Australian and New Zealand Diplomacy

Australian policy resembled that of the United Kingdom except in one respect. Whereas Spender found, on a visit to London in August 1950, that the British wanted to give Taiwan to the People's Republic of China as quickly as possible, he considered it preferable that Taiwan become a ward of the United Nations, at least temporarily. Spender's fear was that an alliance with Chiang Kai Shek would push the PRC into an alliance with the USSR, which could threaten the security of Western Europe. At that time, Spender considered the highest priority of the United Nations to be the forcible removal of North Koreans from that part of the Korean peninsula south of the 38th parallel.[113] His conversion to a northward thrust came later.

Actually, Spender was willing to let the United States lead on that issue. Whether to cross the 38th parallel was a topic which he discussed with British authorities, but Spender's position was this. As U.S. forces were doing most of the fighting, Australia should learn what the U.S. government was planning to do before it took a stand.[114] Professor Robert O'Neill, official historian of Australia's involvement in the Korean War and his country's participation, has suggested that Spender was so deeply involved with other matters that "Australia, unlike Canada, made no contribution to the development of United Nations or American policy regarding the 38th parallel."[115] Spender's primary objective was a military alliance with the United States—ANZUS, among Australia, New Zealand, and the United States—which materialized in 1951. In the interval, he did not want to antagonize the United States over a seemingly less significant matter—whether to cross the 38th parallel. After an examination of the documentary evidence, O'Neill concluded that between 4 August and 8 September, Spender changed his mind. On 4 August, he was still thinking of driving the North Korean army out of South Korea. On 8 September, he indicated to Menzies that he had no objections to a thrust into North Korea if that was what the U.S. government wanted.

There were other considerations. Statements by Australian officials emphasized the importance of collective security, the absence whereof had encouraged Hitler to develop an insatiable appetite for new conquests. If the West did not resist Communist expansion in Korea, there might soon be another victim of Communist aggression somewhere else. In search of his U.S.-Australian security treaty, in September 1950 Spender met President Truman in Washington, where the president sought his support for the northward advance. Truman was not confident that the UN Resolution of 27 June authorized such action, and with the Soviet Union having ended its boycott and returned to the Security Council, it was certain that approval from Security Council was no longer attainable. Approval from the countries fighting alongside the United States had thus become important. On 18 September, UNCOK released its report, which clearly accused North Korea of launching an unprovoked invasion of South Korea. With that, Spender had less reason than ever to justify North Korea's territorial integrity.[116]

On 27 September, with Spender out of the country, Menzies addressed Australia's House of Representatives on the 38th parallel issue. By then United Nations forces had recaptured Seoul and were very close to the former inter-Korean border. Menzies certainly had no objections if the United Nations should decide to proceed beyond that:

> When forces reach the 38th parallel, which after all is not an identifiable land mark but only a line on the map, I, for one, do not assume that they will cease fire when somebody says, "we are now on the 38th parallel." That would not make sense. They might be in the middle of a battle. Armies do not knock off and abandon their advantage in the middle of a battle merely because they have reached a certain parallel of latitude.[117]

Menzies then made another point. If the United Nations Command left North Korea's army "quite intact" on the other side of the parallel, the aggressor might strike again. If North Korea could attack South Korea with impunity, it would have little incentive not to undertake another invasion.[118] From the Opposition benches, Evatt agreed—at least to a point. The United Nations should offer peace terms and indicate the limits of its northward advance, but it would be "absurd and impractical" to stop at an imaginary line.[119]

Four years later, writing after the crossing of the parallel, the advance to the Yalu River, the Chinese intervention, and another thirty-four months of war, Spender's successor, Richard Casey, said that MacArthur had interpreted a UN resolution of 7 October as his authorization to proceed. Those who supported the resolution knew the risks, said Casey.

> But we really had no alternative, when the 38th parallel was reached, except to advance into North Korea. So long as the Communists continued to fight, the United Nations forces had little choice except to pursue the enemy and attempt to destroy them. To have taken any other attitude would have been to accept the principle that an aggressor can at any time launch an attack and, if it is unsuccessful, retire again at will behind his own frontiers, where the victim is obliged to halt. It must be remembered that the Communists did not seek a cease-fire when they were driven back to the 38th parallel late in 1950. On the contrary, they continued to fight against the United Nations forces.[120]

South Korean soldiers entered North Korea 1 October, U.S. forces six days later. British and Australian troops followed,[121] with British forces participating in the capture of Pyongyang.[122] At that point, Australia had no foreign intelligence service of its own; the Australian Secret Intelligence Service dates from 13 May 1952.[123] Under the circumstances, Canberra depended heavily upon British intelligence, and British intelligence appeared to know very little about possible Soviet and Chinese intentions in Korea. Evidence on China was minimal, but that on the Soviet Union suggested (accurately as will be evident below) that Stalin would rather cut his losses and abandon North Korea altogether than fight a war against the United States.

As MacArthur's army advanced northward, Spender remained in Washington, advocating a U.S.-Australian military alliance. Aware that the United States wanted a peace treaty with Japan, Spender did not want to be vulnerable if that former enemy remilitarized. He was unlikely to attack U.S. policy in Korea, and in the Australian House of Representatives, government members had nothing but positive comments about MacArthur's achievements. In the second half of October, Chinese forces entered North Korea. In Spender's absence, early in November Menzies ordered Watt to meet the U.S. Ambassador, Pete Jarman, to express concern over a possible widening of the war.[124] Keith Officer, Acting Head of the Australian Mission at the United Nations, approached the U.S. delegation 10 November and received assurances that the U.S. Air Force would not bomb Manchuria without first consulting Australia. (Any plans to bomb Manchuria were dropped after meetings of U.S., British, and French representatives from 14 to 24 November. Australia did not attend those meetings, but the British government informed Australian authorities as to what was happening.) The Chinese army (Chinese People's Volunteers or CPV) launched its offensive 25-26 November, as a result of which the United Nations Command began its retreat from the Yalu River to a line south of Seoul, let alone the 38th parallel.

Washington's original approach toward the use of soldiers from New Zealand was that they might be too few in number to be of much use. However, in mid-November 1950—after the arrival of the first Chinese soldiers but before the end-of-the-month offensive—the U.S. government decided it wanted the New Zealanders after all. Sidney Holland's government agreed to despatch the 16th Field Artillery Regiment early in December.[125] In all, New Zealand sent 2000 soldiers to Korea.[126] (See Chapter 3.)

New Zealand's National Party government, like that of Menzies in Australia, did not attempt to discourage the UNC from crossing the 38th parallel. As he voted for the UN resolution of 7 October 1950, Berendsen rejoiced that the "good" side was taking decisive action against the "evil." The Holland government contentedly accepted UK leadership on an issue about which it had limited information. The fact that U.S., British, and Australian authorities appeared to agree on a course of action made the crossing of the parallel seem all the more desirable. Inasmuch as the northward thrust was an issue in Wellington, the consensus was that North Korea had committed aggression and deserved punishment. However, events in North Korea clearly were not a burning issue. External Affairs Minister Doidge was out of the country at the time and left policymaking to Sir Clifton Webb, the acting minister of external affairs. In the absence of Doidge, members of parliament ignored the issue throughout the month of October. Modification of U.S. behaviour was not a high priority for New Zealand's political leaders.[127]

VIII   The Northward Thrust: Canadian Diplomacy

When MacArthur turned the tide at Inchon, Canada's Secretary of State for External Affairs, Lester B. Pearson, nevertheless thought that the United Nations Command should remain south of the 38th parallel. As early as 4 July, while South Korean forces were in full retreat, Pearson wrote to Prime Minister St. Laurent:

> This [the Korean War] may result in a prolonged indecisive conflict which would be a drain on United States reserves. The USSR would have every reason to be happy if the United Nations became heavily, but indecisively, engaged in Korea, while the French were deeply involved in Indo-China and the British pre-occupied with Malaya.

> There is, of course, another danger...namely that United States action may prove decisive, and that public opinion in that country will then insist that United Nations forces move beyond the 38th parallel and clean up the whole of the Korean situation. In that case, there may be an unhappy conflict between United States policy and United Nations policy. The latter is pledged merely to defeat an aggression and not...to change the political situation in Korea...[128]

In a private meeting at the United Nations, U.S. authorities, backed by the Turks, argued that to stop there would "throw away our victory" and leave the North Korean aggressor unpunished. Pearson discussed this with the U.S. delegation at the United Nations, as did Hume Wrong, Canada's ambassador in Washington, with Secretary of State Dean Acheson and Assistant-Secretary of State for Far Eastern Affairs, Dean Rusk. In his memoirs, Pearson said when he and Wrong could not persuade U.S. authorities to stop at the 38th parallel, he proposed the Nampo-Wonsan line—across North Korea's "narrow neck" just south of Pyongyang—as a compromise. For a few hours he thought that there was agreement on that point, but in short order he learned otherwise. Pearson did not know whom to blame for the misunderstanding but believed that Acheson acted in good faith.[129]

Pearson was deeply concerned. He had met prominent members of India's government at Commonwealth meetings and had deep respect for them. Unlike Canada, Australia, and New Zealand, India had recognized the PRC and had diplomats in Beijing. India's ambassador in Beijing, Kavalam Madhava Panikkar, warned of PRC intervention in Korea as the war moved closer to the Yalu River. (As early as 2 October 1950, Chinese Foreign Minister Zhou Enlai had warned Panikkar that the CPV would intervene if U.S. forces crossed the 38th parallel.[130]) Pearson was aware of this when he argued with the Americans, first over the 38th parallel, then over the Nampo-Wonsan line.[131]

The record may indicate that Pearson was somewhat more ambivalent than his memoirs indicate. Correspondence of 26 September 1950 indicates his fears that the Soviets or Chinese might intervene if the United Nations Command occupied North Korea. Even if they did not, the presence of Western armies on the Soviet and Chinese borders would hardly be conducive to world peace. However, he also realized that

> Redivision of the country at the 38th parallel would re-create all the old
> military, political, and economic problems that plagued the Republic of
> Korea, and might make many Americans feel that their losses in Korea
> had been in vain.[132]

Also, Canada supported a United General Assembly resolution of 7 October 1950 which authorized the United Nations Command to move north of the 38th parallel.[133] Pearson expressed his reservations to Menzies before the vote,[134] but the cabinet was aware that not only the U.S. government but also the British, which like the Americans already had combat forces in Korea, would think that to stop at the 38th parallel would render "futile" all their actions to date.[135]

Perhaps, however, Pearson was consistent in his opposition to the crossing of the 38th parallel. That was certainly the opinion of Denis Stairs, author of the classic *The Diplomacy of Constraint: Canada, the Korean War, and the United States.*[136] It is difficult to argue that Stairs was wrong. Pearson had every right, even an obligation, to consider all sides of the argument. Moreover, the language of the UN resolution of 7 October—sponsored by Australia, Brazil, Cuba, the Netherlands, Norway, Pakistan, the Philippines, and the United Kingdom (and supported by Canada)—is open to interpretation. The resolution recommended:

(a) That all appropriate steps be taken to ensure conditions of stability throughout Korea.

(b) That all constituent acts be taken, including the holding of elections, under the auspices of the United Nations for the establishment of a unified, independent and democratic Government in the sovereign state of Korea...

(c) That United Nations forces should not remain in any part of Korea otherwise than so far as necessary for achieving the objectives specified in (a) and (b) above.[137]

Even Dean Acheson admitted that General MacArthur stretched the meaning of that resolution in suggesting that it authorized the United Nations Command to annihilate North Korea and send forces as far north as the Yalu River.[138] Prince suggests at least two reasons why Canada supported the 7 October 1950 Resolution. First, Pearson realized that U.S. authorities were so determined to cross the 38th parallel that any opposition would be futile, if not counterproductive; and, secondly, Canadian officials agreed in principle that Korean unification was desirable and that this was a way to achieve unification.[139]

For its part, Australia did not support Pearson's Nampo-Wonsan line; Spender agreed with Bevin on the Chongju-Hungnam line. Even this was too little for Acheson, who indicated that he would accept only a narrow demilitarized zone south of the Yalu River,[140] but too much for the Chinese government, which did not want the United Nations Command north of the 38th parallel. To summarize, in view of the information available to governments whose forces contributed to the United Nations Command, Pearson's reservations were indeed sensible. To go north of Nampo-Wonsan entailed more risks than possible benefits. Given what available Soviet and Chinese forces reveal, even Nampo-Wonsan was too far north. (This point will be discussed later in this chapter.) Certainly the price for an additional twenty-two additional months of fighting proved disproportionate to any benefits for the UNC: thousands of deaths, extensive property damage throughout Korea, for a boundary modified from the 38th parallel to a demarcation line (DML) aligned to geographical features south of the parallel in the west and north of it in the east. Unfortunately, Pearson was less than persuasive, even with his British and Australian allies, but his lack of persuasiveness did not matter. Even Nampo-Wonsan would have been too far north for Mao Zedong and his colleagues.

IX The Significance of British, Canadian, Australian Diplomacy Regarding the Northward Thrust

Co-ordination of strategy was minimal among members of the Old Commonwealth. Not until late August did Bevin begin to think that it might be worthwhile. Spender complained about the lack thereof. Louis St. Laurent's biographer, Dale Thomson, wrote:

> The only serious difference of view between the British and Canadian leaders [in connection with Korea] concerned the most effective way of using the Commonwealth to promote peace and international co-operation. Attlee argued that more formal structures were required, and that a common policy should be adopted by all members of the Commonwealth wherever possible. St. Laurent continued to insist that the greatest value of the Commonwealth was as a bridge between democratic nations in different parts of the world, and a vehicle to reduce misunderstandings between them. The mere impression of attempting to interfere with the right of member nations to determine their own policies on particular issues, he pointed out, would reduce the usefulness of the organization.[141]

However, even if they had co-ordinated, they might not have agreed. As it was, Pearson objected more seriously than did his British or Australian colleagues to the crossing of the 38th parallel. The consequences are clear. South Korea did end the war with more defensible borders than it had at the beginning, but meanwhile the Chinese intervention prolonged the war for more than two and one-half years. The cost was hardly proportionate to the benefit.

Nor would Pearson's "compromise" of a border at the Nampo-Wonsan line have avoided a tragedy. Soviet and Chinese documents now available indicate that the Soviets probably would have lived with such an arrangement, but that the Chinese—at least in the long run—would not.

Stalin was so reluctant to enter a war against the United States—and he saw the Korean War as a war against the "Anglo-Americans," not the United Nations[142]— that in October, 1950, as U.S. and South Korean forces advanced through North Korea toward the Soviet and Chinese borders, he was prepared to accept defeat. He worked furiously to persuade Mao Zedong to send Chinese forces to fight the "Anglo-Americans," but Mao seemed reluctant. Stalin would send the Soviet air force from bases in China to assist the North Koreans, but under no circumstances would he send ground troops.[143]

The spirit of defeatism developed within a matter of days. Late in September, even before South Korean forces had entered North Korea, Shtykov asked permission to repatriate a number of Soviet "specialists." Shtykov explained to his superiors in Moscow that the U.S. Air Force had bombed Pyongyang so extensively that many factories and plants were "not in operation" nor likely to be so in the foreseeable future. The repatriation of the appropriate people, thought Shtykov, would not affect productivity. Anxious to maintain North Korean morale, Gromyko authorized such a repatriation or evacuation only if North Korean authorities proposed such a course of action. The initiative must come from the North Koreans. "You should not display any initiative of your own," Gromyko told Shtykov, "in raising the issue of the evacuation of Soviet specialists before the Koreans do."[144]

Within a week, before U.S. troops had entered North Korea or the United Nations General Assembly had passed its resolution of 7 October, Gromyko changed his tune. On 5 October, Shtykov sent another urgent telegram to Moscow. This time the Soviet ambassador in Pyongyang requested permission to evacuate

> Soviet specialists working in Korea, families of Soviet citizens of Korean nationality, staff of the Soviet air commandants' offices, and, in case of emergency, all Soviet citizens...[145]

This time Gromyko and Soviet Defence Minister A.M. Vasilevsky replied:

> Second. You [Shtyov] must decide the question of the evacuation of families of Soviet citizens of Korean nationality from the territory of Korea on the spot, bearing in mind changes in the situation on the ground.

> Third. All the Soviet personnel of the air commandants' offices and families of Soviet military advisers must be evacuated from the territory of Korea.

> Fourth. We agree with your proposal that, in case of emergency, all the Soviet citizens, including Soviet citizens of Korean nationality, be evacuated to the territory of the USSR and China.[146]

On 12 October, Stalin—through Shtykov—advised Kim Il Sung that in the absence of Chinese assistance, Kim should evacuate North Korea, taking key North Korean political and military people with him.[147]

The timing of the Chinese decision to intervene is less clear. Marshal Peng Dehuai, commander of the Chinese People's Volunteers, says that the Central Committee of the Communist Party made the decision at a meeting in Beijing 5 October, two days before the UN vote of 7 October. Peng offered a number of reasons. China had a moral obligation to help fellow revolutionaries in distress. The problem was especially acute as the collapse of North Korea might bring U.S. forces to the Yalu River, within sight of China, where they would endanger China's security. U.S.

control of Taiwan posed a threat to Shanghai and East China. The U.S. could find a pretext at any time to launch a war of aggression against China. The tiger wanted to eat human beings when it would do so would depend on its appetite. No concession could stop it. If the U.S. wanted to invade China, we had to resist its aggression.[148]

This decision predated the UN Command's advance north of the Nampo-Wonsan line.

There is evidence that Mao Zedong had decided at an even earlier date that China must intervene, but that he had not told Stalin. Perhaps he wanted to extract a maximum of support from Stalin to do what he planned to do anyway, especially as the course of action was one which Stalin favoured. Chen Jian, who has examined Chinese archival sources, says that

early in August 1950, more than one month before the Inchon landing, Mao Zedong and the Beijing leadership had been inclined to send troops to Korea, and China's military and political preparations had begun even a month earlier.

The security of the border along the Yalu River was not the only motivating factor, says Chen. "Mao and his associates aimed to win a glorious victory by driving the Americans off the Korean peninsula."[149] Chen has examined Chinese books and articles based on archival materials from the Chinese Communist Party's Central Collection, although he has not been able to visit that collection himself. He has studied memoirs and published correspondence of Chinese participants and decision-makers, but he has examined unpublished, classified correspondence of Mao, Zhou, and other prominent Chinese leaders.[150]

Professor Michael M. Sheng of Southwest Missouri State University has examined documents from both Soviet and Chinese archives. He agrees with Chen that what determined Chinese intervention was not "what the U.S. did or did not do" but rather what he calls the "inner dynamics" of the Chinese Communist Party, "a combination of the Leninist ideology, revolutionary experience, the 'middle kingdom' mentality, and national security concerns."[151] Sheng too sees the Chinese decision to intervene as an early one. With the outbreak of hostilities 25 June and the U.S. decision to send the Seventh Fleet into the Taiwan Straits a few days later, Mao and his associates began to prepare for war against the United States. By the end of that month,

Beijing shifted its military focus from the Taiwan Straits to Korea. On June 30, Mao informed Xiao Jinguang, the commander-in-chief of the CCP [Chinese Communist Party] navy, that the timing for liberating Taiwan be postponed, and the preparation for encountering the U.S. in Korea took the first priority.[152]

In July, the Beijing government created a Northeast Defence Army (NDA), consisting of four infantry armies and three artillery divisions. The NDA had orders to muster near the Manchurian border by the end of the month, even though North Korea forces were pushing the United Nations Command into the Pusan Perimeter at that time. Its purpose, Mao indicated, was to participate in the Korean War, not to stop unfriendly forces from crossing the Yalu River. Zhou Enlai agreed. There was a consensus that if the "reactionaries" won in Korea, China might be their next target.

Sheng says that on 5 August, Mao told the NDA to be ready to fight in September. Nie Rongzhen, China's Chief of Staff, believed that in pushing toward Pusan, the North Korean army had left North Korea undefended. The U.S. would not readily accept defeat, but given the absence of North Korean soldiers from North Korea, a North Korean defeat was a distinct possibility. Mao and his associates thought that a conflict between China and the United States was inevitable sooner or later, in the Taiwan Straits, in Korea, or in Vietnam. As Mao's air force and navy were not formidable, the Taiwan Straits appeared an undesirable locale for the confrontation. Vietnam was distant from the Chinese heartland, and there France was the principal enemy, not the United States. Hence, to the men in Beijing, Korea seemed the most advantageous battlefield.

Stalin knew none of this. He did not have agents at the meetings of Chinese political and military leaders. Hence, Mao was in a position to ask Stalin for a long list of supplies, some of which Stalin was unwilling or unable to provide. On 2 October 1950, Mao sent Stalin a letter which said that he had originally planned to send the Chinese into Korea when "the enemy advanced north of the 38th parallel." (There was no mention of the Nampo-Wonsan line.) However, further consideration led to the conclusion that "such actions may entail extremely serious consequences." The Chinese forces lacked equipment. Intervention might lead to war between China and the United States, which might escalate into a war which involved the Soviet Union.[153] No copy of that letter, available in the Soviet archives, is available in Beijing. Another letter of the same date, with Mao's handwriting, says that China had definitely decided to intervene. Sheng suggests that Mao drafted but never sent the affirmative letter and that the negative letter had been a bluff. Once he realized that Stalin would give no more, Mao prepared to do what he had planned to do all along: intervene.[154] Accordingly, the Chinese crossed the Yalu into Korea at midnight, 16 October.[155]

On 12 October, Mao Zedong suggested to Zhou Enlai that initially Chinese forces should remain north of the Nampo-Pyongyang-Wonsan line. That could buy time. Hopefully it would prevent a northward thrust by the enemy. The CPV might have to wait behind that line for six months, until the spring of 1951, by which time it would have more training and better equipment and be in position to launch an southward offensive.[156]

David Wolff, who like Sheng has examined Russian and Chinese documents, says that Mao regarded Korea as a distraction from China's civil war, which he wanted to complete before the end of 1950 by attacking Tibet and Taiwan. Like Sheng, Wolff says that Mao and his associates decided at some point in July 1950 that Korea might have to become a higher priority.[157] Shen Zhihua agrees and says that Stalin circumvented Mao once he had given the green light to Kim Il Sung. Soviet sources, according to Shen Zhihua, indicate that Kim, not Stalin, was the one who told Chinese leaders that war was imminent, and he did so while visiting Beijing in May 1950. Kim's hosts were incredulous and sought confirmation from the Soviets. Admittedly, Mao had allowed ethnic Korean soldiers enlisted in his army to return to North Korea in 1949 and early 1950—23,000 in 1950 alone—but he did so before Kim's visit, and he might have done so for economic reasons. Despite his intention to "liberate" Taiwan, it was expensive to maintain a huge army far from the likely site of battle. The departure of the Koreans freed money for higher priorities.[158]

Yet other historians who have studied Chinese sources agree that the die had been cast for Chinese intervention long before it happened. Hao Yufan and Zhai Shihai report that shortly after United Nations forces recaptured Seoul, Bevin sent a message to Zhou Enlai through Nehru. The message was that if UN forces did cross the 38th parallel, they would halt sixty miles (100 kilometres) south of the Yalu River. Mao had little reason, say Hao and Zhai, to trust this promise. Nehru had already forwarded a United States promise not to cross the 38th parallel, and U.S. involvement in Taiwan (Chinese territory)and in Japan (China's perennial enemy) seemed threatening. Moreover, a U.S. client state south of the Yalu would force China to place an army on the opposite shore for an indefinite period of time. Mao believed that if China remained passive when North Korea's survival was at stake, the Soviet Union might not help the People's Republic of China if U.S. forces in Taiwan, Korea, or Vietnam threatened its longevity. If war against the United States was inevitable, perhaps the Korean battlefield was the most advantageous from the perspective of Mao and his colleagues. Korea was closer to Beijing than was Vietnam, and the People's Republic of China could rely exclusively on its army. (A fight involving Taiwan would involve a navy and an air force.) Also, thought Mao and General Peng, Europe remained the highest priority for the United States, and the Soviet Union was America's principal adversary. Korea was only a sideshow. Mao decided to intervene 2 October 1950,[159] ten days before Stalin told Shtykov to prepare for evacuation and at which point United Nations forces were still well south of Wonsan on the east coast and between Seoul and the 38th parallel on the west.[160] The Chinese Politburo confirmed the decision six days later.[161] Conclude Hao and Zhai:

> From Chinese sources...we learn that China's participation was neither a
> long-planned, well-designed operation, nor an action taken as part of the
> Soviet Union's plan for expansion.[162]

It appears probable that a cease-fire at the Nampo-Wonsan line would not have lasted.

Briefly, Pearson's suggestion that the United Nations Command stay south of the Nampo-Wonsan line was a cautious Canadian compromise. If the United States and its allies wanted to punish Kim Il Sung for aggression without frightening the Chinese, a cease fire at the Nampo-Wonsan line seemed sensible. It removed territory from North Korea, but it kept the United Nations Command far from the Yalu River and China's borders. Unfortunately, it was doomed to failure. Chinese documents show that to the political leaders in Beijing, more than the safety of China's northeastern border region was at stake. A halt at the Nampo-Wonsan line would not have prevented Chinese intervention, nor was it likely to have stopped the bloodshed for more than six months. In all likelihood, it really did not matter that Pearson failed to persuade either the Old Commonwealth governments or the Truman administration of its merits.

Yet, no less an authority than historian William Stueck, himself an American, thinks that the Nampo-Wonsan line might have had some positive impact, although even he has his doubts:

> Had UN forces halted in the area of Pyongyang and Wonsan, a major
> clash with the Chinese could have been avoided for months. Conceivably,
> diplomatic action during those months and, most important, the emer-
> gence of a relative balance of military forces in the northern reaches of the
> peninsula would have discouraged either side from taking the offensive on

the battlefield. A stalemate at the narrow neck would have protected the security of China's borders and left some territory under DPRK [Democratic People's Republic of Korea, i.e., North Korean] control, but it would not have achieved Kim's aim of uniting the peninsula under his control; it would not even have left him in a position equal to that before the June attack. Surely he would have pressed for offensive action. No one can say whether Mao, facing divisions at home and a difficult campaign in Korea, which might spark U.S. attacks on China, would have considered his brotherly obligation to Kim or the prestige of his government...or even his nation's physical security and economic development, as requiring an offensive. Presumably, Stalin would have had input on the matter. Although much about his views remain shrouded in mystery, he clearly wanted to avoid a direct military clash with the United States...A year later Mao, unquestionably with his Soviet ally's approval, would accept an armistice line the balance of which was north of the 38th parallel. Yet this was only after China had won some glorious victories on the battlefield and suffered huge losses in manpower.[163]

This, of course, is counter-factual history. Pearson's advice about the Wonsan-Nampo line fell on deaf ears. One can but make educated guesses about the impact of a receptive audience in Washington.

X   The Commonwealth as a Force for Restraint

As early as 11 July 1950, British authorities saw definite advantages to the Old Commonwealth connection. At that time, Younger wrote:

> It is very important for us to line up the Commonwealth as far as possible, particularly Canada and Australia. If their views are like anything the same as ours, collectively we might have a real influence upon the Americans.[164]

Perhaps members of the Old Commonwealth should have co-ordinated strategy rather than strike out in five directions which might or might not be similar. He did encourage Canada, Australia, New Zealand, and South Africa to participate militarily in the Korean War, and the five countries did create a Commonwealth Division. By late August, Bevin was co-opting France as a partner in dealing with the USA.

However, the Old Commonwealth countries did not work together in a co-ordinated attempt to deter the United Nations Command, led by General Douglas MacArthur, from crossing the 38th parallel. Indeed, British and Australian leaders saw definite advantages to crossing the parallel, and all five countries supported the United Nations General Assembly Resolution of 7 October authorizing the crossing. Apart from Pearson, there seems to have been little interest in stopping at the Nampo-Wonsan line, and even if there had been, the People's Republic of China would have intervened on the side of North Korea. (Bevin's Chongju-Hungnam line was totally unrealistic.) The major difference that such a halt might have made appears to have been one of timing. Most of the fighting which took place in bitterly cold North Korea during the winter of 1950–1951 would have taken place in the spring.

Nevertheless, historian Stanley Weintraub does see the Commonwealth as a successful force for restraining General Douglas MacArthur, whose policies might well have provoked full scale war—not limited to Korea—between the United Nations Command and the People's Republic of China. When MacArthur ordered B-29 bombers to destroy the Korean end of a bridge across the Yalu River between Sinuiju in North Korea and Dandong on the Chinese side, General George Stratemeyer of the United States Air Force sent a radio message to his superior in Washington, General Hoyt Vandenberg. At Vandenberg's instigation, the Joint Chiefs of Staff annulled the order on the grounds that the U.S. had agreed to consult the British before carrying the war to Manchuria.[165] On 10 November 1950, the State Department asked U.S. embassies in the United Kingdom, France, Australia, Canada, India, and the Soviet Union for possible reactions should the United States Air Force chase Chinese aircraft into Manchurian air space. Their negative replies had a deterrent effect.[166]

Minutes of the Australian cabinet support Weintraub's contention. The cabinet met 7 November 1950, the very day Americans were electing one-third of their Senators and all members of the House of Representatives. The summary of the minutes reads:

> In the last 10 days there has been an attempt to chase planes into Manchuria. U.S. wanted to give the authority—'hot pursuit'. We thought that we should damp this down a bit...UK was even less enthusiastic than we were...UK has been thinking of a 'demilitarized zone'. Truman and Acheson are trying to take the heat out of it.[167]

Notes

1. *United Nations Yearbook*, 1950, p. 222.

2. *United Nations Yearbook*, 1950, p. 224.

3. *United Nations Yearbook*, 1950, p. 230.

4. As early as August 1950, a speech which General MacArthur delivered to the Veterans of Foreign Wars alarmed State Department officials, who feared its impact on Allies and possible Allies; George Kennan, State Department, Washington, to Secretary of State Dean Acheson, Washington, 23 Aug. 1950; and Acheson's reply, dated 26 Aug. 1950; File: Papers of Dean Acheson [14 of 23], Student Research File (B File), Korean War: Response to North Korean Invasion, 43B, Box 2, HST.

5. Bullock says that they did not (pp. 790-835, especially pp. 791 and 826), but Farrar-Hockley minimizes any differences (I, p. 939; II, pp. 174-175).

6. Steven Hugh Lee, p. 162.

7. Steven Hugh Lee, pp. 18-20.

8. See especially Pearson, p. 140.

9. Steven Hugh Lee, pp. 23-25.

10. Steven Hugh Lee, p. 97.

11. U.S. Ambassador Gallman, Cape Town, to the Secretary of State, Washington, 14 Feb. 1952, File: "Contributions to the UN Effort" [3 of 3], in Staff Members' Official Files (SMOF): Official Records Relating to the Korean War: Topical File Subseries, Box 5, HST.

12. Farrar-Hockley, II, p. 405.

13. Memorandum of Conversation, 3 Aug. 1950, File: The Korean War—The United States Response to North Korea's Invasion of South Korea, Papers of Dean Acheson [14 of 23], Student Research File (B File), KOREAN WAR: RESPONSE TO NORTH KOREA'S INVASION, 43B, Box 2 of 2, HST.

14. *Public Papers of the Presidents*, 1950, p. 492.

15. *Ibid.*

16. Catchpole, pp. 5-7.

17. Chiefs of Staff Committee, 96th meeting, 27 June 1950, CAB 21/1988, PRO.

18. Chiefs of Staff Committee, Joint Planning Staff, 1 July 1950, CAB 21/1988, PRO.

19. Bouchier, Tokyo, to Chiefs of Staff, Ministry of Defence, London, 28 Aug. 1950, CAB 21/1988, PRO. For maps which show the extent of the North Korean advance and South Korean retreat from 30 June 1950 to 1 August 1950, see Joseph C. Goulden, *Korea: The Untold Story of the War* (New York: Quadrangle, 1982), p. 126.

20. Scott, Foreign Office, London, to Younger, London, 29 June 1950, *DBPO*, pp. 13-15.

21. Farrar-Hockley, I, pp. 67-68.

22. Acheson, *The Korean War*, p. 35.

23. Acheson, *The Korean War*, pp. 36-37.

24. Chiefs of Staff Committee, Joint Planning Staff, 1 July 1950, CAB 21/1988, PRO. This is also the source of the information, including the quotation, in the following four sentences.

25. *Ibid.*

26. Michael Hopkins, "The Price of Cold War Partnership: Sir Oliver Franks and the British Commitment in the Korean War," *Cold War History*, I, 2 (Jan. 2001), p. 40.

27. Hopkins, p. 32.

28. Minutes of a Meeting of the Defence Committee of the Cabinet, 6 July 1950, *DBPO*, pp. 36-42. See also Record of a Meeting held in the Minister of State's Room, 15 July 1950, *DBPO*, pp. 68-76; and Extract from the Conclusions of a Meeting of the Cabinet, 25 July 1950, *DBPO*, pp. 81-82.

29. Record of a Meeting held in the Minister of State's Room, 15 July 1950, *DBPO*, p.69.

30. Franks, Washington, to Younger, London, 23 July 1950, *DBPO*, pp. 76-78.

31. Sandler, pp. 75-82.

32. General (Ret.) Bernard Trainor, "Memories and Significance of the Korean War," luncheon speech to conference of the Society for Historians of American Foreign Relations, Toronto, 22 June 2000.

33. See A.W. Martin, *Robert Menzies: A Life, 1944-1978* (Melbourne, Melbourne University Press, vol. II), 1999. This was also the attitude of U.S. diplomats; see Dept. of State Policy Statement, Washington, 21 April 1950, *FRUS*, 1950, VI, p. 190; se also Background Memoranda Prepared in the Dept. of State, 24 July 1950, *FRUS*, 1950, VI, p. 201.

34. Siracusa and Cheong, pp. 26-32.

35. Suggested by O'Neill, p. 20.

36. O'Neill, pp. 36-37.

37. O'Neill, p. 37.

38. O'Neill, pp. 47-48.

39. O'Neill, pp. 48-49.

40. Minutes of the Australian cabinet, Series A 11099/1, Item 1, 25 Aug. 1950, National Archives of Australia, Canberra. Cited hereafter as Minutes.

41. David Lowe, *Menzies and the Great World Struggle: Australia's Cold War*, 1948-1954 (Sydney: University of New South Wales Press, 1999), pp. 64-65.

42. O'Neill, I, pp. 234-235; Lowe, p. 1.

43. Lowe, pp. 87, 91-92, 97-98).

44. Lowe, p. 100.

45. Lowe, p. 152.

46. O'Neill, p. 49.

47. Allison Terry, *The Battle for Pusan: A Korean War Memoir* (Novato, CA: Presidio, 2000), p. 35.

48. O'Neill, p. 65.

49. O'Neill, p. 71.

50. O'Neill, pp. 75-76.

51. O'Neill, p. 128.

52. O'Neill, p. 89.

53. Siracusa and Cheong, p. 28.

54. Memorandum of Conversation, by the Secretary of State, Washington, 28 July 1950, *FRUS*, 1950, VI, pp. 204-205.

55. Memorandum of Conversation, by the Secretary of State, Washington, 31 July 1950, *FRUS*, 1950, VI, p. 205.

56. Acheson to Marshall, Washington, 24 Nov. 1950, *FRUS*, 1950, VI, p. 226.

57. Minutes, 25 Aug. 1950, Item 1/1, NAA.

58. Minutes, 15 Feb. 1951, Item 1/10, NAA.

59. Ian McGibbon, *New Zealand and the Korean War* (Aukland: Oxford University Press, 1992), I, p. 1.

60. McGibbon, I, p. 17.

61. McGibbon, I, pp. 20, 25, 42-43, 45, 86-101.

62. David J. Bercuson, *True Patriot: The Life of Brooke Claxton, 1898-1960* (Toronto: University of Toronto Press, 1993), pp. 209-211.

63. Marc Milner, *Canada's Navy: The First Century* (Toronto: University of Toronto Press, 1999), p. 195.

64. Milner, pp. 201-203.

65. Steven Hugh Lee, p. 85.

66. Pearson, II, pp. 148-149; Denis Stairs, *The Diplomacy of Constraint: Canada, the Korean War, and the United States* (Toronto: University of Toronto Press, 1974), p. 84.

67. O'Neill, p. 92.

68. Prince, p. 141.

69. Grey, pp. 34-35.

70. Pearson, II, p. 148.

71. Pearson, Ottawa, to St. Laurent, Ottawa, 27 June and 4 July 1950, reprinted in Greg Donaghy (ed.), *Canadian Diplomacy and the Korean War* (Ottawa: Department of Foreign Affairs and International Trade, 2001), p. 12.

72. *Public Papers of the Presidents*, 27 June 1950, p. 492.

73. *Ibid.*

74. Pearson to St. Laurent, Ottawa, 27 June and 4 July 1950, *DCER*, 1950, pp. 22-23.

75. Memorandum from A.D.P. Heeney, Under-Secretary of State for External Affairs, to Pearson, Ottawa, 18 July 1950, *DCER*, 1950. pp. 67-69; Draft Statement by Prime Minister, Ottawa, 18 July 1950, *DCER*, 1950, pp. 69-70.

76. Pearson, II, pp. 147-149. What Pearson says in his memoirs is totally compatible with what he said to "All [Canadian] Missions Abroad," 28 June 1950; *DCER*, 1950, pp. 31-32.

77. Pearson, II, p. 157.

78. Pearson to Canada's High Commissioner in London, 24 Aug. 1950, *DCER*, 1950, pp. 115-116.

79. E.g., Pearson, Ottawa; to [Canadian] High Commissioner in United Kingdom, London, 26 Sept. 1950, *DCER*, 1950, pp. 130-131; Secretary of State for Commonwealth Relations of United Kingdom to [Canadian] High Commissioner of United Kingdom, London, 18 Nov. 1950, *DCER*,1950, pp. 149-150.

80. E.g., Lie to Acting Permanent Delegate to United Nations, 14 July 1950, *DCER*, 1950, p. 63.

81. Acting Permanent Delegate to United Nations to Secretary of State for External Affairs, 6 July 1950, *DCER*, 1950, p. 59.

82. Holmes, United Nations, to Pearson, Ottawa, 1 Aug. 1950, *DCER*, 1950, pp. 97-98.

83. Kaufman, p. 32.

84. Simon Foster, *Hit the Beach: The Drama of Amphibious Warfare* (London: Cassell, 1999 [1995]), pp. 105-131; Joseph C. Goulden, *Korea: The Untold Story of the War* (New York: Quadrangle, 1984), pp. 184-232; Burton I. Kaufman, *The Korean War: Challenges in Crisis, Credibility, and Command* (Knopf: New York, 1986), pp. 78-82; William Manchester, *American Caesar: Douglas MacArthur, 1880-1964* (Boston: Little, Brown, and Company, 1978), pp. 578-581; Sandler, 96-97.

85. Milner, p. 202; Farrar-Hockley, I, pp. 149, 155-157.

86. Weintraub, p. 132.

87. A Report to the National Security Council by the Executive Secretary on United Nations Courses of Action with Respect to Korea, 1 Sept. 1950, PSF [17 of 23], Student Research File (B File), Korean War: Response to North Korea's Invasion, 43B, Box 2 of 2, HST.

88. Marshall to Truman, 27 Sept. 1950, ibid.

89. Truman, p. 411. To that end, MacArthur had authorization to cross the 38th parallel "provided that at the time of such operation there had been no entry into North Korea by major Soviet or Chinese Communist forces, no announcement of an intended entry, and no threat by Russian or Chinese Communists to counter our operations militarily in North Korea." See also Acheson, *Present at the Creation*, p. 452.

90. Rusk, p. 167.

91. Ministry of Defence, London, to B.J.S.M., Washington, 30 June 1950, CAB 21/1988, PRO.

92. FK 1015/119 and FK 1022/143, 245, 249, summarized in *DBPO*, p. 74.

93. Document DEFE 4/36, quoted in *DBPO*, p. 145.

94. Acheson, The Korean War, p. 35.

95. Farrar-Hockley, I, p. 21. See also Farrar-Hockley, II, pp. 265, 389.

96. Bevin, London, to Franks, Washington, 14 Aug. 1950, PREM 8/1156, PRO.

97. Franks, Washington, to Bevin, London, 16 Aug. 1950, PREM 8/1156, PRO.

98. Memo of 30 Aug. 1950, "Review of position in the Far East and South East Asia [in 1950] in the light of the Korean battle," PREM 8/1171, PRO.

99. *Ibid.*

100. Memo, 6 Oct. 1950, PREM 8/1171, PRO.

101. Kelly, Moscow, to the Foreign Office, London, 21 Sept. 1950, *DBPO*, fiches 6/6-7.

102. Hutchison, Beijing, to the Foreign Office, 29 and 30 Sept. 1950, *DBPO*, fiches 35-37 and 38-39. The quotation comes from the 3ntry of 30 Sept.

103. Extract from the Conclusions of a Meeting of the Cabinet, 26 Sept. 1950, *DBPO*, pp. 153-154.

104. Jebb, New York, to Attlee, London, 27 Sept. 1950, *DBPO*, pp. 155-157.

105. Ministry of Defence, London, to British Joint Services Mission, Washington, 5 Oct. 1950, pp. 169-171.

106. *DBPO*, note 3, p. 169.

107. Bevin, London, to Franks, Washington, 6 Oct. 1950, *DBPO*, p. 174.

108. Bevin, London, to Franks, Washington, 14 Nov. 1950, *DBPO*, pp. 202-204.

109. Roe. p. 148. Shu Guang Zhang, who has made an extensive study of China's military role in the Korean War on the basis of Chinese and Soviet sources, is convinced that once the United Nations Command crossed the 38th parallel, there was no way to avoid Chinese intervention. See Shu Guang Zhang, *Mao's Military Romanticism: China and the Korean War, 1950-1953* (Lawrence: University Press of Kansas, 1995), pp. 9, 55-85.

110. Roe, p. 199.

111. Roe, pp. 200, 202, 208-210, 213.

112. Roe, p. 216.

113. O'Neill, p. 109.

114. O'Neill, p. 110.

115. O'Neill, p. 113.

116. O'Neill, pp. 114-117.

117. O'Neill, p. 124.

118. O'Neill, pp. 121-122.

119. *Ibid.*

120. O'Neill, p. 126.

121. Alexander, p. 250; Catchpole, pp. 57-58.

122. Weintraub, pp. 172, 196.

123. Commission of Inquiry into the Australian Secret Intelligence Service, *Report on the Australian Secret Intelligence Service* (Canberra: Australia Government Publishing Service, 1995), p. xix.

124. O'Neill, p. 136.

125. O'Neill, pp. 130-139.

126. Keith Sinclair, *A History of New Zealand* (Aukland: Penguin, 1984 [1959]), p. 304.

127. McGibbon, I, pp. 139-152.

128. Pearson, Ottawa, to St. Laurent, Ottawa, 27 June and 4 July 1950, in Donaghy, p. 16.

129. Pearson, II, pp. 158-160.

130. O'Neill, p. 127.

131. Pearson, II, p. 162.

132. Pearson to Chairman, Delegation to United Nations General Assembly, 26 Sept. 1950, *DCER*, 1950, p. 166.

133. *New York Times*, 8 Oct. 1950; *Globe and Mail*, 9 Oct. 1950.

134. Pearson to Chairman, Delegation to United Nations General Assembly, *DCER*, 1950, p. 168.

135. Extract from Cabinet Conclusions, Ottawa, 4 Oct. 1950, *DCER*, 1950, p. 170.

136. Stairs, p. 121.

137. Stairs, pp. 121-122.

138. Acheson, *Present at the Creation*, p. 454.

139. Prince, pp. 41-42.

140. O'Neill, p. 143.

141. Dale Thomson, *Louis St. Laurent, Canadian* (Toronto: Macmillan, 1967), p. 304.

142. This is the terminology used throughout the *CWIHP* documentation.

143. Alexandre Y. Mansourov, "Stalin, Mao, Kim, and China's Decision to Enter the Korean War, September 16-October 15, 1950: New Evidence from the Russian Archives," *CWIHP*, VI-VII (Winter 1995-1996), pp. 94-95.

144. Memorandum Gromyko, Moscow, to Stalin, Moscow, 30 Sept. 1950, with draft cable form Gromyko to Shytkov, Pyongyang, *CWIHP*, VI-VII (Winter 1995-1996), pp. 113-114. The quotation is from p. 114.

145. Summary of Shtykov's 5 Oct. 1950 letter to Moscow appears in a letter from A.M. Vasilevsky and A. Gromyko, both in Moscow, to Stalin, 6 Oct. 1950; *CWIHP*, VI-VII (Winter 1995-1996), p. 117.

146. Vasilevsky and Gromyko, Moscow, to Shtykov, Pyongyang, 6 Oct. 1950, *CWIHP*, VI-VII (Winter 1995-1996), p. 117.

147. Stalin, Moscow, to Kim Il Sung, Pyongyang, 13 Oct. 1950, , VI-VII (Winter 1995-1996), p. 119. That letter reverses a message which Stalin had sent Kim the previous day and summarizes the contents of the earlier letter.

148. Peng Dehuai, *Memoirs of a Chinese General* (Beijing: Foreign Language Press, 1984), pp. 472-474. The quotation comes from p. 473.

149. Chen Jian, "China's Road to the Korean War," *CWIHP*, VI-VII (Winter 1995-1996), p. 41. Chen is also author of the book *China's Road to the Korean War: The Making of the Sino-American Confrontation* (New York: Columbia University Press, 1994).

150. Chen, *CWIHP*, p. 85.

151. Michael M. Sheng, "The Psychology of the Korean War: The Role of Ideology and Perception in China's Entry into the War," paper presented to the Annual Meeting of The Society for Historians of American Foreign Relations, Toronto, June 2000, pp. 1-2.

152. Sheng, p. 3.

153. Mao, Beijing, to Stalin, Moscow, 2 Oct. 1950, *CWIHP*, VI-VII (Winter 1995-1996), pp. 114-115.

154. Jennifer Milliken agrees with Sheng's account of Sino-Soviet diplomacy; pp. 142-168.

155. A summary of Sheng's paper.

156. Sheng, p. 15.

157. David Wolff, "'One Finger's Worth of Historical Events'; New Russian and Chinese Evidence on the Sino-Soviet Alliance and Split, 1948-1959," Cold War International History Project, Working Paper #30 (Aug. 2000), pp. 8-9, and related documents, pp. 39-40.

158. Shen Zhihua, pp. 65-66.

159. Hao Yufan and Zhai Zhihai, "China's Decision to Enter the Korean War: History Revisited," in Kim Chull Baum and James I. Matray (eds.), Korea and the Cold War: Division, Destruction and Disarmament (Claremont, California: Regina, 1993), pp. 141-166.

160. Map in Burton J. Kaufman, The Korean War: Challenges in Crisis, Credibility and Command (New York: Knopf, 1986), p. 79.

161. Hao and Zhai, p. 160.

162. Hao and Zhai, p. 165.

163. Stueck, p. 120.

164. Younger, London, to Bevin, London, 11 July 1950, DBPO, p. 48.

165. Weintraub, p. 216.

166. Weintraub, p. 226.

167. Minutes, 7 Nov. 1950, Item 1/8,NAA. See also the Anglo-Australian correspondence in Series A 816/1, Item 19/323/24; and Series A 5954/69, Item 1693/2, NAA.

Chapter Three

Did The Old Commonwealth Leaders Persuade President Truman
Not To Use The Atomic Bomb In Korea? Were They Wise To
Challenge U.S. Policy Toward China?

I   Nuclear Weapons in the Korean War?

The Chinese launched their offensive 25 November, two days after the American Thanksgiving. Before the offensive ended in February, South Korean and United Nations forces had retreated—from regions near the Yalu River, from Pyongyang, south of the Nampo-Wonson line, then south of the 38th parallel and south of Seoul itself. For some time it appeared as though the Chinese would chase the United Nations command completely off the Korean peninsula, with some Dunkirk-like evacuation from Pusan itself.[1] Korea would be united under North Korean leadership backed by, if not dominated by, the People's Republic of China.

After victory had seemed so close, retreat was a disappointment, to say the least. President Truman commented on the developments of 30 November at a press conference in Washington:

> The Chinese Communist leaders have sent their troops from Manchuria to launch a strong and well-organized attack against the United Nations forces in North Korea. This has been done despite prolonged and earnest efforts to bring home to the Communist leaders of China the plain fact that neither the United Nations nor the United States has any aggressive intentions toward China...
>
> If the United Nations yields to the forces of aggression, no nation will be safe or secure. If aggression is successful in Korea, we can expect it to spread throughout Asia and Europe to this hemisphere. We are fighting in Korea for our own national security and survival...[2]

After further comments, questions and answers on the deteriorating situation in Korea, the President said, "We will take whatever steps are necessary to meet the military situation, just as we always have."

One reporter then asked, "Will that include the atomic bomb?"

Truman responded, "That includes every weapon that we have."

In order that there might be no misunderstanding, the reporter asked:

Mr. President, you said "every weapon that we have." Does that mean that there is active consideration of the use of the atomic bomb?

Truman answered:

There has always been active consideration of its use. I don't want to see it used. It is a terrible weapon, and it should not be used on innocent men, women, and children who have nothing to do with this military aggression. That happens when it is used.

After some discussion about Yugoslavia, the press conference returned to the issue of nuclear weapons in Korea. Merriman Smith of United Press asked, "Did we understand you clearly that the use of the atomic bomb is under active consideration?" Truman's biographer, David McCullough, has suggested that Smith, an experienced reporter, suspected that Truman had spoken impromptu, and not really meant what his words indicated.[3]

Truman replied: "Always has been. It is one of our weapons."

Robert Nixon of the International News Service, another experienced White House reporter, said, "Does that mean, Mr. President, use against military objectives, or civilian—"

The President interrupted him:

It's a matter that the military people will have to decide. I'm not a military authority that passes on those things...

Frank Bourgholtzer of NBC spoke next:

Mr. President, you said this depends on United Nations action. Does that mean that we wouldn't use the atomic bomb except on a United Nations authorization?

Truman denied that:

No, it doesn't mean that at all. The action against Communist China depends on the actions of the United Nations. The military commander in the field will have charge of the use of the weapons, as he always has.

Lest anyone interpret those words as indicating that General Douglas MacArthur—hero of Inchon but the general as responsible as any single individual for the march to the Yalu and the subsequent debacle—might have *carte blanche* to use nuclear weapons, the White House issued a statement of clarification that very afternoon:

> The President wants to make it certain that there is no misinterpretation of his answers to questions at his press conference today about the use of the atom bomb. Naturally, there has been consideration of this subject since the outbreak of the hostilities in Korea, just as there is consideration of the use of all military weapons whenever our forces are in combat.
>
> Consideration of the use of any weapon is always implicit in the very possession of that weapon.
>
> However, it should be emphasized, that, by law, only the President can authorize the use of the atom bomb, and no such authorization has been given. If and when such authorization should be given, the military commander in the field would have charge of the tactical delivery of the weapon.
>
> In brief, the replies to the questions at today's press conference do not represent any change in this situation.[4]

British, Canadian, and Australian[5] leaders voiced their alarm, and President Truman reassured them that there would be no use of nuclear weapons as long as he was president. However, it does not appear likely that Clement Attlee, Lester Pearson, or any other Commonwealth authority changed the president's mind. It appears much more probable that Truman had chosen his words carelessly at the press conference, without realizing their significance. By his own account, he had little trouble reassuring Attlee, who almost immediately flew to Washington for talks with the president.[6]

This is certainly the opinion of serious commentators. McCullough says that Truman "said far more than he ever intended and had been inaccurate besides, but the reporters had their story...Truman's answers had been devastatingly foolish, the press conference a fiasco."[7] Two other authors of articles about the use of nuclear weapons during the Korean War, Daniel Calingaert and Roger Dingman, share McCullough's opinion. Weintraub uses the words "presidential misstep," "gaffe," and "blunder" to explain what Truman said.[8] Truman never seriously intended to use nuclear weapons in Korea and misspoke himself at the press conference.[9]

Calingaert catalogues the reasons why the Truman administration would not use nuclear weapons in Korea. Few military targets in Korea were large enough that their destruction required nuclear weapons. The Joint Chiefs of Staff doubted whether the deaths of civilians in Manchurian cities would deter the People's Republic of China from pursuing its campaign in Korea. Moreover, Americans rejected on principle any "terror attack on civilian populations." Other arguments were that a nuclear attack on China, which at the time lacked nuclear weapons of its own, would unite world opinion and opinion within China against the United States. Few regarded China as a threat to their own security the way millions of Asians and Europeans feared the Soviet Union. Also, the U.S. arsenal contained a finite number of nuclear weapons. The more the U.S. used against China, the fewer it would have if the primary adversary, the Soviet Union, misbehaved. Almost certainly the use of nuclear weapons would lead to the expansion of the Korean War, perhaps on the Chinese mainland, perhaps against the Soviet Union. Such expansion would inhibit the ability of the United States to defend Western Europe, a higher priority for President Truman than the mainland of northeast Asia.[10] Dingman adds that key generals thought that nuclear weapons were quite unnecessary. There could be an acceptable outcome without them.

Both official British and official American records give the impression that Attlee went to Washington to deal with a problem which appeared to be but which did not actually exist. Attlee had considerable moral authority as he spoke with President Truman, because between Truman's unfortunate press conference and his departure for Washington, the British prime minister spoke with French Prime Minister René Pléven and French Foreign Minister Robert Schuman, as well as with representatives of Commonwealth countries. He knew that they agreed with him, as did the Dutch, Belgian, and Danish foreign ministers.[11] The U.S. Ambassador in France confirmed that British and French policies on Korea in general and the use of nuclear weapons there were similar.[12] However, the record shows that when Truman and Attlee met, the use of nuclear weapons was only one of several items which they discussed, despite word from Ambassador Holmes in London that fear of the use of nuclear weapons in Korea was what had prompted Attlee's trip.[13]

The British cabinet was not under any illusions as it pondered the Chinese offensive in Korea. The Chinese could threaten, perhaps overwhelm, British interests in Hong Kong and Malaya.[14] On 29 November, four days into the offensive and one day before President Truman's notorious press conference, it noted "that the intervention of these Chinese troops in Korea had not been provoked by the latest movements of the United Nations forces, and went beyond anything necessary for the limited purpose of protecting the hydro-electric installations or the frontier zone." Hydro-electric installations in the Yalu River provided electricity to both the People's Republic of

China and North Korea. If the United Nations Command destroyed them even from the North Korean side of the border, many Chinese homes, schools, hospitals, and factories, would have felt the effect. Understandably too, Chinese authorities might have wanted more than the Yalu River between the PRC and the United Nations Command, and a Chinese occupation of North Korean territory close to the border might have been acceptable. However, the Chinese army was penetrating beyond North Korea's border region. Bevin warned that the advance of Chinese forces into Korea required "greater vigilance in Europe," where the Soviets might exploit Western preoccupation in Korea and create trouble in Austria or Berlin.

Attlee told his cabinet ministers that the Truman administration had consulted its British ally as much as was reasonable given the disproportionate military burden which the United States had shouldered in Korea. Moreover, he said, it would be unfair and unwise to hold the United States responsible for what had happened:

> We had fully supported the proposal that the United Nations forces should advance beyond the 38th Parallel, despite India's warning that this would provoke Chinese intervention. We, as well as the Americans, had taken the risk of proceeding on the assumption that the Chinese would not in fact fulfil their threat. Finally, any strong divergence of policy between ourselves and the Americans over the Far East would involve a risk of losing American support in Europe. The ultimate threat to our security came from Russia, and we would not afford to break our united front with the United States against our main potential enemy.[15]

On the whole, then, Attlee and Bevin supported U.S. policy in Korea, from conviction and from necessity, even as MacArthur's triumph on the banks of the Yalu visibly disintegrated. The following afternoon, however, as news of Truman's press conference arrived, the British cabinet met in special session. Bevin wrote to Sir Oliver Franks that the ministers wanted Attlee to meet Truman, face to face, "as soon as possible." On 2 December, Bevin informed Franks that the Chiefs of Staff and the cabinet believed that there must be greater British input into decisions regarding the Korean War.

> Chiefs of Staff also consider and Ministers agree that the time has come to *press for coordinated* system of higher direction of operations in Korea and on closer control of General MacArthur by United States Government in consultation with Governments' members of the Security Council which have forces in Korea.[16]

Spender of Australia, they thought, agreed with them (and O'Neill confirms this[17]), and at a cabinet meeting on 4 December, Bevin said that "The Canadian Government were now showing less anxiety to conform with United States policy."[18] What Bevin, Franks, and the Chiefs of Staff did not realize was that key people at the State Department and the Pentagon had also lost confidence in General MacArthur and sought his dismissal there and then. One of these people was General Matthew Ridgway, who, after President Truman did dismiss MacArthur in April 1951, became MacArthur's successor.[19] According to British historian Peter Lowe, President Truman was not pleased that Attlee was inviting himself to Washington but felt that he had no choice but to receive him.[20]

When Attlee went to Washington and met members of the Truman administration, including the President himself, the atom bomb was but one of many items of conversation. The president and the prime minister first spoke to each other 5 December 1950. Omar Bradley, Chairman of the Joint Chiefs of Staff, told Attlee in Truman's presence that friendly forces would almost certainly have to withdraw from all areas north of the 38th parallel nor were they likely to avoid defeat in South Korea. The two men then discussed China.[21] They met again the next day aboard the presidential yacht and again discussed the possibility of a total military defeat in Korea. Again they discussed the direction of relations with China in the event of such a defeat. Attlee was willing to be much more conciliatory to a victorious China than was Acheson,[22] but since the Chinese never did manage to chase the United Nations Command out of South Korea and the problem remained hypothetical, it is difficult to assess Attlee's impact. At their fifth meeting, which took place 7 December, China was the second item on their agenda. Nuclear matters came fourth, the last issue of substance that day. According to the British version,

> The President said that he had reaffirmed to the Prime Minister that the Governments of the United Kingdom and Canada were partners with the United States in the atomic weapon [as they had been since World War II] and that the United States Government would not consider its use without consulting the United Kingdom and Canada. The understanding on this point was clear even though it depended upon no written agreement.[23]

The American version is totally compatible but more vivid:

> The President said he had just talked with the Prime Minister and that they had discussed the atomic bomb and its use. The President reminded Mr. Attlee that the Governments of the United Kingdom and the United

States had always been partners in this matter and that he would not consider the use of the bomb without consulting with the United Kingdom. The Prime Minister asked whether this agreement should be put in writing, and the President replied no that it would not be in writing, that if a man's word wasn't any good it wasn't made any better by writing it down. The Prime Minister expressed his thanks.[24]

"Consultation," of course, is a far cry from "agreement," and President Truman thus left open the door for the use of nuclear weapons at some future date. He could then inform Attlee and Canadian authorities of his intentions, hear and then reject their advice, and claim that there had been "consultation." Happily, as Truman apparently never had any serious intention of using nuclear weapons in Korea, Attlee probably did not persuade him not to use them. That is not to say that Attlee's Washington visit was entirely fruitless in that respect. When Stuart Symington, Chairman of the National Security Resources Board, referred to the atomic bomb as America's "political ace," Truman encouraged Secretary of State Acheson to label it a "political liability...[which] frighten[ed] our allies to death."[25]

II Anglo-American Differences over the People's Republic of China

The U.S. record of the Attlee-Truman talks also indicates that the possible use of nuclear weapons consumed very little time. Both parties agreed that, for the foreseeable future at any rate, the atomic bomb had no role to play in the Korean War.[26] However, there was much consideration of alternative courses of action. After 25 November, the war was going very badly, and high level U.S. military officers envisioned the possibility of a Korean "Dunkirk." If the Chinese offensive continued, there was a very strong possibility that all soldiers of the United Nations Command and as many South Koreans as possible might face evacuation from the Korean mainland through Hungnam, Inchon, or even Pusan.[27] In such an eventuality, Truman and Attlee could not agree as to what would happen next.

As far as Attlee was concerned, it was "game over." British strategists agreed that Korea had little strategic importance for the defence of vital Western interests in the rest of the world. To maintain a hostile relationship with the People's Republic of China might jeopardize more serious Western interests. First, it would absorb the energy of Western military establishments to such a point that they could not defend Western Europe if the USSR, a more formidable enemy than China, were to attack. Similarly, it would leave the oil fields of the Middle East more vulnerable to Soviet pressure. Secondly, it would encourage the People's Republic of China to attack Hong Kong or to assist rebels in Malaya, places of greater importance than South Korea or Taiwan. Thirdly, it would push the People's Republic of China into an alliance with the Soviet Union, the ultimate enemy. If given a little encouragement, thought Attlee, Mao and his associates would prove as independent of the Soviet Union as had Yugoslavia's Marshal Josip Broz Tito.

For Attlee, the Korean War had become a matter of damage control, and he had solutions. Admit the People's Republic of China into the United Nations and stop treating it as an outlaw or rogue state. Then Mao's government would feel some obligation to respect international law. Also, assure Mao that Taiwan was legally a part of the People's Republic of China, which, after a period of trusteeship, would be his to govern—in accordance with the 1943 Cairo declaration of Prime Minister Winston Churchill (Attlee's predecessor) and President Franklin Delano Roosevelt (Truman's predecessor). Finally, allow Asians to determine the future of Asia. Asian members of the Commonwealth indicated that the People's Republic of China was the government which the Chinese people wanted.[28]

Truman and his advisers disagreed strongly. It would be difficult to persuade the American public to exert much energy in defence of Western Europe as Asia was being abandoned. A policy of strength across the Atlantic could not credibly co-exist with one of appeasement in Asia. Voters would not understand why they should spend blood and treasure on one continent and sacrifice what they had earned on the other. Even if the United Nations Command had to abandon South Korea, the United States must remain in a hostile relationship with the Chinese who had defeated the Western armies. Secondly, successful Communist aggression in Korea would encourage further attempts at aggression throughout Asia—in Hong Kong, Malaya, French Indo-China, and the Philippines. Soon even the Japanese would come to believe that it was dangerous to rely for their defence on the West and that some accommodation with China was necessary. Thirdly, Truman's advisers believed that Mao and his associates really were Soviet surrogates. Defense Secretary George Marshall remembered a dinner with Zhou Enlai when the Communists and the United States were allied militarily against Japan. Zhou was proud that he and Mao were Communists, and pictures of Lenin and Stalin were ubiquitous. For their part, Truman's political and military advisors totally rejected Attlee's "solutions." To allow the People's Republic of China to represent China at the United Nations would be to reward aggression. To deliver Taiwan to Mao would also be to reward aggression and would jeopardize the security of the Philippines and make more difficult flights of the United States Air Force between the Philippines and Okinawa. Taiwan in unfriendly hands would endanger the defence of vital Western interests on the islands off the eastern coast of Asia. Finally, when Roosevelt and Churchill had issued their Cairo Declaration which declared Taiwan to be Chinese territory, they had done so in an entirely different context. In 1943, Japan controlled Taiwan, as it had since the Sino-Japanese War of 1894-1895. The Chinese government of Generalissimo Chiang Kai Shek was an ally in the war against Japan. By 1950, people who appeared to be Soviet surrogates controlled the Chinese mainland.

The Truman administration, then, was much more willing than Attlee's government to risk a confrontation with Mao and his associates. At the very least, the United States wanted the United Nations to vote an economic embargo against the People's Republic of China. Western countries would not buy its products nor sell on its market. British authorities had long opposed such a policy as catastrophic to the prosperity, if not the very survival, of Hong Kong and Malaya.[29]

Farrar-Hockley thinks that the Truman-Attlee talks were useful. Each party gained a better understanding of the other's position. Truman saw the futility of pushing too hard on the sanctions issue.[30]

III Canadian Concerns Regarding Nuclear War

From Washington, Attlee flew directly to Ottawa, where he could anticipate a friendly reception. He and Lester Pearson agreed on the essential issues regarding Korea. Like Attlee, Pearson regarded the Korean War as a side-show. Western countries should not divert their military resources from Western Europe, where there was a danger of a Soviet invasion, to a fight against China. "The only country whose interests would be served by a war with China would be the Soviet Union," said Pearson.[31] Like Attlee, he did not want the United States to use the atomic bomb in Korea.

On 4 December, the day before Attlee's first meeting with Truman, Pearson wrote a lengthy memo to Hume Wrong, Canada's ambassador in Washington. He had been thinking about the use of the atomic bomb in the Korean War, said Pearson, since Truman's press conference of 30 November. What he called "the rapidly deteriorating military situation in Korea" made it imperative, he thought, to tell the U.S. government that under no circumstances should it resort to the atomic bomb. There should not even be a threat to use it. Psychologically, said Pearson, the atomic bomb was not "just another weapon." The possibility it might be used was driving people to support the "cynical Communist 'peace campaign'." Europeans were particularly vulnerable to nuclear warfare, and if they thought there was an in-creased danger that their homeland might be a target, Western allies might well de-fect and become neutrals. After Hiroshima and Nagasaki, the use of such weapons against Asians would irreparably damage relations between Asians and Westerners. The bomb had some value as a hypothetical weapon as last resort, but it would lose some of its effectiveness once its use in combat clarified its limitations. Canada, as one of the nuclear partners of the Western alliance since 1943 (along with the United States and the United Kingdom), had the right to be consulted before any usage of nuclear weapons.[32]

Wrong replied the same day that Pearson was unduly worried. Chances that the United States would "soon," on its own unilateral accord, use the atomic bomb in Korea, were minimal. Wrong agreed that the destruction of "several hundred thou-sand lives" in various Manchurian cities would have little impact upon the course of the Korean War, given the human resources at the disposal of the ruthless govern-ment of the People's Republic of China.[33] To that end, he worked on revisions to Pearson's statement so that it might have the maximum impact on U.S. authorities.[34]

Notwithstanding Wrong's message, official Ottawa did have grounds for con-cern. In August 1950, Prime Minister St. Laurent had permitted the United States Air Force to position nuclear weapons at Goose Bay, Labrador. What the U.S. gov-ernment might do with those weapons was, however, unclear.[35] The Canadian gov-ernment agreed that the Strategic Air Command could use them without permission if the Soviet Union attacked a NATO country, but Soviet attacks on U.S. forces elsewhere would be another matter. The Truman administration wanted a blank cheque to use the weapons automatically in such circumstances, but Ottawa would not agree. That same issue remained contentious throughout 1950.[36]

On 6 December, while Attlee was still in Washington and without waiting for a joint planning strategy with Attlee, the Canadian Embassy in Washington delivered the Pearson/Wrong message to the State Department.[37] George Ignatieff, Counsellor at the Canadian Embassy, spoke to R. Gordan [sic] Arneson, Special Assistant to the Secretary of State on Atomic Energy. Arneson said that he could understand why President Truman's words at the 30 November press conference had created concern over the use of atomic weapons, and he confirmed that the President and Prime Min-ister Attlee had discussed the issue. In the hypothetical event that it should become advisable to use the atomic bomb and if time permitted, the U.S. government would certainly be willing to consult its British and Canadian allies, said Arneson. Mean-while, the Joint Chiefs of Staff, who normally would recommend the use of nuclear weapons, had not done so. Even if the Chiefs were to do so, several other key officials would have to approve before forwarding the advice to the President, the ultimate decision-maker. As far as Arneson was concerned, the use of the atomic bomb against a target in Manchuria or Korea would be overkill. Such a weapon could make a significant difference over an industrialized Soviet city, but not one on the Korean peninsula or the adjacent mainland. The U.S. would not want to waste such a weapon on any Asian target south of the Soviet Union. The number of atomic bombs in the U.S. arsenal was limited. Only if the Soviet Union were to launch an "overt" attack on the United States itself was the United States likely to respond use nuclear weapons without consulting its allies.[38]

Hence, even before Attlee's arrival in Ottawa, Canadian authorities were aware that he had discussed with President Truman the possible use of nuclear weapons in Korea and that the United States government was unlikely to use them there. On 8 December, before departing Washington, Attlee, Sir Oliver Franks, and other British officials had briefed delegations from the Canadian, Australian, New Zealand, South African, Indian, Pakistani, and Ceylonese embassies, but the issue of nuclear weapons had not arisen. Pearson and South Africa's T.E. Donges, Minister of the Interior, attended alongside their ambassadors, and heard that "the military situation [in Korea] was not as hopeless as some people might think." In response to a question from Canadian ambassador Hume Wrong, Attlee said that aerial bombardment of Manchuria was unlikely. It "would be ineffective and would lead to most serious and undesirable complications."[39]

IV British Prime Minister Attlee Visits Ottawa

In Ottawa, the British prime minister informed St. Laurent and Pearson of events in Korea and his talks in Washington. He did not attempt to co-ordinate a joint Commonwealth approach toward the Korean War. In a cable from Ottawa to Bevin, Attlee explained that Commonwealth leaders would resent any effort on his part to speak for more than the United Kingdom. Moreover, U.S. authorities had dealt with him as leader of the United Kingdom, not as voice of or gateway to the Commonwealth. Any effort to use the Commonwealth as a counter-weight to the United States must await the meeting of Commonwealth prime ministers, scheduled for January 1951.[40]

Field Marshal Sir William Slim, Chief of the Imperial General Staff (the United Kingdom's top military officer), accompanied Attlee, and like his prime minister, he was a bearer of good news. Although the United Nations must withdraw its forces from Hamhung almost immediately and from the Seoul-Inchon area some time thereafter, there would not be a Korean Dunkirk. Slim was confident that it would be possible to maintain a line well north of the earlier Pusan Perimeter.[41] Slim's projections stood in stark contrast from the defeatist memoranda which Pearson's subordinates had been writing. They feared total defeat in Korea, and saw no easy solutions. Europeans would not want another Munich (triumph for the aggressor) in Korea, but they would not want the United States so over-committed in Korea that it could not defend Western Europe. While Korea's salvation was a lower priority than that of Western Europe, there might be a domino effect (although nobody used that word). A Chinese victory in Korea might lead to victories by pro-Chinese governments in Burma (now Myanmar) and Vietnam.[42] Now, according to Slim, such a worst case scenario was unlikely.

While Attlee outlined Anglo-American differences on China's independence from the Soviet Union and the importance of its admission to the United Nations, he was reassuring on the use of nuclear weapons. "[The] President's recent remark concerning the use of the atomic bomb," he said, "was apparently an unpremeditated answer to a question at a press conference. He had evidently never seriously considered use of the bomb in Korea." Pearson interjected that he had received "a reassuring interim reply to the Canadian note to the U.S. government on the use of the atomic bomb." On balance, thought Attlee, the United Kingdom and the United States enjoyed an "underlying unity...so great...that...they could continue to act together."[43] Both Canadian and British sources indicate that Attlee had greatly reassured Canadian leaders.[44]

V   The Royal Canadian Navy Goes to Korea

The pessimism of Pearson's advisers—Jules Leger, Herbert Norman, and Escott Reid—had not arisen in a vacuum. They had good reason to fear a Korean Dunkirk. Early in December, the three destroyers of the Royal Canadian Navy assigned to Korean waters had played a major role in the evacuation of Chinampo (now Nampo), the port of Pyongyang on the Yellow Sea. The Cayuga, the Sioux, and the Athabaskan, had led three other destroyers, one from the United States, two from Australia, up the Taedong River. In the process, the Sioux and the Warramunga from Australia became temporarily trapped by the shallowness of the water. Nevertheless, the flotilla protected United Nations forces as they retreated and destroyed oil depots and other facilities which might be useful to the enemy.[45] Although the naval operation was a success in that evacuation is preferable to capture, evacuations are hardly grounds for optimism.

VI Australian and New Zealand Diplomacy Late in 1950

From Canberra, Menzies and Spender monitored Korean developments. The two principal makers of Australian foreign policy operated from somewhat different perspectives. Menzies was an anglophile, who cared what British authorities thought. Spender wanted a bilateral U.S.-Australian military alliance and did not want to do anything to jeopardize its creation. Spender was, outwardly at least, less worried than Attlee and Bevin about extension of the war to China. In his opinion, the Security Council should make clear that United Nations forces would not necessarily regard Chinese territory as sacred. For his part, the Chinese were Soviet surrogates.[46]

There were mixed signals from Australian authorities. At the United Nations, Sir Keith Officer informed the U.S. delegation on 10 November—after the Chinese had entered North Korea but before they launched their offensive—that his government thought it would be dangerous to bomb Manchuria. Indeed, he thought he had a commitment that no such bombing would take place without U.S.-Australian consultation.[47] On the eve of the Chinese offensive, Menzies broadcast that "none of the Democracies have any designs upon Manchuria," but he also warned that conflicts could have unforeseen consequences.[48] Spender had returned to Australia from a trip to the United States and Canada on 15 November, and on 21 November delivered an address on foreign policy to the House of Representatives. That speech emphasized the need for a U.S.-Australian military pact (like NATO) and the importance of working closely with the United States.[49]

On 30 November, five days into the Chinese offensive, Ambassador Sir Keith Officer cabled Canberra from the United Nations that MacArthur had requested permission to bomb Manchuria. Officer thought it possible that Truman might agree to that request. Officer maintained close contact with the British and Canadian delegations at the United Nations, and all of them noted Truman's comments about the possible use of the atomic bomb at his 30 November press conference. As soon as Spender heard the news, he cabled Australia's High Commissioner in Ottawa, Francis Michael Forde, to enquire about Canadian opinion. (Forde replied that Canada's views closely resembled Australia's.) The British High Commission in the Australian capital quickly notified Menzies and Spender that Attlee would be going to Washington. Spender then instructed Norman John Makin, Australia's Ambassador in Washington, to promote Australia's views as forcibly as possible while they might still make a difference.

Before Attlee left for Washington, he met the Commonwealth High Commissioners. Sir Eric John Harrison, Australian High Commissioner in London, stressed that the war must not expand beyond Korea and that Truman should exert better control over MacArthur. Dana Wilgress, Canada's High Commissioner, agreed, as did India's Krishna Menon. Harrison thought that Attlee and the Australian government had similar views regarding the use of the atomic bomb.

Spender then made a public announcement that Harrison had stated the Australian government's position to Attlee before his departure for Washington:

(a) to give effect to the principles and purposes of the Charter of the United Nations in accordance with which members of the United Nations had sent forces to Korea to resist aggression;

(b) to limit the area of conflict;

(c) to express the special Australian point of view, as distinct from a purely European point of view, in determining what action was necessary to resist aggression in the Far East;

(d) to exhaust political negotiation before undertaking new and irrevocable commitments in the military field;

(e) to devise, from time to time, the best methods of giving effect to these principles.[50]

At the same time, Spender deplored "loose speculation as to the possible use of the atomic bomb" and warned that the Chinese must take responsibility for whatever developments might occur. Professor Robert O'Neill, Australia's foremost historian of the Korean War, wrote that Spender's words comforted both the British and Canadians, who sought to limit the war and to extend the area of discussion, and to the Truman administration, which wanted reliable allies. In this sense, thought O'Neill, Spender served as a bridge between London and Ottawa on the one hand, and Washington on the other, and demonstrated to Washington that Australian views were closer to American views than were those of the British and Canadians. This constituted good politics for Spender at a time when he was desperately promoting the U.S.-Australian military alliance.[51]

Prince agrees with Rosemary Foot's contention that Allied protests persuaded the Truman administration not to send the United States Air Force over Manchuria. Using U.S. sources, he says that the United Kingdom and Australia took the lead, and that the Canadian government supported them.[52]

It was during the Chinese offensive that the United States government decided that the United Nations Command really could use soldiers from New Zealand.

They went to Korea in December.[53] New Zealand's government had taken no initiatives regarding the use of nuclear weapons in Korea. In the aftermath of the Truman-Attlee talks, Holland and Doidge expressed delight that the two leaders had reached an agreement and that nuclear weapons would not be used. Ian McGibbon, New Zealand's primary historian of the Korean War, suggests that his country maintained its low profile for four reasons: its isolated geographical location; its lack of soldiers yet upon the ground in Korea; its relative lack of vulnerability (as compared to Western Europe) to nuclear attack even if the Korean War should expand; and its lack of ambition for a major role on the world stage. Nevertheless, Holland and Doidge were full of admiration for what Attlee had accomplished in Washington. Closer to the scene, Berendsen was less impressed. He referred to Attlee as a "rabbity little man" and "stupid in the extreme."[54]

When it appeared that the UNC might face total defeat in Korea, the U.S. Joint Chiefs of Staff (JCS) made contingency plans for the evacuation of some 328,000 South Koreans. Their new home, thought the JCS, could be Western Samoa, a trust territory which New Zealand had been governing since World War I on behalf of the League of Nations and then the United Nations. Maintenance of amicable relations between the new arrivals and the 70,000 Samoans who already lived there would have been a challenge—to say the least—for New Zealand authorities. Happily, the UN did not suffer total defeat, evacuation proved unnecessary, and the New Zealand government did not know about the JCS plans, let alone discuss them with other members of the Commonwealth.[55]

VII Should the People's Republic of China Be Punished as an Aggressor?

There was one further Anglo-American disagreement before the start of the Korean truce talks of 1951-1953. Should the United Nations condemn the People's Republic of China as an aggressor? The Truman administration favoured such a course of action, while the Attlee government did not. Despite a meeting of Commonwealth Prime Ministers 4-12 January 1951, British authorities discovered that they could not depend upon even the "Old Commonwealth" for support and faced the danger of isolation from their Western Europe and Commonwealth allies, not to mention the United States itself.

Bevin had considered the possibility of an "agreed Commonwealth policy" for the Prime Ministers' Conference,[56] but it was not to materialize. From Washington Sir Oliver Franks said that from the point of view of dealing with the Americans and influencing their policy we should be in a much stronger position if you [Bevin] were able to secure an agreed Commonwealth policy about Korea.[57]

Whatever its desirability, such an "agreed Commonwealth policy about Korea" proved unattainable.

Bevin was by no means an appeaser, soft on Communism or indifferent to the fate of South Korea. An extract from a cable which he sent to Franks at the end of 1950 outlines his position succinctly:

I would like to see a good defensive line selected and fortified at whatever place in South Korea the Military Commanders may select and then stubbornly held by every means in our powers, with maximum air effort within Korean limits to harass opposing forces.

At the same time, I am strongly averse to any extension of the issue beyond Korea. Though the Chinese have not so far responded to any of the efforts so far made to negotiate a settlement, I do not believe that the door is yet entirely closed.

Bevin wanted to clarify British objectives in Korea with three declarations to be issued to the Prime Ministers:

(a) a declaration that we intend to stand fast and hold our ground in Korea and will support the United Nations efforts to that end;

(b) a declaration that our objective remains the establishment of a unified, free and independent Korea and that we are determined not to extend the conflict beyond Korea;

(c) a declaration that we are at all times ready to attain these objectives by means of negotiation.

Point (c), Bevin told Franks, would require a negotiated cease-fire in Korea, accompanied by the staged withdrawal of Chinese and United Nations forces; the admission of the People's Republic of China to the United Nations; and "acceptance of the Cairo Declaration in principle" with regard to Taiwan.[58] (In November 1943, President Roosevelt, Prime Minister Churchill, and China's Chiang Kai Shek had met in Cairo and agreed that Japan must evacuate all Chinese territory, which would then be restored to China.[59]) Political conditions in the United States precluded the termination of Chiang Kai Shek's government on Taiwan and that island's handover to the People's Republic of China, an event which, almost sixty years later, has not yet happened. On point (b) there would be partial success; the division of Korea also remains a fact of life, but hostilities did not extend beyond Korea. Point (a) proved a total success. but it was one with which the United States Government would agree.

Bevin realized that none of his ideas had more than academic value unless he could convince President Truman and Secretary Acheson of their merit. Without support from the United States, the Chinese simply would not take the ideas seriously. Gaining that support, Bevin told Franks, would not be easy. "I realise...that the Commonwealth and in particular the United Kingdom will come in for much criticism from the American press for our part in what they will no doubt call 'appeasement'." That was a risk Bevin was willing to take, on the assumption that with sober second thoughts American authorities would decide that they were realistic after all.[60]

When the Commonwealth leaders met, they sang from different hymn books. At the opening session 4 January 1951, the very day the advancing Chinese army occupied Seoul, Attlee—the first speaker—made no attempt to hide his differences from those of the Truman administration. He expressed fear of a war against China, which would then "give a free hand to Russia in Europe." India's Pandit Jawaharlal Nehru, the next speaker, launched a blistering tirade against U.S. policy in Asia. China, he said, was a great power and was not a Soviet satellite. "The moment you named China an aggressor," he said, "this would lead you very close to a general war." Canada's Louis St. Laurent, who spoke next, said that Asia-watchers should not confuse Communist expansion with legitimate Nationalist developments. They were separate entities. The United Nations had not committed aggression in Korea, but there certainly had been aggression in Korea. Nevertheless, "he hoped that there would not be an early necessity to brand China as an aggressor." New Zealand's Sidney Holland suggested that some of the Prime Ministers should go on a goodwill tour of the United States, and he volunteered to be one of them. He defended U.S. foreign policy,[61] as did Menzies.[62]

The next day it became clear that no co-ordinated Commonwealth approach was possible. Australia's highest priority was a military alliance with the United States—which materialized as the ANZUS (Australia, New Zealand, United States) Pact a few weeks later. Menzies could not afford to antagonize the U.S. at that point.[63] St. Laurent argued that any joint message would emphasize differences between the Truman administration and the Commonwealth. Dr. T.E. Donges, South Africa's Minister of the Interior—who was substituting for Dr. Daniel Malan—agreed that each separate Commonwealth government should send a separate message to Washington. There was no agreement on China and Taiwan. Nehru wanted the People's Republic of China to assume China's seat in the United Nations at once.

Donges disagreed and said that his country would not be recognizing Mao's regime for the foreseeable future.[64]

On 8 and 9 January, the leaders again discussed Korea. According to Dana Wilgress, Canada's High Commissioner in London, "There was unanimous agreement that the objective is to get the United States Government and the Central People's Government of China to a conference table." However, the delegates had to admit that they did not know how best to do this, and Wilgress asked Pearson for suggestions which might prove acceptable to Washington.[65] The Middle East and the defence of Western Europe then moved to the top of the agenda, and there were no further discussions on Korea until 11 January. Then the Commonwealth leaders discussed cease-fire proposals newly arrived from the United Nations Cease Fire Committee.[66]

By 12 January, the final day of the conference, Pearson had replied to Wilgress, but there was still little consensus about how best to proceed. Nehru stood at one end of the continuum, Donges and Holland at the other, closest to the United States.[67] The conference ended on an acrimonious note, with India's Jawaharlal Nehru complaining that a speech of Sir Gladwyn Jebb at the United Nations the previous day had ignored all attempts by the prime ministers to find common ground between China and the United States.[68]

The Declaration by Commonwealth Prime Ministers at the end of the conference said very little that was specific about Korea.

> We do not seek to interfere in the affairs of the Soviet Union or China or any other country; we are simply determined to retain the mastery of our own affairs without fear of aggression.

> It is with these considerations in mind that in the last few days we have directed our efforts to the securing of a cessation of hostilities on Korea, so that around the conference table the Great Powers concerned may compose their differences on a basis which will strengthen the United Nations and fulfil the purposes of the charter.[69]

The Final Communiqué was even more vague.

> There was agreement on the urgency and importance of promoting a satisfactory settlement in the Far East.[70]

It would be less than convincing to argue that this gathering had hastened an end to the conflict in Korea by a single minute. One American who sees merit in Commonwealth diplomacy, especially Canadian diplomacy, early in 1951 is historian William Stueck. Stueck refers to a "quadrilateral relationship...Within this group," he says, were America's two closest allies (Canada and the United Kingdom), a soon-to-be ally (Australia), and a neutral harboring strong suspicions toward the West (India). While India...split with the other three on the aggressor resolution, the UN and commonwealth formats proved useful in...blunting America's rage against China. Throughout the process, Canada's Pearson played the deft hand of mediator. When the commonwealth prime ministers in London moved dangerously far from the U.S. position on principles for a cease-fire in Korea, it was Pearson from New York, through St. Laurent, who persuaded them (Nehru in particular) to move back on track. Lacking the imperial past of the British or the reflexive condescension toward dark-skinned peoples of the Australians, the Canadians achieved an intimacy with the Indians surpassing that of other allies.

Canada did so without compromising its relationship with its allies. Despite the U.S. State Department's occasional irritation over Pearson's maneuvering behind its back, Canadian-U.S. relations never reached a crisis, thus testifying to Pearson's keen sense of how far he could go in pursuing an independent course. Ambassador Franks in Washington paid... [Pearson] a rare compliment on 27 January when he advised the British Foreign Office that "it still remains a good first rough check on what will really inflict serious damage on Anglo-American relations and see whether Canada is with us or with the United States. If the former, the situation is nearly always under control; if the latter, this may not be so."[71]

Stueck explains that Australia's leaders played a less significant role at this point. Menzies invariably followed the British lead, while Spender was so anxious for a military alliance with the United States that he would agree to anything from Washington.[72] Stueck does not consider the diplomacy of New Zealand and South Africa in any way significant.

Throughout January, Bevin's primary concern was that the United States would insist that the United Nations adopt a resolution which would brand the People's Republic of China as an aggressor. As far as he was concerned, such a resolution would serve no useful purpose. At best it would discourage the Chinese from negotiating a cease-fire. At worst it would jeopardize Hong Kong and cement the Sino-Soviet alliance.

The British cabinet met 2 January 1951, and Bevin expressed concern that President Truman might paint himself into a corner when he delivered his State of the Union message before Congress the following week. Naming China an aggressor, warned Bevin, would lead to economic sanctions which "would give China strong provocation to take action against us in Hong Kong and elsewhere in the Far East."[73] Hume Wrong, Canada's Ambassador in Washington, confirmed Bevin's worst fears. Wrong had seen a State Department memorandum which noted that the United States government had placed a total embargo upon trade with the People's Republic of China and wished that "all members of the United Nations would do likewise." Aware that this was unlikely, the State Department said that its "irreducible minimum" was a "selective embargo" on such strategic materials as petroleum products, munitions, as well as equipment and commodities directly employed in the production of munitions.[74] Happily, when Truman delivered that speech 8 January, he restricted himself to a condemnation of appeasement. The United States, he said, would not repeat in Korea the policies which had tolerated Japanese aggression in Manchuria in 1931, Italian aggression in Ethiopia in 1935, or Hitler's annexation of Austria in 1938.[75] However, Bevin feared that the issue would arise at the United Nations. The Cabinet agreed with Bevin and instructed him and Attlee "to seek Commonwealth support...at the forthcoming meeting of Commonwealth Prime Ministers."[76]

A Chinese initiative at the end of 1950 and the beginning of 1951 created a new situation, at least as far as Canada was concerned. The Chinese launched their offensive the morning of 31 December and by 4 January they had captured Seoul and moved south to a line which extended from Pyongtaek on the Yellow Sea through Wonju to Samchok on the Sea of Japan. The new line proved militarily defensible for the United Nations Command, and logistical problems would limit the Chinese capacity to advance further south. However, the Chinese had for the first time penetrated south of the 38th parallel, occupied the South Korean capital, and advanced some thirty-five miles (between fifty and sixty kilometres) beyond that.[77] At the time, nobody could foresee that this would be the Chinese army's finest hour, the moment of its maximum extent. On 15 January 1951, in correspondence to Sir Oliver Franks, Bevin was still speculating that the Chinese might oust the United Nations Command from Korea altogether.[78] That same day, the Canadian government repudiated a memo which it had sent Bevin 30 December. Circumstances had changed, observed Pearson, and given the new realities "the entire Commonwealth [must] vote for (repeat for) a condemnatory resolution. Any other course...would never be forgotten or forgiven in the United States."[79]

Franks met Acheson the afternoon of 4 January and confirmed Washington's grim determination. The very fact that Chinese forces had advanced south of the

38th parallel, emphasized Acheson, made it imperative to declare China "an aggressor." He thought that any negative consequences would be minimal. According to Franks, Acheson said:

> It was essential that Britain and the United States should be able to act together in this. On our joint action together with our friends depended the future of the United Nations and all confidence in the free world that aggression would be resisted. It was especially important in the United States that people should not come to think through failure to act in this case that collective security meant nothing and therefore transfer the lesson learned in the Far East to Western Europe. He begged me to impress upon you the importance he attached to abiding by the principle of collective security in the case of the Chinese as we had done in the case of the North Koreans.[80]

The Republicans had made gains in the congressional elections of 7 November, when MacArthur still appeared to be winning the war! The Democrats still controlled both Houses of Congress, but by the narrowest of margins: two in the Senate, twelve in the House of Representatives. It did not require much imagination to envision what might happen in the event of a total defeat, especially as Republicans were already blaming the Democrats for the "loss of China" in 1949 and the isolationist Senator Robert Taft of Ohio appeared to be the most probable Republican presidential candidate in 1952. An administration led by Robert Taft would definitely not be interested in British opinions and would almost certainly reduce American commitments in Europe.[81] Pressures on Acheson were considerably different from those upon Bevin, concerned as he was about Hong Kong and Malaya. Perspectives also differed. Whereas Bevin feared that an obsession with Korea lessened the West's ability to defend Western Europe, Acheson predicted that if Korea appeared expendable American voters might also decide that Western Europe was expendable. The question was whether the Truman administration could convince the American electorate that Commonwealth governments were useful allies whose opinions Americans ought to heed.

On 5 January, Bevin addressed the Commonwealth Prime Ministers, who had assembled at 10 Downing Street. He explained that while China was not a Soviet satellite like Poland or Hungary, it was for the moment an ally of the Soviet Union. China's population combined with the USSR's industrial power created a formidable force. Together they could involve "large numbers of the troops of the democracies" in Asia and thereby jeopardize the defence of Western Europe. What he was saying as

British Foreign Minister, explained Bevin, was not what he would be saying as a Professor of Political Science:

> If, for instance, he were asked whether China were in the ordinary sense of the word an aggressor, his answer would be "yes." If he were asked formally to declare China and aggressor, and to shape his policy on that basis, his answer would be "no." A declaration by the United Nations that China was an aggressor carried many implications, and involved just the consequences which we wished to avoid.[82]

Bevin explained what those consequences were. The Chinese might respond with even greater intransigence. The Soviets might increase their assistance to the Chinese. The war might extend to China on the grounds that it was the source of Korea's problems. Bevin was not optimistic about the good will of Mao and his colleagues. Despite early British recognition of the People's Republic of China, said Bevin, China was fomenting trouble in Malaya.[83] Bevin's goal was to keep a bad situation from becoming worse.

Some twenty months later, the CIA would confirm Bevin's analysis. National Intelligence Estimate 58 of 10 September 1952, declassified in March 1993, stated:

> We believe that Moscow will try to extend and intensify its control over Communist China. However, we believe it unlikely that, at least during the period of this estimate, the Kremlin will be able by nonmilitary means to achieve a degree of control over Communist China comparable to that which it exercises over the European Satellites. We believe it is almost certain that the Kremlin will not attempt to achieve such control by military force.[84]

In the aftermath of the Commonwealth Conference, Bevin thought that the Heads of Government had become aware of the complexity of the issues. In a telegram to the British Ambassador in Ankara, circulated to other British ambassadors as well, Bevin explained:

> 3. Commonwealth Prime Ministers felt that formal condemnation by the United Nations of the Central People's Government of China as an aggressor would have serious and far reaching implications, and that further efforts must yet be made to find a peaceful solution on lines acceptable both to the Chinese and the Americans.
>
> 4. They have now reached general agreement that the immediate objective is to try to bring representatives of the United States Government and of

the Central People's Government of China to a conference table. This is clearly not possible unless the proposal is presented in a way which will commend it both to the Americans and to the Chinese.[85]

Worthy these goals certainly were, but their implementation was another matter. More fighting would have to take place before the Americans and Chinese would talk to teach other. As long as either adversary thought that it might make gains on the battlefield, it did not want to settle for less than what might be necessary. Meanwhile, the Truman administration—responsive as it had to be to the political realities of the United States—pushed forward with its resolution condemning the People's Republic of China. Franks outlined American thinking in a letter of 13 January to the Foreign Office. Most Americans considered it "unrealistic" to fight a war unless there was some legal declaration that the adversary had committed aggression. They also suspected that if the Chinese were to attack Hong Kong, British authorities would want support from the United States.[86] The best that Bevin could hope to achieve was some limited damage control.

To that end, Bevin told Franks that any United Nations resolution must limit its condemnation of China to "her act of aggression in Korea." Bevin indicated to Franks that he would seek the support of other Commonwealth governments in this matter.[87] On 17 January, Sir Gladwyn Jebb, British Ambassador at the United Nations, said that the Americans were proceeding with their resolution, and that they wanted all United Nations member states with combat forces in Korea to join in its sponsorship.[88] Bevin refused to be one of the sponsors, and on 22 January he informed Attlee's cabinet:

> that it had not proved possible to restrain the United States Government from putting forward in the Political Committee of the United Nations a resolution condemning Chinese aggression in Korea. After consulting the Prime Minister he had instructed the United Kingdom representative at the United Nations not to join in sponsoring the resolution. On 20th January the United States Government had abandoned their [sic] attempts to persuade other countries to join them in proposing a condemnatory resolution, and had tabled one on their own responsibility...[89]

The only decision left to British authorities was whether to vote in favour of that resolution. The cabinet agreed with Bevin.[90]

That decision would not be an easy one. The following day, Sir Pierson Dixon at the Foreign Office drafted a telegram to Franks, which Kenneth Younger, the Minister of State, approved. It lamented that the American resolution was premature. "It might close a door which now appears to be slightly opening." If the Americans refused to delay their resolution, warned the telegram,

> I am afraid that it will be necessary for us to engage in some plain speaking with the United States in an attempt to drive home to them that we regard their present tactics towards both China and the United Nations as ill-conceived in the interests of us all.[91]

The telegram accused the Truman administration of "steamroller tactics" and of "neglecting the views of many friendly governments...[in order] to impose on the United Nations a policy which is the direct result of past American failures in the Far East and which does not at all spring from the needs of the United Nations or of other member states." The telegram charged the Americans with "high pressure tactics" and accused Secretary Acheson of lack of consultation. Acheson ought to realize "that it is not the rest of the world which is out of step...but their own public opinion which is out on a limb by itself."[92] Acheson's memoirs indicate that his contempt for British, Canadian, and Indian diplomacy throughout January 1951,[93] at which point United States forces were bearing most of the effort and by which point the Canadian army had not yet begun to fight.[94] (The Indians, of course, remained non-combatants throughout the Korean War.)

How would the British vote? From the United Nations, Sir Gladwyn Jebb said that he "earnestly hope[d]" that he would not receive instructions to abstain. If he did, he feared, he would be in the company of Arabs, Asians, and "only one or two Western Europeans." He had confirmed that Canada, Australia, New Zealand, and South Africa would definitely support the American resolution and that most Western European countries would probably do so.[95] (As far as Canadian Prime Minister Louis St. Laurent was concerned, the matter was fairly straightforward. Canada had no choice but to vote for the resolution "since the fact could not be avoided that Communist China had aided the aggressor in Korea."[96]) The British cabinet considered Jebb's message, and pondered its dilemma at length. In the absence of Bevin, who was seriously ill to the point that he would soon resign as Foreign Secretary, Younger explained the situation. The resolution was indeed counterproductive, but the United Kingdom did not want to appear to be "dissociating ourselves from the older members of the Commonwealth or from the United States and France." A negative vote might seriously endanger Anglo-American relations, to the point that the morale of British troops in Korea might suffer. Also, a negative vote might "be widely misrepresented as condoning Chinese aggression." Yet, abstention would be "a weak course for a great Power to take on a major issue."[97]

Within the Foreign Office itself, debate continued. One official who had had experience at the League of Nations wrote to Younger that abstention might not be such a bad course of action:

> I was brought up on the League of Nations and have very little direct knowledge of the United Nations and its ways; but I am told that an abstention has come to be regarded as a proper method of expressing disapproval when you do not wish to be unnecessarily offensive, whereas to give an adverse vote is a very strong step to take. We do not really yet know for certain which other Delegations, if any, other than the Soviet bloc, are certain to vote against. Do we really want to risk a position in which we might be almost the only Power other than the Soviet bloc giving an adverse vote? Would it not meet our position if we instructed Sir G. Jebb to abstain? Would not abstention also translate more accurately our attitude to a resolution parts of which we accept and parts of which we do not?[98]

Happily, the British won some minor concessions which enabled them, in the end, to vote in favour of the American resolution. It had not been easy to do so. Acheson's mood of determination, not to mention the pressures upon him, are evident from the language he used in a telegram to the U.S. embassy in London:

> In spite heavy U.S. losses Korea, and resulting public pressure for quick and effective action, U.S. has acquiesced in desire other Powers defer measures during attempts negotiate cease-fire arrangements. This forbearance has evidenced our desire explore all reasonable possibilities for peaceful settlement. It is now clear that failure to condemn Commie aggression would seriously damage UN prestige and influence and jeopardize U.S. public and congressional support for UN.[99]

The Attlee government wanted some modifications to paragraphs 2 and 8. The former indicated that China had "rejected all United Nations proposals" for an end to the fighting, but the British preferred wording about a "disappointing" Chinese response. If the resolution contained any threat of sanctions against China, Sir Gladwyn Jebb would receive instructions to vote against the resolution.[100] Right to the end, the Foreign Office insisted on a change to the wording of paragraph 2. On 29 January, the day before the first of two votes at the United Nations, Jebb received instructions not to support the resolution if paragraph 2 included the word "rejected."[101] After intense Anglo-American negotiations at the United Nations, U.S. and British officials reached a compromise. Instead of the words "rejected all," paragraph 2 would say "not accepted."[102] The version of Paragraph 2 which appeared in Resolution 498 (V) read:

> Noting that the Central People's Government of the People's Republic of China *has not accepted* [italics: the author's] United Nations proposals to bring about a cession of hostilities in Korea with a view to peaceful settlement, and that its armed forces continue their invasion of Korea and their large-scale attacks upon United Nations forces there...[103]

Sir Oliver Franks in Washington and Sir Gladwyn Jebb at the United Nations warned the Attlee cabinet about certain unpleasant realities. Franks had spoken to Acheson, who in turn spoke to President Truman, both of whom agreed to some of the changes which British authorities wanted in paragraph 8. They would accept these additional words:

> it being understood that the committee is authorized to defer its report if the Good Offices Committee referred to in the following paragraph reports satisfactory progress in its efforts.[104]

Beyond that they would not go, especially as they knew that the "white dominions of the Commonwealth and [most] western European countries" would support them. Franks wanted the British cabinet to support an initiative by Canada's Lester Pearson, outlined in a speech of 26 January 1951 to the United Nations Political Committee. Pearson suggested "a seven-power conference be convoked within a week after adoption of his plan" to discuss a cease-fire. The seven powers would be the People's Republic of China, France, Egypt, India, the Soviet Union, the United Kingdom, the United States,[105] Franks hoped that Jebb could "say with the Canadians, who agree with us on nearly everything else, that quite simply we think China has aggressed in Korea."[106] For his part, Jebb expressed concern that the United Kingdom might find itself in a minority alongside "Arabs, Asians, and Slavs."[107]

At the same time, Attlee was discovering that no matter what he did, he could not maintain the unity of the Commonwealth. From New Delhi, India's government was warning that even if the U.S. delegation accepted all the amendments sought by London, it would vote negatively. Younger told Attlee that the latest American concessions "represented a substantial advance," but that the United Kingdom should still "try to extract a price for our agreement." The price was that the White House and the State Department would not "oppose the action which Mr. Pearson would take after the [amended] resolution...was passed." Some Foreign Office officials disagreed and thought that for the sake of American good will, the United Kingdom must support the amended American resolution regardless of U.S. actions regarding the Pearson initiative. Attlee agreed that Jebb would definitely not vote against the amended resolution but said that he might have to abstain if the Americans objected to what Pearson was doing. Younger warned that if the British would not support the amended resolution, the Americans would return to the harsher original version.

Sir Pierson Dixon at the Foreign Office made a case for British capitulation, support for the amended American resolution even without removal of the word "rejected." In a memo of Sunday, 28 January, the date before the vote, Sir Pierson wrote:

> We consider that American Far Eastern policy is wrong-headed, will unnecessarily add to the hostile forces ranged against us, and may precipitate a world war. There can be little doubt that we are right.

Under the circumstances, said Sir Pierson, it was arguable that the United Kingdom should oppose the American resolution. However,

> it is not the case that the Americans feel a great compulsion to carry us with them in the Far East: they are prepared, & indeed determined, to go their own way in that part of the world. The threat of our disagreement over their Far Eastern policy is therefore not as potent as we might suppose. If we were ready to tell them that we should have to reconsider our European & world policy if they continued with a F.E. policy of which we disapprove, that might have some effect, because in the West it is true that they are dependent on us just as we are dependent on them. This would mean that we should have to threaten to reconsider our policy of opposition to Communism & the USSR and of support of Atlantic Defence. Clearly we are not prepared to go to those lengths.[108]

Given that British arguments could not change U.S. policy, said Sir Pierson, the best the Attlee government could do was "resign ourselves to a role of counsellor and moderator. We have already had considerable effect in this role." Otherwise, there was no choice but to accept U.S. leadership in Asia, and this meant that there was no choice but to vote in favour of the American resolution despite its flaws.[109]

The Australian government took a similar position. On 23 January 1951, Spender told the cabinet that he had instructed Keith Shann, Australia's Ambassador at the United Nations, not to label the People's Republic of China an "aggressor." The British thought the term inappropriate, as did Spender. Menzies agreed that both the term "aggressor" and the imposition of sanctions against the People's Republic of China would lessen the chances of a negotiated settlement in Korea. However, as a last resort, if the Truman administration were to prove adamant, Menzies thought that "Shann should not vote against USA without further instructions."[110]

British historian Farrar-Hockley credits Australian, Canadian, and New Zealand diplomats in narrowing the Anglo-American differences. They persuaded the British government to accept the word "aggressor," while the Truman administration accepted the creation of a Good Offices Committee to find common ground with China. Iran chaired the committee, formed in February, and India, Mexico, and Sweden served on it.[111] The United States resolution then passed through the committee stage 30 January by a margin of 45 in favour (including the United Kingdom, Canada, Australia, New Zealand, and South Africa), 7 opposed (the USSR, the Ukrainian SSR, the Byelorussian SSR, Burma, Czechoslovakia, India, and Poland), and 8 abstentions (Afghanistan, Egypt, Indonesia, Pakistan, Sweden, Syria, Yemen, Yugoslavia). On 1 February, the General Assembly gave its approval by a similar margin.[112]

As it was, Dean Rusk—Assistant Secretary of State for Far Eastern Affairs—met Hume Wrong at the end of January and told him that he would welcome trilateral U.S.-British-Canadian discussions to implement Pearson's ideas as expressed 26 January.[113] (On 23 February, Rusk told Wrong that he and other officials of the Truman administration preferred dealing with Pearson to dealing with British authorities.[114] For his part, Acheson in his memoirs refers highly to both Pearson and Hume Wrong, as well as to Franks, but not to Attlee, Bevin, or Morrison. Among British officials whom he admired were their successors after the election of 25 October 1951: Prime Minister Winston Churchill and Foreign Secretary Anthony Eden. He also mentioned Richard Casey, who would succeed Spender as Australian Minister of External Affairs in 26 April 1951,but not Spender. No New Zealander or South African appeared on Acheson's list of favourites.[115]) Subsequently, Wrong and Rusk did have discussions, whose contents Wrong then discussed with Pearson, his superior.[116] Unfortunately, General MacArthur's shenanigans alarmed Ottawa as well as London and Canberra,[117] and progress proved impossible until Ridgway replaced him and ousted the Chinese from South Korea, and both sides in the conflict accepted that there really was a military stalemate.[118]

Stueck thinks that "Allied opinion probably influenced Truman and his advisers" when the President decided to fire MacArthur.[119] While prominent Republicans and the Daughters of the American Revolution supported MacArthur, "Minimally, the Allied viewpoint reinforced the concerns of U.S. leaders as they gingerly approached a most difficult decision."[120] Stueck does not suggest that the Old Commonwealth leaders persuaded Truman to turn against MacArthur, but that they encouraged him to stay the course at a time when others disagreed.

There certainly is evidence that negotiations among Commonwealth countries could make a difference. By March, the Additional Measures Committee of the United Nations was debating further sanctions against China, and there were differences of opinion between Washington and London. Australian authorities agreed with Washington. Despite voluminous correspondence which the British government sent to Canberra, Australian authorities found the U.S. position on sanctions more credible.[121] On 14 March 1951, Shann cabled Spender:

> I understand that the Commonwealth Relations Office has been keeping you in touch with the discussions in Washington between the United States and the United Kingdom. We find the United Kingdom line a little hard to follow as they seem to prefer a definite list of commodities in any resolution, i.e., petroleum products, atomic energy materials, arms and other military equipment and vehicles and materials going into the making of the foregoing. The United States on the other hand seem [sic] to prefer a general appeal not to aid the Chinese leaving it to individual States to make their own interpretation. I should have thought the latter was preferable.[122]

Officials at the Department of External Affairs agreed.[123]

Nevertheless, Richard Casey—who replaced Spender as Minister of External Affairs 26 April 1951—instructed his country's UN delegation to keep Sir Gladwyn Jebb up-to-date on Australian thinking. The Australian High Commissioner in Ottawa also informed Canadian officials. U.S. authorities listened, and a compromise proved feasible. On 18 May 1951, the General Assembly voted solidly in favour of a selected embargo resolution. In favour were 47 countries, including all Western allies of the U.S., among them all countries of the Old Commonwealth. No delegation cast a negative vote, although eight abstained (Afghanistan, Burma, Egypt, India, Indonesia, Pakistan, Sweden, Syria) and the Soviet-bloc refused to participate.[124]

New Zealand's role in the debate over sanctions was that of a concerned bystander. For emotional reasons, Holland wanted to support the British, but he knew that his country's long term security might depend on the U.S. and did not want to antagonize it. He also had happy memories of trips he had taken there both as a private citizen and as a backbencher in parliament. In Washington and at the United Nations, Berendsen believed that the U.S. could do no wrong. He forwarded a warning after former President Herbert Hoover delivered a speech 20 December 1950 against military commitments outside the Western Hemisphere. Other Republicans, most notably Ohio Senator Robert Taft—a presidential prospect—shared this opinion. Hoover complained that his country lacked "foul weather friends" and might have greater strength if it would consolidate its military resources. Forced to make a choice between New Zealand's powerful mentors, New Zealand sided with the U.S. against the United Kingdom in a UN Political Committee procedural vote of 22 January. The U.S. side lost 27:23. Later that month, New Zealand and Australia voted "with the majority" on a twelve-nation Afro-Asian resolution regarding cease-fire talks. The United Kingdom and Canada abstained. New Zealand authorities were greatly relieved when the U.S. compromised on the sanctions issue and the U.S. and UK delegations could vote the same way.[125]

Nevertheless, McGibbon sees whatever role New Zealand played as one of bridging the gap between the United States and the rest of the Commonwealth, not as persuading U.S. authorities to modify their policies. In his words,

> Forced to choose [between the U.S. and the United Kingdom], New Zealand had opted for the United States relationship—as had Britain in the end. The New Zealand approach, firmly grounded in a perception of the strategic requirements of a small, isolated power, helped to ensure with Australian support, that Commonwealth diplomacy did not lead inexorably to a breach with the United States. New Zealand and Australia provided a counterpoise to India...[126]

Soon even the CIA came to see the futility of a UN embargo against the People's Republic of China. Special Estimate 20 of 17 December 1951, declassified in 1993, noted that an embargo against Chinese ports "would be largely nullified" if trade through Hong Kong and Macao continued. Also, Soviet-bloc states plus many others "would not respect" the embargo. A naval blockade to enforce the embargo "would not in itself force the Chinese Communists to end the Korean War or threaten the stability of the Chinese Communist regime." However, the Chinese might attack blockading ships with mines, aircraft, and submarines, and the USSR could increase overland shipments to China.[127]

VIII   The Battlefield in the First Half of 1951

The situation over the next several months was serious on the battlefield. Members of the Kayforce from New Zealand took their position 23 January as part of the 27 Commonwealth Brigade.[128] In February the Princess Patricia's Canadian Light Infantry from Canada joined the 27 British Commonwealth Infantry Brigade, just as the Chinese launched an offensive. The Commonwealth Division which resulted—including Britons, Canadians, Australians, and New Zealanders—fought a formidable action near Kapyong and reversed the offensive.[129] There were no major differences of opinion between the Truman administration and Commonwealth leaders during this period (February-April 1951).

A Foreign Office memo of 1 February summarized British policy. The Chinese

are not and never will be mere satellites of Russia. They achieved their revolution by themselves, and intend to stay independent...The American analysis of what is happening in China is wrong. They are not mere satellites of Moscow, the Chinese Government is firmly entrenched, he opposition is inconsiderable, and the Nationalists have no prospects.

Yet the basic American strategy is probably right. The new China is a menace to the peace of Asia and a formidable ally of Russia in a bid for world domination, and it would be very unwise of us to allow our irritation at the stupidity of American tactics to blind us to this.[130]

In other words, the United Kingdom should continue as a forceful member of an American-led coalition.

On 6 February, the British Chiefs of Staff ordered Lord Tedder in Washington to express the strategic objectives of the United Kingdom to the U.S. Chiefs of Staff. The United Nations, they said, should regain control of "as great an area of...[Korea] as possible up to the 38th parallel." A move beyond the 38th parallel would be unwise because the Chinese would react and negotiations would not begin. There was no point in repeating the mistake of the previous year.[131] The Canadian government agreed.[132] (The Australians did not want a deep thrust into North Korea, but they were not committed to the 38th parallel itself.[133])

In his memoirs, Secretary Acheson confirmed that there was little discrepancy between the British position of a stalemate "approximately on the line of the 38th parallel" and U.S. objectives. "Despite some illusions to the contrary," said Acheson,

United Nations and United States war aims had not included the unification of Korea by armed force against all comers, and Chinese intervention had now removed this as a practical possibility...The line to be sought and held should be north of the parallel and chosen for its tactical defensive possibilities and practicality of attainment. As April opened, General [Matthew] Ridgway [the ground commander who on 11 April would replace MacArthur] entered the area over which he was to fight for two years...In this area he found and held the line which became that of the ultimate cease-fire.[134]

Also, at their meeting of 31 January 1951, Dean Rusk confirmed to Hume Wrong that the United States government anticipated the 38th Parallel as the inter-Korean boundary.[135]

Yet, throughout February, U.S. authorities refused to make a commitment to stay south of the 38th parallel. Any such commitment, they indicated to British officials, would be "premature." (Given the realities of the battlefield, they might have said "academic.") However, they did promise consultation with the allies before undertaking any northward thrust. Pearson expressed alarm over a mid-March statement by General Ridgway indicating that the 38th parallel might not be the limit after all.[136] For its part, the Foreign Office predicted what actually did materialize: "a...stalemate...approximately on the line of the 38th parallel."[137] On 24 March Bevin's successor as Foreign Secretary, Herbert Morrison, instructed his embassy in Washington to inform the United States government in no uncertain terms that United Nations forces should not advance north of the 38th parallel. To move north, Morrison warned, would have two serious consequences. It would delay the truce negotiations, and it would shorten the Chinese supply lines, thereby enabling them to fight more effectively.[138] General MacArthur was making public statements about an expanded war and causing alarm,[139] but the alarm existed in Washington as well as London, Ottawa and Canberra. On 11 April, President Truman relieved General MacArthur of his command.

IX Co-operation among the Commonwealth Belligerents

Even in the face of battlefield conditions, the Commonwealth was less than cohesive. In July 1950, the U.S. Secretary of Defense, Louis A. Johnson, had suggested that given their small numbers, the British, Australian, and New Zealand ground troops in Korea might unite into a British Commonwealth Division (BCD). Menzies agreed. However, when the St. Laurent government agreed to send soldiers to Korea, it was less than enthusiastic about adding the Canadians to the BCD. This seemed anachronistic, a throwback to the colonial era. St. Laurent's government preferred a "1st United Nations Division" which would include soldiers from twelve countries, only some of whom were members of the Commonwealth. This proved quite impractical, especially as all the non-Commonwealth participants except Belgium used U.S. military hardware. According to Farrar-Hockley, the Australian government persuaded Canada to swallow its doubts and participate in the BCD.[140]

According to Farrar-Hockley, the integrated Commonwealth military effort was a total success.

Australian, Canadian, and New Zealand naval and ground contingents integrated so rapidly within the British formations that it was difficult to tell one from another—nor did it matter to the Americans what came from where to join the United Nations Command.[141]

Commonwealth forces distinguished themselves against Chinese troops, particularly at the April 1951 Battle of Kapyong.[142]

X   Thoughts on the Diplomacy of the Commonwealth Belligerents to Mid-1951

Happily, the pessimistic projections of the Truman-Attlee talks did not materialize. The United Nations command did manage to hold the line south of Seoul, then early in 1951 recapture the South Korean capital and establish a new front somewhat south of the 38th parallel near Kaesong in the west and north of the 38th parallel in the east. There were limits to the length of the supply lines which the People's Liberation Army (the Chinese army) could maintain.

Some of the concerns expressed at the Truman-Attlee talks now appear somewhat exaggerated. The Western world thrived in the 1990s despite the triumph of Communist forces in what had been French Indo-China, against the French in 1954 and the Americans in 1975. In 1997, the last British forces departed from Hong Kong, which became part of the People's Republic of China—albeit with its own autonomous legal and economic system. Hong Kong continues to play a major role in the global economy. The Philippines and Japan remained consistently outside the orbits of the Soviet Union and China.

With regard to Sino-Soviet relations, Attlee was correct. Mao really was an Asian Tito. Declassified Soviet and Chinese documents confirm that Mao's one meeting with Stalin had been an unhappy experience. When Mao went to the Soviet Union in December 1949, where he stayed until February 1950, he felt that Stalin treated him like a prisoner and that Stalin was an uncultured boor.[143] By 1969, the People's Republic of China and the Soviet Union were shooting at each other over a boundary dispute.

Most of the other arguments remain untested. The issue of Taiwan is unresolved. (The status of Taiwan may yet provoke bloodshed, and while Taiwan is important to the global—and even the mainland Chinese—economy, it is certainly not a positive factor in Sino-American relations. However, relations between Beijing and Washington are much more friendly one than they were in 1950.) Fortunately, Stalin had no intention of invading Western Europe in 1950 or 1951, nor did his successors after 1953. The Soviet Union disintegrated and disappeared in 1991. Whether the

United States and its allies could have handled simultaneous confrontations with the Soviet Union and the People's Republic of China is now largely academic.

With regard to the United Nations resolution which declared the People's Republic of China guilty of aggression, there was some justification for the support given the U.S. resolution. It was also wise to have a bottom line with regard to the contents, and it was fortunate that Truman and Acheson were willing to respect that bottom line. There were logical and well-founded reasons for the British objections. However, the Truman administration found itself caught between American opinion and the opinions of its most important Allies, and siding with the former made sense. After all, Americans were the ones who voted in American elections, and Americans were doing most of the fighting on behalf of South Korea. Americans were paying the taxes and sustaining the casualties. In the end, the United Kingdom needed American support in Europe more than the United States required British support in Asia. Given the perceived military threat from the Soviet Union, unilateralism would have jeopardized British interests more seriously than American ones. Happily, a public Anglo-American confrontation proved unnecessary, as did British capitulation to American terms.

Did it matter that the British government persuaded Truman and Acheson to amend their United Nations resolution? Would it have mattered if the original resolution had passed without amendments or gone down to defeat? Certainly, sanctions against the People's Republic of China might have endangered Hong Kong, which would remain a British colony for yet another forty-six years and retain its own identity after 1997. Defeat of the American resolution might well have angered American opinion to the point that a Republican administration, elected in 1952, might have lost interest in working with trans-Atlantic allies. When the resolution passed, even the liberal *New York Times* editorialized:

> The General Assembly of the United Nations has now acted to put the aggression of the Chinese Communists in Korea formally on the record. This seems to us to have been the only possible course if the United Nations valued its survival.[144]

However, it is doubtful whether passage of the resolution, amended or unamended, would have had much impact on the timing of the cease-fire talks. Battlefield conditions determined when they would take place. Once both sides had become convinced that they had achieved all that they were likely to achieve in the shooting war, the talks could—and did—begin.

Finally, there was the matter of General MacArthur, whom President Truman relieved of his command in April 1951. Attlee's government had lost confidence in him by late November 1950,[145] but there is little evidence that Truman dismissed him because of British pressure. Truman's memoirs indicate that MacArthur's refusal to obey the civilian authority (the duly elected President of the United States, Truman himself) was reason enough.[146]

Notes

1. Acheson, p. 475.

2. David McCullough, *Truman* (New York: Simon and Schuster,1992), p. 821.

3. *Ibid.*

4. *Public Papers of the Presidents*, 1950, pp. 724-727.

5. O'Neill, pp. 145-148.

6. Harry S. Truman, *Memoirs: Years of Trial and Hope, II* (New York: Signet, 1956), pp. 449-469.

7. McCullough, p. 822.

8. Weintraub, pp. 259, 261, 318.

9. Daniel Calingaert, "Nuclear Weapons and the Korean War," *The Journal of Strategic Studies*, XI (June 1988), pp. 177-202, especially pp. 179-183; Roger Dingman, "Atomic Diplomacy during the Korean War," *International Security* XIII, 3 (Winter 1988/89), pp. 50-91, especially pages 66-69. This is also the opinion of Prince; p. 143.

10. Calingaert, pp. 178, 181-183.

11. Calingaert, p. 180; Record of a Meeting of the Prime Minister and Foreign Secretary with the French Prime Minister and Minister for Foreign Affairs at 10 Downing Street on Saturday, 2 Dec. 1950, *DBPO*, pp. 229-230, 235.

12. The Ambassador in France (Bruce) to the Secretary of State, 5 Dec. 1950, *FRUS*, 1950, VII, pp. 1387-1389.

13. Holmes, London, to the Secretary of State, Washington, 1 Dec. 1950, 3:p.m., 3:19 p.m., and 7:20 p.m. (separate messages), File: Reactions to President's Statement re Use of Atomic Bomb, : Selected Records Relating to the Korean War, Dept of State: Topical File Subseries, Box 8, HST.

14. Steven Hugh Lee, p. 105.

15. Extract from the Conclusions of a Meeting of the Cabinet, 29 Nov. 1950, *DBPO*, pp. 215-218.

16. Bevin, London, to Franks, Washington, 2 Dec. 1950, *DBPO*, p. 226.

17. O'Neill, pp. 145-148.

18. Re Spender: endnote 6, *DBPO*, p. 228; re the Canadian government, CAB 128/18, *DBPO*, p. 237.

19. McCullough, p. 823-824; Acheson, pp. 471-473.

20. Peter Lowe, pp. 49-50.

21. B.J.S.M., Washington, to Ministry of Defence, London, 5 Dec. 1950, *DBPO*, p. 241.

22. Franks, Washington, to Bevin, London, 6 Dec. 1950, *DBPO*, 242-244.

23. Extract from the UK Record of the 5th Meeting between President Truman and Mr. Attlee and the White House, 7 Dec. 1950, *DBPO*, pp. 245-249. The quotation comes from p. 249.

24. Memorandum for the Record by the Ambassador at Large (Philip C. Jessup), Washington, 7 Dec. 1950, *FRUS*, 1950, VII, p. 1462.

25. Dingman, p. 69.

26. *FRUS*, 1950, VII, pp. 1348-1461.

27. Memorandum of Conversation by the U.S. Ambassador at Large, Philip C. (Meeting at the Pentagon), 3 Dec. 1950, *FRUS*, 1950, VII, pp. 1324, 1329. Among those who foresaw the possibility of a Korean Dunkirk were General Omar Bradley, Chairman of the Joint Chiefs of Staff, and General George Marshall, Secretary of Defense. Secretary of State Dean Acheson, a civilian, shared their concern. The Joint Chiefs of Staff actually advised President Truman to discuss a "forced evacuation" from Korea when he met Attlee; *FRUS*, 1950, VII, pp. 1348-1349; When they met, Truman and Attlee actually did discuss the possibility of a Korean Dunkirk; Memorandum of Conversation, Truman Attlee Talks, 4 Dec. 1950, *FRUS*, 1950, P. 1376.

28. U.S. Delegation, Minutes of the 1st Meeting of President Truman and Prime Minister Attlee, *FRUS*, 1950, VII, 4 Dec. 1950, pp. 1365, 1368-1370. Also, Memorandum of Conversation by U.S. Ambassador at Large (Jessup), 5 Dec. 1950, *FRUS*, 1950, VII, p. 1391; U.S. Delegation, Minutes of the 2nd Meeting of Truman and Attlee, 5 Dec. 1950, *FRUS*, 1950, VII, p. 1397; Memorandum of Conversation by the Ambassador at Large (Jessup), 7 Dec. 1950, *FRUS*, 1950, VII, p. 1437; Memorandum of Conversation by U.S. Ambassador at Large (Jessup), 7 Dec. 1950, *FRUS*, 1950, p. 1438; U.S. Delegation, Minutes of the 5th Meeting of Truman and Attlee, 7 Dec. 1950, *FRUS*, 1950, VII, pp. 1451, 1453, 1452; Memorandum of Conversation by the Director of the Executive Secretariat (W.J. McWilliams), Washington, 5 Dec. 1950, *FRUS*, 1950, VII, p. 1384.

29. Memorandum of Conversation by the Ambassador at Large (Jessup), 4 Dec. 1950, *FRUS*, 1950, VII, p. 1374; Memorandum of Conversation by the Director of the Executive Secretariat (McWilliams), Washington, 5 Dec. 1950, *FRUS*, 1950, VII, pp. 1382-1383; U.S. Delegation, Minutes of the 2nd Meeting of Truman and Attlee, 5 Dec. 1950, *FRUS*, 1950, VII, p. 1404. Records of the Truman-Attlee talks appear in *FRUS*, 1950, VII, pp. 1269-1479; and in *DBPO*, p. 222-252. For earlier documentation on British concerns about Anglo-American differences over treatment of the People's Republic of China, see *DBPO*, pp. 53-57, 65-66, 88-89, 100-101, 142-143, 160, 209-211.

30. Farrar-Hockley, I, p. 368.

31. Telegram by Pearson to Canadian embassies and high commissions in London, Washington, Paris, Brussels, The Hague, Oslo, Ankara, Canberra, Wellington, Cape Town, New Delhi, and Karachi, 2 Dec. 1950, *DCER*, 1950, pp. 250-251.

32. Pearson, Ottawa, to Wrong, Washington, 4 Dec. 1950, *DCER*, 1950, pp. 253-355.

33. Wrong, Washington, to Pearson, Ottawa, 4 Dec. 1950, *DCER*,1950, pp. 255-256.

34. Wrong, Washington, to Pearson, Ottawa, 4 Dec. 1950, *DCER*, 1950, pp. 256-257.

35. John Clearwater, *U.S. Nuclear Weapons in Canada* (Toronto: Dundurn, 1999), pp. 125, 128.

36. Edelgard E. Mahant and Graeme S. Mount, *Invisible and Inaudible in Washington* (Vancouver: UBC Press, 1999), p. 21.

37. Wrong, Washington, to Pearson, Ottawa, 7 Dec. 1950, *DCER*, 1950, p. 264.

38. Memorandum of conversation between R.G. Arneson and G. Ignatieff, *DCER*, 1950, pp. 265-268.

39. Record of a Meeting at the British Embassy, Washington, between Attlee and Commonwealth Representatives, 8 Dec. 1950, *DBPO*, fiche 8/50-51.

40. Attlee, Ottawa, to Bevin, London, 10 Dec. 1950, *DBPO*, p. 257.

41. Extracts from Cabinet Conclusions, 9 Dec. 1950, *DCER*, 1950, pp. 285-286. Cited hereafter as Extracts.

42. Memorandum by Deputy Under-Secretary of State for External Affairs (Escott Reid), 9 Dec. 1950; Memorandum by Head, American and Far Eastern Division (Herbert Norman), 8 Dec. 1950; Memorandum by Head, European Division (Jules Leger), 9 Dec. 1950; *DCER*, 1950, pp. 269-281.

43. Extracts, pp. 286-289.

44. Extracts, pp. 288-289; Attlee to Bevin, 10 Dec. 1950, *DBPO*, p. 257.

45. Milner, pp. 202-203.

46. Siracusa and Cheong, pp. 30-31.

47. O'Neill, p. 137.

48. O'Neill, p. 140.

49. O'Neill, p. 141.

50. O'Neill, pp. 143-148. The quotation comes from p. 148.

51. *Ibid.*

52. Prince, p. 142.

53. O'Neill, p. 137.

54. McGibbon, I, p. 183.

55. McGibbon, I, p. 187.

56. Bevin, London, to Franks, Washington, 31 Dec. 1950, *DBPO*, p. 274.

57. Franks, Washington, to Bevin, London, 1 Jan. 1951, *DBPO*, Fiche 9/19.

58. Bevin, London, to Franks, Washington, 31 Dec. 1950, *DBPO*, pp. 274-275.

59. For a report on the Cairo Conference, see Winston S. Churchill (Toronto: Thomas Allen, 1951), pp. 325-341.

60. Bevin, London, to Franks, Washington, 31 Dec. 1950, *DBPO*, p. 276.

61. Dana Wilgress, Canada's High Commissioner in London, to Pearson, Ottawa, 4 Jan. 1951, *DCER*, 1951, pp. 1019-1021.

62. Lowe, p. 87.

63. Farrar-Hockley, p. 26.

64. Wilgress, London, to Pearson, Ottawa, 6 Jan. 1951, *DCER*, 1951, pp. 1023-1024. See also Meeting of Prime Ministers: Minutes of the Fourth Meeting, 5 Jan. 1951, *DBPO*, fiche 10/1-10/5.

65. Wilgress, London, to Pearson, Ottawa, 9 Jan. 1951, *DCER*,1951, pp. 1031-1032 (source of the quotation). For British records of the meetings of 8 and 9 Jan., see *DBPO*, fiches 10/6-11 and 10/12-15.

66. Meeting of Prime Ministers, 11 Jan. 1951, *DBPO*, fiches 10/26-27.

67. Appraisal of the Commonwealth Prime Ministers' Meeting, written in Ottawa, 24 January 1951, *DCER*, 1951, pp. 1038-1041.

68. Records of the 10th meeting (11 Jan. 1951) and the 11th meeting (12 Jan. 1951) are available in *DBPO*, fiches 10/16-19 and 10:20-22. Nehru's complain appears on 10/22.

69. Declaration by Commonwealth Prime Ministers, released 13 Jan. 1951, *DBPO*, fiches 10/28-29.

70. Final Communique, released 13 Jan. 1951, *DBPO*, fiches 10/19-30.

71. Stueck, p. 165. For further insights on the Commonwealth and the People's Republic of China, see pp. 171, 173, 177-178.

72. Stueck, pp. 165-166.

73. Extracts from the Conclusions of a Meeting of the Cabinet, 2 Jan. 1951, *DBPO*, p. 279.

74. Wrong, Washington, to Pearson, Ottawa, 20 Jan. 1951, *DCER*, 1951, pp. 68-70. The quotations come from p. 69.

75. *Public Papers of the Presidents*, Truman, 1951, pp. 6-13.

76. Extracts from the Conclusions of a Meeting of the Cabinet, 2 Jan. 1951, *DBPO*, p. 280.

77. Goulden, p. 433.

78. Bevin, London, to Franks, Washington, 3 Jan. 1951, *DBPO*, p. 305.

79. Reprinted in *DBPO*, p. 285.

80. Franks, Washington, to Bevin, London, 4 January 1951, *DBPO*, pp. 286-289. The quotation comes from p. 288.

81. Goulden, pp. 388-389.

82. Bevin, London, to Sir N. Charles, Ankara, 12 Jan. 1951, *DBPO*, p. 301.

83. Extract from the Third Meeting of Commonwealth Prime Ministers, *DBPO*, pp. 289-292. The quotation comes from p. 291.

84. National Intelligence Estimate 58, "Relations between the Chinese Communist Regime and the USSR: Their Present Character and Probable Future Course," 10 Sept. 1952, R.G. 26, Box 1, File 32, NARA.

85. Bevin, London, to Sir N. Charles, Ankara, 12 Jan. 1951, *DBPO*, p. 301.

86. Franks, Washington, to Sir Roger Makins, Foreign Office, London, 13 Jan. 1950, *DBPO*, p. 307.

87. Bevin, London, to Franks, Washington, 15 Jan. 1951, *DBPO*, p. 306.

88. Jebb, New York, to Bevin, London, 17 Jan. 1951, *DBPO*, p. 308.

89. Extracts from the Conclusions of a Meeting of the Cabinet, 22 Jan. 1951, *DBPO*, pp. 318-321. The quotation comes form p. 318.

90. Ibid.

91. Foreign Office, London, to Franks, Washington, *DBPO*, pp. 322-326.

92. *Ibid.*

93. Acheson, *Present at the Creation* (New York: Norton, 1969), pp. 512-513.

94. David J. Bercuson, *Blood on the Hills: The Canadian Army in the Korean War* (Toronto: University of Toronto Press, 1999), especially pp. 83-111.

95. Jebb, New York, to Foreign Office, London, 24 Jan. 1951, *DBPO*, pp. 327-329. Quotations and paraphrasing come from p. 328.

96. Extract from Cabinet Conclusions, 24 Jan. 1951, *DCER*, 1951, p. 85.

97. Extract from the Conclusions of a Meeting of the Cabinet, 25 Jan. 1951, *DBPO*, pp. 330-333.

98. Sir W. Strang, Foreign Office, London, to Younger, 25 Jan. 1951, *DBPO*, p. 334.

99. Secretary of State, Washington, to Embassy in the United Kingdom, 24 Jan. 1951, *FRUS*, 1951, VII, pp. 122-123.

100. Conclusions of a Meeting of the Cabinet, 26 Jan. 1951, *DBPO*, pp. 335-338.

101. Foreign Office, London, to Franks, Washington, 29 January 1951, pp. 344-346.

102. Editorial note, *FRUS*, 1951, VII, pp. 145-146.

103. *United Nations Yearbook*, 1951, p. 225.

104. *Globe and Mail*, 27 Jan. 1951.

105. *Ibid.*

106. Franks, Washington, to Foreign Office, 27 Jan. 1951,*DBPO*, pp. 339-341.

107. A summary of Jebb's telegram of 27 Jan. 1951 to the Foreign Office appears in *DBPO*, p. 341.

108. Minute by Sir Pierson Dixon, Foreign Office, London, 28 Jan. 1951, *DBPO*, pp. 343-344.
109. *Ibid.*

110. Minutes, 23 Jan. 1951, Item 1/10, NAA,

111. Farrar-Hockley, II, p. 27.

112. *United Nations Yearbook*, 1951, p. 224.

113. Wrong, Washington, to Pearson, Ottawa, 1 Feb. 1951, *DCER*, 1951, p. 101.

114. Wrong, Washington, to Pearson, Ottawa, 23 Feb. 1951, *DCER*, 1951, p. 121.

115. Acheson, Present at the Creation, p. 272.

116. Lester B. Pearson, *Mike: The Memoirs of the Rt. Hon. Lester B. Pearson* (Toronto: University of Toronto Press, 1973), II, pp. 171-179.

117. O'Neill, p. 208.

118. Pearson, II, pp. 179-183.

119. Stueck, p. 181.

120. Stueck, p. 182.

121. See correspondence in Series A621 (A621/1), Item 5789, Part 1, NAA.

122. Australian Mission to the United Nations to Minister and Department of External Affairs, Canberra, 15 March 1951, Series A621 (A621/1), Item 5789, Part 1, NAA.

123. Doig, Canberra, to Secretary, Department of Commerce and Agriculture, Canberra, 20 March 1951, Series A621 (A621/1), Item 5789, NAA; J.G. Crawford, Canberra, Memorandum, 2 April 1951, ibid.

124. Secretary, Department of External Affairs, Canberra, to Australian Delegation to the UN, 3 May 1951; Australian High Commissioner in Ottawa to Casey, Canberra, 7 May 1951; Australian delegation to the UN to Casey, 11 May 1951; Australian delegation to the UN to Casey, 18 May 1951; all in Series A621 (A621/1), Item 5789, Part 1, NAA.

125. McGibbon, I, pp. 189-205.

126. McGibbon, I, p. 203.

127. Special Estimate 20, "The Probable Consequences of Certain Possible U.S. Courses of Action with Respect to Communist China and Korea," 17 Dec. 1951, R.G. 263, Box 1, File 24, NARA.

128. McGibbon, p. 200.

129. Bercuson, pp. 83-111.

130. Memorandum by Mr. R. Scott, Foreign Office, London, 1 Feb. 1951, DBPO, pp. 346-351.

131. Summarized in DBPO, p. 354.

132. Pearson, Ottawa, to Wrong, Washington, 13 Feb. 1951, DCER , 1951, p. 111.

133. O'Neill, I, pp. 203-208.

134. Acheson, Present at the Creation, pp. 517-518.

135. Wrong, Washington, to Pearson, Ottawa, 1 Feb. 1951, DCER, 1951, p. 101.

136. Pearson, Ottawa, to Wrong, Washington, DCER, 1951, p. 130.

137. Memorandum by Younger, Foreign Office, London, 1 March, 1951, DPBO, pp. 364-367. The quotations comes from pp. 364-365.

138. Morrison, London, to Steel, Washington, pp. 382-383.

139. Steel, Washington, to Morrison, London, 24 March 1951, DBPO, pp. 383-385. See also Franks, Washington, to Morrison, London, 6 April 1951, DBPO, pp. 399-402; Morrison to Franks, 9 April, DBPO, pp. 403-404. See the correspondence, most of it between Pearson in Ottawa and Wrong in Washington, in DCER, 1951, pp. 112-136.

140. Farrar-Hockley, II, pp. 59-64.

141. Farrar-Hockley, II, p. 405.

142. Bercuson, pp. 83-111; Peter Gaston, Thirty-Eighth Parallel: The British in Korea (Glasgow: A.D. Hamilton, 1976), especially pp. 30-57; Government of New Zealand, Ice and Fire: New Zealand and the Korean War (Wellington: Government of New Zealand, c. 2003), pp. 19-20; Grey, pp. 81-85.

143. Mark Kramer, "The USSR Foreign Ministry's Appraisal of Sino-Soviet Relations on the Eve of the Split, September 1959," CWIHP, VI-VII, pp. 170-173.

144. New York Times, 2 Feb. 1951.

145. Weintraub, p. 249.

146. Harry S Truman, Memoirs, II: Years of Trial and Hope (New York: Signet, 1956), especially p.. 501. Secretary of State Acheson (Present at the Creation, pp. 512-528) and historian David McCullough (pp. 834-843) agree.

Chapter Four

What Should Have Been The Cease-Fire Terms?

I Churchill Replaces Attlee in the United Kingdom

Winston Churchill's Conservatives defeated the Labour government of Clement Attlee in the British parliamentary elections of 25 October 1951. According to Peter Lowe, the Truman administration welcomed this development but soon came to realize that differences between Washington and London would remain.[1] Another historian, Steven Hugh Lee, thinks that the differences actually widened.[2] During his time in Opposition, Churchill addressed the President as "Harry."[3] At the same time, Churchill feared that too deep a U.S. commitment in Asia might jeopardize the security of Europe, which for him was a higher priority.[4] Once he became prime minister, much more of Churchill's correspondence dealt with Iran, where the United Kingdom had extensive petroleum interests, than with Korea.

Churchill shared Attlee's views on foreign relations and particularly valued friendly relations with the U.S., which had assisted him so significantly during World War II. Churchill's Secretary of State for Commonwealth Relations was a general, Lord Ismay, and his Minister of Defence, Lord Alexander, had been Governor General of Canada until his appointment to the cabinet.[5] That is not to say that there was complete harmony between London and Ottawa. Like Acheson, Selwyn Lloyd— who had replaced Sir Gladwyn Jebb as British Ambassador to the United Nations— thought that Pearson could be incredibly naïve. Lloyd marvelled that Pearson, who at the time was President of the United Nations General Assembly, could suggest a unilateral cease-fire while the Chinese considered a peace proposal sponsored by India. "He thinks once the shooting stops it will not begin again," wrote Lloyd in amazement.[6]

Members of the Truman administration kept the Commonwealth Relations Office (CRO) informed about the talks at Panmunjom. At first they also briefed the Australian and Canadian governments directly, although—to the dismay of Canberra and Ottawa—not as thoroughly as they briefed the CRO.[7] They then began to inform individual Commonwealth governments.[8] Dean Acheson appreciated support from the Commonwealth and France.[9] For their part, says Steven Hugh Lee, British and Canadian authorities weRe most reluctant to disagree publicly with the U.S. government, but neither did they want the Korean War to continue, let alone expand.[10]

II   The Truce Talks

The most extensive commentary on the truce talks of 1951-1953 is that by Rosemary Foot, *A Substitute for Victory*.[11] Drawing extensively on U.S. and British—but not Canadian or Australian—sources, Foot makes several points. The talks began because neither side thought that it could force the enemy to unconditional surrender. Indeed, neither side thought that it had the capacity to seize much more territory than it already had without paying a higher price—in blood, in money, in risk of a wider war—than it was willing or able to pay. The opinions of British, Canadian, and Australian leaders *did* matter to members of the Truman administration, but President Truman and Secretary Acheson had other considerations as well. If the Commonwealth belligerents would pay a higher price for peace than seemed reasonable to the White House and the State Department, the government of South Korea leaned (to say the least) in the opposite direction. Syngman Rhee preferred a military victory to a negotiated settlement, and if he had to settle for the latter, he wanted to make as few concessions or compromises as possible. Within the United States itself, the Truman administration faced criticism—above all from Republicans—who equated concessions to or compromises with Communists as close to treason. This was the heyday of Wisconsin Senator Joseph McCarthy, and 1952 would be a presidential election year.[12]

Under those circumstances, talks began at Kaesong, south of but within easy walking distance of the 38th parallel. The principal negotiators were General Nam Il, a North Korean, and Vice Admiral Charles Turner Joy, an American. Negotiations at the military level could avoid such issues as the diplomatic recognition of enemy governments. Kaesong had been capital of mediaeval Korea, a seat of royalty from the tenth to the fourteenth century.[13] British writer M.L. Dockrill has noted the absence of a negotiator from any United Nations Command country other than the United States and assumed a corresponding lack of influence by other countries. Dockrill does, however, admit that "Britain, France, Australia and Canada received regular but often out of date briefings from the State Department on the progress of the talks."[14] Despite problems, there were some major developments in 1951. The two sides agreed on a demilitarized zone (DMZ) four kilometres in width (two either side of the demarcation line [DML], the inter-Korean boundary) once the truce took effect. Although when the talks began 10 July, the Chinese and North Koreans anticipated that the DML would be the 38th parallel, within weeks they accepted the Kansas Line, the place where the two sides actually confronted each other at the time. (Admiral Joy had proposed, probably as a bargaining chip, that the DML be far north of the Kansas Line, from Pyongyang to Wonsan.) The Kansas Line was slightly north of the 38th parallel except in Korea's far west, and it was militarily more defensible than the 38th parallel had been.[15] It also allowed for more efficient transportation across the northern part of South Korea. With North Korea's archives still unavailable for scholarly research, one can only surmise, but it seems plausible that North Korean control of Kaesong helped to make the Kansas Line acceptable in Pyongyang. There was a suspension of talks 23 August when the Chinese and North Koreans accused the United Nations Command of military action near Kaesong, but negotiations resumed at a new location, Panmunjom, a few kilometres to the east, on 25 October. Both sides adopted the United Nations agenda and readily agreed that the new inter-Korean boundary should be the actual battlefront, which moved very little for the rest of the war, rather than the 38th parallel itself.[16]

Despite these achievements there were disagreements, which would require 575 meetings (until 27 July 1953).[17] While the talks continued, casualties did as well. Some 45% of U.S. battle casualties occurred after the truce talks had begun in Kaesong.[18] More Canadians died between August 1951 and the end of the conflict—that is, during the Kaesong and Panmunjom talks and the various interruptions—than had died in the earlier battles.[19] (This was not the case for all participants in the United Nations command, for while the Canadians had fought fierce battles, most notably at Kapyong, Canadian soldiers had begun to fight only on 21 February 1951.[20])

The ongoing talks would affect the new British government of Winston Churchill. Churchill's Foreign Secretary was Anthony Eden who, in his memoirs, wrote favourably of Secretary Acheson and General Matthew Ridgway, the superior of Vice Admiral Joy. "I was impressed by General Ridgway's handling of his command and of the armistice negotiations," said Eden.[21] Eden, like Bevin, had no doubt that the Korean War was a just war. His memoirs indicate his belief that appeasement in the face of apparent Soviet aggression in Korea would have encouraged Soviet aggression elsewhere. "That was the lesson of Europe in the 'thirties," he said.[22] Peter Lowe says that Churchill and Eden hoped, in vain, that John Foster Dulles would not become Eisenhower's Secretary of State.[23]

According to Denis Stairs, a Professor of Political Science at Nova Scotia's Dalhousie University, by the beginning of 1951 British, Canadian and Australian diplomats were meeting frequently in Washington to discuss developments in Korea. As of January 1951, diplomats from the sixteen countries rendering military support in the United Nations Command formed what is known as the Committee of Sixteen. High-ranking U.S. officials from the Pentagon and the State Department informed those in attendance as to what was happening in Korea. The State Department often solicited opinions from others, and the diplomats from the fifteen other belligerents frequently raised questions of their own. Stairs wrote:

> There was considerable *esprit de corps* among the non-American participants, but there was never advance collusion against the American officials. The Canadians, British, and Australians were especially close and often lunched together beforehand for general discussion, but the views even of these three were seldom unanimous. The principal Canadian participant [P.G.R. Campbell, second secretary of the Canadian embassy in Washington] can recall only one occasion on which there was advance agreement upon a tactic to be adopted during a committee session, and this was merely in support of a request for further information on a specific issue.[24]

Governments of the five Old Commonwealth countries communicated regularly with each other on Korea. Frequently they also involved the government of India, because of the contacts which India's ambassador in Beijing, Kavalam Madhava Panikkar, had with the Chinese leadership.[25] The government of India also contacted Lester B. Pearson, still Canada's Minister of External Affairs, not so much because of a Commonwealth connection but because in 1952-1953, during the last phases of the Korean War, he was President of the United Nations General Assembly.[26]

Significantly, although the United Kingdom had its Commonwealth Relations Office which co-ordinated strategy among the Old Commonwealth countries, and the State Department occasionally invited ambassadors of the Old Commonwealth countries to joint meetings, Canada appears to have taken few initiatives involving only the Commonwealth. Most of the Korean War-related correspondence appearing in the *Documents on Canadian External Relations* (1953) consists of letters between Ottawa and Washington or Ottawa and the United Nations. Indeed, there is more correspondence between Ottawa and New Delhi than between Ottawa on the one hand and all the other Old Commonwealth capitals combined. One of the few exceptions concerned a U.S. proposal to try and to punish North Korean and Chinese POWs who committed criminal acts while in captivity. Pearson questioned the legality of such questions and sought advice from British Foreign Secretary Anthony Eden. Eden shared Pearson's concerns but advised against making trouble with the United States over that issue. Pearson accepted Eden's advice.[27]

That is not to say that Ottawa was satisfied with bilateral consultations between the United States and Canada. As far as Dana Wilgress, who had become Canada's Under-Secretary of State for External Affairs, was concerned, they had not occurred with sufficient frequency during the Truman years. On 30 April 1953, Wilgress complained to Pearson

> that the United States Government, during the past two and three-quarter years, has very literally interpreted these resolutions [of the Security Council, 27 June and 7 July 1950] which gave it a blank cheque in Korea. For example, the United States Government did not consult its Allies when it recessed the Armistice negotiations at Panmunjom in October, 1952... Canada was not directly consulted when the full Armistice negotiations were recently resumed...Canada was neither consulted nor informed in advance when the United States authorized the bombing of Communist power installations on the Yalu River in June, 1952, at a time when delicate negotiations were under way to break the prisoner-of-war deadlock Canada was not consulted...when President Truman issued his order to the Seventh Fleet, on June 27, 2950, "neutralizing Formosa [Taiwan]; nor was Canada consulted...when President Eisenhower rescinded part of this order, and "deneutralized" Formosa in February of this year. Most important of all, neither Canada nor the other Allies of the United States were consulted, or informed in advance, when the United Nations Command interjected the principle of "voluntary repatriation" into the prisoners-of-war question in January 1952, a principle which was rapidly developed by the United States into an inflexible position.

Wilgress noted that Canada's greatest impact in Korean War diplomacy had taken place at the United Nations

> where we have been instrumental, together with other delegations, in persuading the Americans to accept proposals which they have not favoured originally—e.g., the Indian Resolution adopted last December by the General Assembly.[28]

Wilgress did not claim that Canada had used the Commonwealth or any part of the Commonwealth as an instrument for influencing the United States.

III   The Prisoner-Of-War Issue

By January 1952, the only unresolved issue was the question of prisoners-of-war who did not wish to return to their homeland. This became a major issue, which prolonged the conflict until 27 July 1953, more than four months after the death of Joseph Stalin, who had insisted at the Yalta conference in February 1945 that all Soviet prisoners-of-war must return home, voluntarily or involuntarily. The United Nations Command questioned the morality of such repatriations, especially when there were 183,000 North Korean and Chinese POWS at camps throughout South Korea and only 83,000 chose to return to China or North Korea. The remaining North Koreans wanted to stay in South Korea, while the dissenting Chinese preferred Taiwan. The United States was prepared to allow the twenty-two Americans who wanted to stay in China or North Korea to do so. The North Koreans and the Chinese demanded that all POWs must return to their country of origin.[29]

Dockrill found that differences between the Commonwealth governments and official Washington were minimal, despite Article 118 of the 1949 Geneva Convention (which required the repatriation of all POWs).[30] As will be clear, authorities in London, Ottawa, and Canberra did not think that the North Koreans and Chinese should be repatriated against their will. Nor did the government of New Zealand, although from Opposition benches some Labour MPs were to argue that the lives of soldiers of the United Nations Command were more important than the fate of Chinese and North Korean POWs.[31] At the same time, leaders of the UK, Canada, and Australia wanted a cease-fire at the earliest possible moment, not only to save the lives of their own soldiers but to win the release of their own prisoners of war. Eden wrote in his memoirs:

> I supported the determination of the United Nations command that we could not agree to a cease-fire which left the fate of our prisoners in suspense. The position was about as unsatisfactory as it could be. As I put it to the House of Commons, "We have not even had contact with our prisoners, we do not even know where they are. We do not know how many there are. The Red Cross have [sic] never been allowed to see them. All this must be cleared up before we can agree to an armistice."[32]

Red Cross sources confirm Eden's statement.[33]

Despite what Eden said, Prime Minister Churchill appears to have been the deciding factor with regard to the official British position on POWs. Like the Opposition MPs in New Zealand, prominent Foreign Office officials regarded the speedy return of British POWs as a higher priority than the fate of POWs from North Korea and China. Cabinet Minister Selwyn Lloyd agreed, and Eden wavered. In the end, it was Churchill's opinion that mattered.[34]

Commonwealth-U.S. differences over repatriation of unwilling POWs lay in the details, not in the principle. On 28 April 1952, Ridgway offered Nam Il and his team a package deal, which included the principle of voluntary repatriation in exchange for certain United Nations concessions to the Chinese and North Koreans.[35] Foot notes quite rightly Australian interest in the repatriation issue.[36] At first Australian authorities had serious doubts whether rulers of North Korean and the People's Republic of China would execute tens of thousands of their own soldiers.

In April 1952, Australia's ambassador to the United States, Sir Percy Spender, replaced 26 April 1951 as Australia's Minister of External Affairs by Richard Casey, had serious doubts on that score. Based on the track record of Mao's army as it defeated Chiang Kai Shek's forces, British authorities also had their doubts.[37] However, both governments soon became convinced that North Korean and Chinese soldiers should not have to return home against their will. On 8 May 1952, Casey told the Australian House of Representatives that the Menzies government supported the principle of voluntary repatriation. Casey agreed with Evatt, still Leader of the Opposition, that Australia's opinions deserved be taken more seriously than they were and that the veto-proof United Nations General Assembly ought to have a greater say in the Panmunjom negotiations than was currently the case. Yet, Casey told Evatt, "Australia was expressing her views as much as possible through the UN negotiators in the truce talks."[38]

Unresolved details remained, and the Commonwealth governments debated them. Should POWs of the United Nations Command also undergo rescreening to determine whether they wanted to return home, or should their unanimous desire for repatriation be taken for granted? Should screening of POWs "under neutral auspices" take place before or after an armistice? Casey thought that both sides ought to accept the principle of voluntary repatriation, and he thought that the screening could take place before the armistice, if the timing stood in the way of a cease-fire. In mid-June 1952, Casey rejoiced that Acheson appeared to be softening his opposition on both issues and accepting the Australian proposals.[39]

The Commonwealth initiative on the POW issue was clearly Australian, not British. Menzies and Casey had fewer qualms than St. Laurent and Donges about appearing to be sycophantic colonials. Early in June 1952, Casey instructed Australia House in London to approach the Foreign Office. Would Churchill's government be interested in a common front with Australia and other Old Commonwealth governments regarding POWs? Would it agree that the screening of the POWs might take place (a) before an armistice? (b) on a reciprocal basis?

There already had been a first screening in the sense that some North Korean and Chinese POWs had told their captors that they wanted to remain in South Korea or go to Taiwan, but that first screening had no credibility in Pyongyang or Beijing. That there had to be a second, more credible, screening seemed a reasonable assumption. The Australian initiative dealt with the second screening. Australian authorities proposed that the second screening be carried out by either the International Red Cross, a combination of national Red Cross groups, or a "small commission...of neutral nations such as Switzerland, India and Sweden (with possibility of observers from other States if need be)."[40]

The British government agreed with Canberra on the principle of reciprocity. Unlikely, even insulting though it might be that POWs of the United Nations Command might want to stay in North Korea or move to China, there was no harm in giving them the option to do so. (The Australians suggested that reciprocity would allow the other side to save face.[41]) However, regarding the timing of the screening, a Foreign Office memorandum expressed reservations:

2. We share the Australian Government's view that there is room for compromise and manoeuver within the framework of General Ridgway's proposal of 28th April...We doubt however whether a simple offer of a second screening before the armistice would be sufficient in itself. The centre of our problem is, we suggest, not in the method or timing of screening but in the principle of voluntary repatriation itself. The American view is that the offer of a second screening would only be possible on condition that the Communists would agree in advance to abide by the results. We agree with this if it is assumed that the re-screening would take place after the conclusion of an armistice and immediately before the return of the prisoners. It is, however, difficult to see how any screening carried out in advance of an armistice and possibly well before the actual exchange of prisoners could be regarded as final. In order to preserve the principle of voluntary repatriation, it seems to us that it would certainly be necessary for the prisoners to be able to take their final decision at the last moment...

3. The idea of a commission of neutrals to carry out screening seems promising. It would be acceptable on our side; and it seems from the latest information through the Indian channel that it might be acceptable to the Chinese Government.

4. As regards the suggestion of an offer of a further screening on a reciprocal basis, it would be difficult for the United Nations Command to accept the implications that any of their own men could elect to remain in Communist hands. But if reciprocity is necessary for an agreement we should most reluctantly be prepared to consider it...

6. We understand that the Australian Government have [sic] now discussed their proposals with the State Department. The Minister of State [Selwyn Lloyd] who is informed of our views on the latest developments will now also have a general discussion with the State Department, and we shall hope then to have a further exchange of views with the Australian and other Governments.[42]

Churchill's government had its reasons, expressed above, for doubts about a second screening before an armistice. Possibly reinforcing and certainly not challenging those doubts was a message of 19 May from Sir Oliver Franks in Washington. The State Department disliked the idea said Franks, in part because Nam Il and his team might interpret such a concession as an indication of weakness on the part of the United Nations Command.[43]

Spender did not wait for London—let alone Ottawa, Wellington, and Cape Town—to respond. On what was a unilateral Australian initiative, he approached the State Department. The British Foreign Office subsequently concluded that the State Department quietly and informally accepted at least some of Spender's ideas, incorporating them without attribution.[44] Indeed, the commission of neutrals eventually evolved into the Neutral Nations Repatriation Commission (NNRC) which included the three nations suggested by Australia along with Poland and Czechoslovakia. Unfortunately, another thirteen months would elapse before the cease-fire and the NNRC would materialize.

It appears that Menzies, Casey, and Spender had a more sympathetic audience in Washington than in some of the Commonwealth capitals. New Zealand and South Africa would accept but not try to influence the outcome. While Spender rushed ahead and the British government offered qualified support, New Zealand's government adopted a wait-and-see approach. Prime Minister Holland's government advised the Australian High Commission in Wellington that "before expressing a definite view...we should like to know more of the United States and United Nations reactions."[45] The South African government also refused to take a stand, on grounds of ignorance. A.M. Hamilton, South Africa's High Commissioner in London, informed Major-General W.H.A. (Alex) Bishop at the CRO—that the Malan government simply did not "possess sufficient information on the latest developments in Korea to enable it to reach any definite conclusions in the immediate future."[46]

IV Sanctions Against the People's Republic of China?

Despite differences among the Old Commonwealth governments, U.S. authorities continued to extend the courtesy of consultation. In mid-August 1952, Franks forwarded to London position papers of the United States government: one on the Panmunjom talks, which appeared to be going nowhere; and a second on possible additional economic reprisals against North Korea and the People's Republic of China. John D. Hickerson, Assistant Secretary of State for United Nations Affairs, said that the only countries whose advice the State Department was seeking were the five from the Old Commonwealth and France. "For the time being," said Franks, Hickerson did not want the privileged six to discuss the contents of the position papers with anyone else. A leak in the *Times of London* was to prove somewhat embarrassing.[47]

Franks saw at once what the difficulty would be. Sanctions against China could affect the prosperity, if not the very survival, of Hong Kong. Franks told Hickerson that as far as the British government was concerned,

> it was of no small importance that Hong Kong remain a part of the free world. In practice, Hong Kong could only hope to feed its inflated refugee population by trade with the Chinese mainland. The colony could hardly survive indefinitely if all trade with the Chinese mainland were cut off.[48]

Hickerson agreed and said that the U.S. certainly did not want to destroy Hong Kong. Perhaps Hong Kongers could find food somewhere else. Franks dismissed that idea as "quite impracticable." Having told Hickerson informally what he thought of his ideas, Franks wanted confirmation to that effect from London, "the sooner...the better."[49]

The Foreign Office responded with the support which Franks had sought. It advised Franks to thank the State Department "for consulting us at this early stage" but said that the U.S. "proposals for action in the [United Nations General] Assembly would cause us the greatest difficulty."

> 3. General embargo on trade with China would be against the economic interests of the UK and would mean the ruin of Hong Kong. It would be futile unless supported by a naval blockade, and a blockade to that effect would have to include Port Arthur, Dairen and Vladivostok as well as Soviet and satellite shipping. Such a course would entail very serious risks.

4. Severance of diplomatic relations would not harm or frighten the Communists, but would have disadvantages for us and in particular lose us our Embassy in Peking, which still has value as an observation post.[50]

With regard to tactics, if the State Department decided to ignore British objections, the Foreign Office was prepared to show restraint. It would operate behind the scenes but not in public. The Foreign Office instructed Franks:

> We are...most anxious to minimise our differences with the Americans over China. We certainly should not be in the forefront of opposition to the Americans over policy in the Assembly. The essential thing is to avoid an open Anglo-American disagreement while the Assembly is still sitting, and that is why we think you should make our position to [the] State Department as soon as possible...[51]

American policy alarmed British authorities on another front as well. At the Panmunjom talks on 19 August, Nam Il launched a tirade against United Nations intransigence. General William K. Harrison, who in May 1952 had replaced Joy as the chief United Nations negotiator, accused the other side of insincerity in its quest for an armistice. Franks told London:

> Nam Il replied vigorously repeating that delay in securing an armistice was entirely the fault of the United Nations...It was a lie that communist prisoners did not wish to be repatriated...[52]

The Foreign Office agreed with the State Department that a temporary adjournment in the Panmunjom talks was probably advisable, but it questioned whether the delay should be as prolonged as Washington seemed to want. C.H. Johnston, British Secretary of State for Foreign Affairs, told Franks that the State Department might have decided that delays at Panmunjom would translate into votes for the Democrats in the U.S. elections of November 1952. Johnston said that London would be turning to the other Old Commonwealth governments for support, and it did so.[53] In his response to Johnston's comments, Franks registered disagreement. An armistice before the presidential election would be advantageous to the Democrats, and they knew it.[54] Franks' assessment was correct. Negotiations at Panmunjom would continue.

If Churchill's government did not need Old Commonwealth support on the delay, it received that support on the embargo. The British High Commissioner in Ottawa noted that "Canadian thinking is broadly in line with ours."[55] More specifically, like the British, the Canadian government supported the British idea of a United Nations General Assembly resolution which would commend the patience and determination with which the United Nations negotiators have conducted the armistice negotiations, endorse the offers and concessions made by them and call upon the Chinese and North Korean authorities to avert further bloodshed in Korea by responding favourably to the outstanding proposals of the United Nations negotiators.[56]

To that the Canadian government would add the United States resolution, minus the threat of sanctions. Official Ottawa believed that it would take so long for sanctions to make a measurable difference to the North Korean and Chinese economies that they would do more harm than good. The embargo "would widen the gulf in the United Nations between Asian and non-Asian states" but do little to break the deadlock at Panmunjom over the fate of POWs.[57]

Governments of France, South Africa, and New Zealand—the other governments which the State Department had approached—thought like the British, Canadians, and Australians.[58] Hamilton at South Africa House said that South Africa's economy would not suffer if there were a "Total Trade Embargo" against North Korea and the People's Republic of China, for his country had no trade with either of them. However, Hamilton wondered about the consequences for Hong Kong "to the maintenance of which we attach much importance" and asked the Foreign Office for advice.[59] According to the British High Commissioner in South Africa, the Malan government wondered whether the Truman White House was deliberately disrupting the Panmunjom talks in order to win support for a UN embargo against China.[60]

In Wellington, the Holland government decided that total sanctions were premature. They might be advisable if the Chinese launched a new offensive in Korea or committed aggression against some other country, but for the moment they would not change the "military situation [but] might increase already serious division among non-Communist (especially Asian) states. Nor did the Holland government appreciate any suggestion of bilateral talks between New Zealand and the United States. "On matters of such significance," it said, "[New Zealanders] are not accustomed to committing themselves in consultations to which the United Kingdom is not a party in [the] fullest sense."[61]

On 23 September the British Embassy in Washington said that the State Department would "very shortly be embarking on bilateral [emphasis mine] talks with the French and the four old commonwealth countries as well as ourselves on the question of additional measures." The State Department had not changed its mind on the desirability of a total embargo against North Korea and the People's Republic of China, but it was willing to consider alternatives.[62] Certainly the resolution which went before the United Nations Additional Measures Committee for approval two days later called for considerably less.[63] It appears that the five countries of the Old Commonwealth plus France had scored a victory![64]

The victory, however, might be less than it first appeared. There might even be "political sanctions," whereby UN members would withdraw their diplomats from the People's Republic of China. On 27 September, a Foreign Office memorandum noted:

> The State Department have [sic] not abandoned their [sic] wish to introduce a resolution calling for political and financial sanctions against China if the terms offered by the UN for an armistice are not accepted, despite the objections to further sanctions which we and the old Commonwealth and French governments have put to them. The State Department have, however, agreed to consider action in the forthcoming session of the Assembly in two parts, the first being a "hortatory" resolution on lines generally acceptable to us, without prejudice to decisions on the second stage, which would be taken later.[65]

Johnston at the Foreign Office liked a suggestion from Sir Gladwyn Jebb that in return for British support, the Truman administration try to postpone the United Nations debate on Korea until after the presidential election.[66] Acheson agreed.

V   Proposals from Mexico and India

In September 1952, the State Department and the five Old Commonwealth countries also considered a Mexican proposal, which turned out to be little more than a red herring. The government of President Miguel Alemán, whose mandate would expire in December, suggested that the reluctant POWs might go to some third country, not South Korea nor the Republic of China (Taiwan). That way, they would not be able to serve in armies hostile to North Korea and the People's Republic of China. Churchill's government thought the proposal worthy of consideration by the Commonwealth Five,[67] who—like the State Department[68]—found the proposal harmless but unlikely to resolve the deadlock at Panmunjom. Pearson agreed. The merit of the Mexican proposal, he wrote, was

> that it would afford an opportunity for participation in the United Nations action in Korea by those countries which have not sent military forces. On the other hand, its defect is that it presupposes that the Com-

munist authorities will compromise on the question of non-forcible repatriation and, for this reason, avoids the central issue...[I]t nevertheless would provide a method of ensuring that non-repatriated Chinese prisoners were not taken into the Nationalist forces on Formosa. For this reason the Mexican proposal might have some appeal to the Communists...

[If] the resolution is placed before the Assembly, the [Canadian] Delegation should not oppose it.[69]

Delegates from Bolivia, Brazil, Canada, Costa Rica, El Salvador, Israel, Lebanon, Nicaragua, Panama, the Philippines, and the United Kingdom spoke in favour of the Mexican resolution.[70] Government officials in Australia and New Zealand said that the issue in dispute was the right of POWs to refuse repatriation, not their domicile after refusal.[71] Given its attitude toward non-Europeans, Malan's government was not willing to accept Chinese or Korean settlers, but if others wanted to take them, South Africa had no objections.[72] The sceptics were right. The Mexican proposal was unacceptable to the North Koreans and Chinese. There was no confrontation between official Washington and the Old Commonwealth about President Alemán's suggestion.

The British government continued to agree that the POWs must not be repatriated against their will, but it endeavoured to soften certain U.S. language and policies. Sir Gladwyn Jebb, British Ambassador at the United Nations, wondered what useful purpose might be served by referring to Mao's government as "the Chinese Communist...authorities" instead of what Beijing wanted, "the Central People's Government of the People's Republic of China."[73] Such caution was to prove quite academic. Then followed the row over a proposal submitted to the United Nations by India's ambassador, Krishna Menon, and supported by the Old Commonwealth governments.

In his memoirs, Acheson refers to Menon and Lester Pearson as "two adroit operators." Their proposal, said Acheson, would "give the appearance, without having the effect," of supporting the right of POWs to refuse repatriation.[74]

Acheson's account is that on 28 October, exactly one week before the U.S. presidential election, Selwyn Lloyd, the British Minister of State, informed him of Menon's plan. According to Acheson, Lloyd pretended to have doubts about it, "though I soon discovered that he was deep in it too." Menon refused to put his proposals into writing but suggested that the reluctant POWs become the responsibility of a specially constituted commission. As the fate of the POWs would then rest with their North Koreans, the Chinese, and the commission—but not the United Nations Command—the other side would probably agree to a cease-fire. Acheson feared that any POW who refused repatriation would remain a prisoner until he accepted repatriation. The Mexican proposal was more responsible than this, thought Acheson.[75]

Writing in what seems to have been a very deep anger, Johnston —Lloyd's immediate subordinate—wrote:

5. The responsibility for the difficult course which the discussions took lies entirely with the United States Delegation. Both in strategy and in tactics their attitude toward the Indian resolution can only be called inept.

6. Their strategy was singularly unimaginative and impervious to the wider advantage of the Indian proposal...

Their use of the press, as exemplified both in the press conference of Nov. 18th and the Associated Press message on me on November 22nd, was clumsy in the extreme. By thus giving publicity to their own "tough" line and to a dramatised version of our disagreement with them, they evidently hoped to frighten the United Kingdom and Canadian Delegations into accepting their views. When this attempt failed, they themselves became alarmed at the extent of the press interest which they had created in our disagreement and did what they could to damp it down...They found themselves obliged to approve an amended version of the Indian resolution after having given so much publicity to the view that it was unacceptable as a basis.

I have narrated...on these proceedings at some length because...they provide an encouraging example of Commonwealth cooperation. The basis of the Commonwealth front was a close Anglo- Canadian understanding and a determination by both Delegations to stand up to the "tough" tactics adopted by the United States representatives. The Australian and New Zealand Delegations rallied to the views of their United Kingdom and Canadian colleagues, not without some personal hesitations on the part of Sir Percy Spender, the head of the Australian Delegation, in whose mind Australia's new relationship to the United States following the ANZUS Pact, was doubtless uppermost. I understand that it was only on direct instructions from his Government that he aligned himself with us. What seemed to me particularly satisfactory was that the Indian Delegation should have been willing to let an initiative of theirs be adopted to conform with the views of the "Old Commonwealth" countries, and on this basis we should have been able to make a concerted Commonwealth effort which gave an effective lead to the entire Assembly.[76]

Nevertheless, Anthony Eden and Lester Pearson went to work as mediators and found language acceptable to the governments of both India and the United States.[77] Peter Lowe thinks that this was possible only because Acheson knew that Vyshinsky would reject the outcome, thereby rendering the whole process academic.[78] Dockrill agrees,[79] and evidence from the Truman Presidential Archives supports their contention. On 21 November 1952, the U.S. Ambassador in New Delhi, Chester Bowles, wrote of the U.S. position:

> Our position thus far has appeared to be one of virtual rejection of India's efforts to find a solution. It would seem to me therefore that we have a splendid opportunity to capitalize on the present situation. Then if the Soviet and the Commi Chi[nese] themselves decide to reject the Ind[ian] proposal, all Ind[ians] will know we have done our best and will know where opposition to peace in Korea really lies.[80]

Soviet Foreign Minister Andrei Vyshinsky indeed did criticize the results, and the Soviet-bloc—contrary to everyone else in the General Assembly—voted negatively when the revised resolution came to a vote.[81] (Chiang Kai-Shek's China abstained.)

For their part, New Zealand authorities breathed more easily once they discovered that the U.S. and the United Kingdom would be voting the same way. New Zealand played the role of follower, not leader. In mid-August 1952, the Truman administration gave a working paper to the five Old Commonwealth governments and explained that it was soliciting advice from "close friends." Thinking that the U.S. was making a direct approach and circumventing the British, the Holland government replied:

> In general...on matters of significance and importance, we are not accustomed to committing ourselves in consultations to which the United Kingdom is not a party in the fullest sense.[82]

Sir Clifton Webb, who had succeeded Doidge as Minister of External Affairs, deeply regretted Anglo-American differences over the Indian proposal, and Sir Leslie Monroe—Berendsen's successor at the United Nations and in Washington—recommended that if Wellington had to make a choice, it should side with the U.S. Webb disagreed. To side with the Americans against the Indians, said Webb, would leave the impression "that we are thinking more of saving face than of the men dying on the battlefield."[83] The cabinet agreed with Webb but realized that without U.S. support, the Indian proposal would be moribund. The compromise was a great relief.

No compromise on the POW issue seemed possible. The Korean War, which had cursed the Truman administration, became the responsibility of the Eisenhower administration, which assumed office 20 January 1953. If the Old Commonwealth governments had risked their credibility with Acheson by supporting the Menon initiative, with Eisenhower's inauguration they would be dealing with a new Secretary of State, John Foster Dulles. In 1953, with the Republicans in the White House, the Indian Resolution would revive and prove relevant in ending the Korean War.[84]

VI Eisenhower Replaces Truman

During his successful election campaign for the U.S. presidency, Republican candidate General Dwight David Eisenhower had promised that if elected, he would go to Korea. As President-elect he did so late in November, but he spent no time with the Commonwealth Division or with Major J. Plimsoll, Australian representative on the United Nations Commission for the Unification and Rehabilitation of Korea.[85]

Eisenhower's inauguration took place 20 January 1953. Six months and seven days later (six days later by Washington time), both sides signed a cease-fire agreement in Panmunjom. One major factor was Stalin's death early in March 1953, which opened the door to peace. Xiaoming Zhang of Texas A&M University has said that Kim Il Sung was ready for a cease-fire in 1952. Mao disagreed, thinking that another year of hostilities would strengthen his cause. However, Stalin's death 5 March 1953 and the policies of the new administration led by Georgi Malenkov convinced Mao and the People's Republic of China to try to end the Korean War.[86] Vladislav Zubok and Constantine Pleshakov, who have studied the Soviet archives, definitely feel that Stalin was an impediment to peace. In their words,

> Stalin was determined to fight until the last drop of blood had been shed
> by Chinese and North Korean soldiers. He also insisted, as a precondition
> of peace, that all North Korean and Chinese POWs be returned by the en-
> emy. Otherwise, he said, the Americans would use them as spies.[87]

Zubok and Pleshakov also note that on the very day of Stalin's funeral, Malenkov spoke to Zhou Enlai, Mao's envoy to the funeral, about ways to end the Korean War. Stalin, they say, "was the main obstacle to a compromise between the West, Peking, and Pyongyang on the Korean armistice. But his death unleashed he peace process."

Indeed, Zhou was very supportive of a cease-fire as rapidly as possible, and both the Soviets and the Chinese began peace initiatives at once.[88]

Wolff agrees that China anticipated a military victory until April 1951 but certainly was ready for peace in 1952. However, because of their less than trusting relationship with the Soviets, the Chinese did not want Stalin to know how eager they were.[89] Not everyone agrees. In his book published one year earlier than that of Zubok and Pleshikov, Stueck advises that Stalin's death was not the only factor conducive to peace in 1953. Mao expected Eisenhower's policies to be "more aggressive" than Truman's and the price of continued conflict would be greater than it had been.[90] A recent biographer of Stalin's, Dimitri Volkogonov,[91] says that a few days before his death, Stalin "had decided to advise his Chinese and Korean allies to seek the best deal they could to try to bring the war to an end."[92] Stalin did not have time to act before he died, but Malenkov did when he approached Zhou at Stalin's funeral. Apart from fear of what Eisenhower might do, Eastern Europe's economy was a cause for instability. (Indeed, East Germany revolted in June 1953.) There were better outlets for Communist funds than the Korean War, thought a number of Soviet officials—at least according to Stueck.[93] Nevertheless, a report in the most recent issue of the Cold War International History Project Bulletin says bluntly, "We have good evidence suggesting that Stalin's death was the critical factor in bringing the war to an end."[94]

Unaware of the Kremlin's thinking, let alone the thoughts of leaders in Beijing and Pyongyang, the Eisenhower administration tried to frighten the Chinese and North Koreans into a settlement. The Eisenhower administration threatened to expand the war beyond the boundaries of Korea, into China itself, and to use nuclear weapons.[95] Zubok and Pleshakov report that Malenkov, Zhou, and Soviet Foreign Minister Vyacheslav Molotov—who had returned to his old post when Malenkov succeeded Stalin—had heard the nuclear threat and took it seriously.[96] Perhaps the threats of expansion and nuclear warfare were quite unnecessary given the changed realities after Stalin's death. Even full disclosure of Russian, Chinese, and (eventually) North Korean archives will probably leave grounds for debate. Some historians will continue, like Stephen Ambrose, to sing the praises of the Eisenhower administration and its policies.[97] Others will argue that Eisenhower benefitted from a changes in circumstances beyond his control or the control of any other American.

Regarding nuclear weapons, whose possible use in Korea happily never became more than hypothetical, key members of the Eisenhower administration did take the opinions of U.S. allies into account—but only to a point. At the 131st meeting of the

National Security Council (NSC), which took place 11 February 1953, three weeks into Eisenhower's presidency, Secretary of State John Foster Dulles and General Omar Bradley, Chairman of the Joint Chiefs of Staff, discussed the use of "atomic weapons" in the Kaesong area, where the Chinese were massively reinforcing their troops. The President said that the U.S. should not use such weapons until there had been discussions with allied countries, "and if they objected to the use of atomic weapons we might well ask them to supply three or more divisions needed to drive the Communists back, in lieu of use of atomic weapons."[98] Not everyone agreed that there were "good strategic targets" for nuclear weapons on the Korean peninsula, but as late as 13 May, President Eisenhower thought that they might be useful "in dislodging the Chinese from their present positions in Korea.

> The President…thought it might be cheaper, dollar-wise, to use atomic weapons in Korea than to continue to use conventional weapons against the dugouts which honeycombed the hills along which the enemy forces were presently deployed.[99]

Eisenhower also thought that to break the stalemate, it might prove necessary to expand the war beyond Korea and to use nuclear weapons in the expanded battle zone. "His one great anxiety, said the President, was that if the U.S. used them against China, the USSR might drop some on Japan."[100] The NSC minutes of 20 May 1953, the 145th meeting, indicate that the Allies would not favour the expansion of the war or the use of nuclear weapons, but Eisenhower responded that the time had come "to infiltrate these ideas into the minds of our Allies." Assistant-Secretary of State Walter Bedell Smith told the NSC that he had already held a special meeting with "the British and Dominion Ambassadors" and told them that the current stalemate was intolerable.

Secretary of State John Foster Dulles in particular was inclined to demand the Nampo-Pyongyang-Wonsan line as the boundary and to use nuclear weapons to achieve his ends. In brief, key members of the NSC saw merit to the use of nuclear weapons, but within the NSC itself the counter-arguments were considerations. Among those considerations was opposition from America's allies.

Some historians certainly believe that the thought of a rupture with other nations of the United Nations Command was a deterrent. Edward Keefer says that in meetings of 28 April and 6 May 1953, Assistant-Secretary of State Walter Bedell Smith warned Eisenhower that if the United States carried the war to China, other nations of the United Nations Command would probably withdraw their forces in protest.[101] Dingman says that Dulles softened his positions on nuclear weapons and the Pyongyang-Wonsan line "in deference to the trepidation of the allies, especially the British."[102] Differences of opinion within the Pentagon also assisted the allies' promotion of restraint, says Dingman.[103] Given her access to British sources, it is hardly surprising that Foot emphasizes the relevance of the allies. On 30 March 1953—weeks after Stalin's death—Zhou Enlai offered a concession on the POW issue. Exchange those who wished to be exchanged, he said, and hand the others "to a neutral state so as to ensure a just solution to the question of their repatriation." Along with General Mark Clark, who on 12 May 1952 had succeded Ridgway as head of the United Nations Command, the British, Canadian, Australian, and Indian governments regarded Zhou's statement as an important concession.[104] On 20 May 1953 the National Security Council noted the "disinclination" of the allies to expand the war or use nuclear weapons. Walter Bedell Smith, substituting for Dulles who had gone abroad, advised the staff at the British embassy that theirs was not the only opinion which the U.S. government had to heed. Syngman Rhee had a powerful lobby in Washington. Foot notes that Eisenhower had serious problems with his European and Canadian allies. By May 1953, Pearson wanted greater appreciation of what he had considered a major concession on the part of the Beijing and Pyongyang governments, a willingness to allow dissident POWs to remain in South Korea, not to be forced to relocate elsewhere. (If they stayed in South Korea, they might join the South Korean army and become a threat to North Korea.) The British government agreed with Pearson, and on the floor of the House of Commons, Prime Minister Churchill criticized the unwillingness of the Eisenhower administration to accept Zhou's proposals with greater enthusiasm or to engage in high level talks with the new Malenkov administration. Both Opposition Leader Clement Attlee and the Paris newspaper, *Le Monde*, thought that Senator Joseph McCarthy was intimidating the Eisenhower administration. The Dutch government also expressed an opinion. It agreed that POWs should not be forcibly repatriated, but it thought that there were more grounds for manoeuvre than the White House was admitting. Ward P. Allen of the European desk at the State Department noted criticism from Australia, Belgium, Canada, Italy, the Netherlands, New Zealand, and the United Kingdom. Robert Murphy, the U.S. ambassador in Japan (with which the United States had concluded a peace treaty in 1951), agreed.[105]

More recently, three American writers expressed similar opinions. Writing in 1989, Phil Williams, Donald M. Goldstein, and Henry L. Andrews Jr. wrote:

> The allies and neutrals were...running out of patience [with the slow progress of the Panmunjom talks]. Among the members of the UNC coalitions,

Britain had become one of the staunchest supporters of U.S. anti-Communist policies and, with occasional reservations, America's Korean War strategy. But even the British were not enthusiastic about the expansions of the war advocated by Dulles in the spring of 1953. By May, they began to withdraw their prior endorsement of the "Greater Sanctions Statement," which threatened China with military attacks by the allies if an armistice was concluded, then broken. Dulles acknowledged allied disaffection when he concluded that the war "caused friction within NATO"...[106]

Even the Holland government of New Zealand had its doubts about Eisenhower's hard line, although it muted its criticism. On 3 February 1953, when he first addressed the issue publicly, Holland expressed agreement with British Foreign Secretary Eden, who had warned that escalation of the conflict could result in "very unfortunate political repercussions without compensating military advantages."[107] From the Opposition side of the House, Walter Nash—a former Labour cabinet minister and future Prime Minister of New Zealand (1957-1960)—complained of the Eisenhower administration's failure to consult its allies on so significant a matter—although Nash said that on the whole he supported U.S. policies regarding Korea.[108]

Quite apart from Commonwealth considerations, Eisenhower had reasons of his own for seeking a truce. A CIA report of 8 April 1953 (declassified in 1994) warned that the military stalemate might continue for some time. There was no easy end in sight.[109] On 24 April, the CIA produced another study, arguably the most optimistic to date. In the aftermath of Stalin's death, said Special Estimate 42 (declassified in 1993),

There have...been developments...which may prove to be of profound significance for Soviet foreign policy...In Korea, we estimate that the Communists are now prepared to make some concessions in order to reach an armistice.[110]

Quite apart from whatever the Communist leaders thought, Eisenhower and his cabinet were receiving advice that the struggle could last a long time, but that the opportunities for ending it were better than they had been.

Nevertheless, it was logically impossible to satisfy South Korean President Syngman Rhee and the United States Congress on one side, and the Old Commonwealth and European allies on the other. Eisenhower indeed faced a formidable challenge in finding an acceptable armistice agreement. It is hard to disagree with Stephen Ambrose's comment:

Just as [General Charles] de Gaulle almost nine years later was the only
Frenchman whose prestige was enough to allow him to end the war in Al-
geria without himself being overthrown, so too was Eisenhower the only
American who could have found and made stick what Eisenhower called
"an acceptable solution to a problem that almost defied...solution."[111]

Another writer who thinks that British, if not Commonwealth, diplomacy proved helpful was Farrar-Hockley. He credits Eden with taking action on the matter of captured
diplomats and missionaries as well as of sick and wounded POWs. Eden spoke in February 1953 to Paul Ruegger, President of the International Committee of the Red Cross,
and the exchanges materialized 9 and 20 April.[112] Stalin's death on 5 March was a critical factor, without which Eden's initiative would almost certainly have been stillborn.

VII The Proposal (continued)

If a consensus was developing that the North Korean and Chinese POWs should not
face forcible repatriation, there was still scope for argument about their fate. Where
would they live? (Pearson appreciated the North Korean/Chinese concession of May
1953 that they need not move to a neutral country so that they could not join the
armed forces of South Korea or Nationalist China.[113]) What would they do? How
soon would they begin their new lives? Who would have the credibility to satisfy all
concerned parties that the dissident POWs really were selecting the option which
they wanted? By May 1953, U.S. and Commonwealth authorities were discussing
these points in earnest.

The United States government, which had responsibility for co-ordinating the
coalition which was the United Nations Command, favoured a speedy release with a
minimum of red tape. South Korean President Syngman Rhee opposed any armistice
which left Kim Il Sung's government in charge of North Korea, and he had sufficient
forces at his disposal to create problems. If South Korean soldiers ignored the
cease-fire, other nations of the United Nations Command would have little choice
but to continue the fight or abandon their efforts of the previous three years. Nor
would South Koreans willingly transfer control of the unwilling North Korean
POWs to Polish and Czechoslovakian soldiers of the Neutral Nations Supervisory
Commission. Those North Koreans might themselves resort to violence, and the
South Korean soldiers certainly would not shove them into the jurisdiction of the
Poles and Czechoslovakians.

When the Panmunjom talks resumed 26 April 1953, the North Koreans and the
Chinese demanded that the dissident POWs could not remain in South Korea,

where conceivably they might join the South Korean Army. They must go to a neutral country, and Switzerland did not qualify as a possible host. There they would remain until all concerned parties could decide their fate. General Harrison, still the chief negotiator for the United States, said that there was no reason to remove them from Korea and he thought that the POWs should have their freedom after a maximum of sixty days. Indefinite confinement was simply unfair and intolerable.[114] Nam Il broke the impasse 7 May. The non-repatriates could stay in South Korea after all, he proposed, and a Neutral Nations Repatriation Committee (NNRP) consisting of five countries (Czechoslovakia, India, Poland, Sweden, and Switzerland) would look after them. Again, however, they would remain in confinement until and unless an international conference could agree on their fate. The United Nations Command thought that the NNRP might be too large to be practical and that the prospect of indefinite confinement was intolerable.[115]

The State Department and General Clark were willing to share information on the Panmunjom talks with Sir Percy Spender in Washington. They were convinced that they had nothing to hide, no sinister motives, and they wanted to retain Australian support. They did not want publicity for every last detail of every last bargaining position, but if Spender would promise to "keep quiet about it"—and he promised that he would—they would include him within the loop. Spender had questioned a U.S. "proposal to release North Koreans immediately after [the] armistice," and U.S. officials sought to explain their position to him.[116]

That Australian officials should have access to information which other allies could not have appears to indicate an American partiality for the Old Commonwealth allies above all, or at least most of, the others. On 19 May 1953, Sir Roger Makins—who had replaced Franks as British Ambassador in Washington—informed his government about a meeting at the State Department. General Walter Bedell Smith, the Under-Secretary of State, had phoned the embassy and issued an invitation for a meeting that same day. He explained that he "wanted to consult the major allies in Korea in regard to the next move in Panmunjom." When Makins arrived at the State Department, the only other invited guests were diplomats from the Australian, Canadian, New Zealand, and South African embassies. Assuring the assembled company that their opinions *did* matter, General Bedell Smith

> went on to emphasize the necessity for the Allies to stand together at this
> point, either to achieve an armistice...or to fail honourably with an agreed
> and unanimous point of view...[117]

Bedell Smith confided to his listeners that he could not ignore Congressional critics. "Congressional leaders" felt very strongly that no North Korean or Chinese who had objected to repatriation should return to North Korea or the People's Republic of China without a unanimous decision by the Neutral Nations Repatriation Commission (NNRC). A simple majority would allow the Poles, Czechoslovakians, and Indians to determine the fate of these people.[118]

This explanation did not entirely satisfy Canada's Minister of External Affairs, Lester B. Pearson. The Indian resolution adopted by the United Nations General Assembly 3 December 1952[119] when the Truman administration still governed the United States had not required unanimity. The Eisenhower administration was creating a new obstacle. While Canadian authorities were grateful that General Bedell Smith was consulting them, they did not want the United Nations Command to insist on unanimity among NNRC members. Nor would Canada want to insist on a requirement that at least four NNRC members would have to support a decision. One solution, thought Pearson, would be to settle for a simple majority on the NNRC, with an "outstanding" Indian who had the confidence of both sides in a position to cast the deciding vote.[120]

The Menzies government took a stance somewhere between those of Washington and Ottawa. It regretted that

> many nations do not agree that even for bargaining purposes [the] United States might seek [a] more favourable settlement than [the] Indian resolution. Communists are aware of this and consequently have more confidence in rejecting any American proposals which deviate from that resolution.[121]

One compromise, thought Australia's Department of External Affairs, might be to insist on a majority of four rather than unanimity at the NNRC. That way, India could not join forces with the Czechoslovakians and Poles to impose a decision. However, that compromise would have its problems. Quite apart from the probability that the North Koreans and Chinese would reject it, it would give the Czechoslovakians and Poles an effective veto over NNRC decisions. Canberra instructed the Australian Embassy in Washington:

> You might explore with [the] Americans possibilities of finding a formula for a majority of 4 on all matters of substance (including decisions to repatriate individuals) and a simple majority on questions of procedure (including questions of administration and certain questions relating to maintenance of discipline in camps)...[122]

From Wellington, New Zealand's Minister of External Affairs, Sir Clifton Webb, told his High Commissioner in London that New Zealand still supported the Indian resolution which the United Nations General Assembly had adopted in December. New Zealand would not create problems for the United States, but the closer the Eisenhower administration would stay with the original bargaining position of the United Nations, the sooner a cease-fire was likely to happen. Webb agreed that the Czechoslovakian and Polish NNRC members

> should not interview the prisoners individually and in the absence of representatives from both sides, and we support the United States on this position.

Webb added an additional suggestion. Dubious cases could become the responsibility of the United Nations General Assembly. The General Assembly, which had adopted the Indian resolution, was representative of the United Nations membership, and the General Assembly was trustworthy. "The prisoners should not be left in complete doubt as to their ultimate fate," said Webb.[123]

South Africa was a special case. Its leaders demonstrated little interest in the Korean War, and U.S. officials returned the favour. Officials at the British Embassy in Washington agreed that most officials at the South African Embassy were mediocrities. The South Africans had fewer combat forces in Korea than did the Turks. Nor could any South African government reasonably grant the same priority to Korea as could the United Kingdom (a world power), Canada, or Australia (both of which had extensive coastlines on the Pacific Ocean). One officer at the British Embassy reported to the Commonwealth Relations Office that despite, this situation, the State Department treated the South African Embassy much as it treated the French. The briefings were neither as thorough nor as prompt as those for the other Old Commonwealth governments, but they were more thorough than those for most embassies of countries serving under the United Nations Command. To treat everyone equally, explained R.H. Belcher at the British Embassy to Bishop at the Commonwealth Relations Office, would "complicate matters." To treat South Africa as an ally of primary importance would create "embarrassments [sic] vis-a-vis those countries who are not brought in."[124]

Four days after Bedell Smith's meeting with the Commonwealth representatives, he summoned Sir Roger Makins to the State Department. The United Kingdom and Canada, said the Under-Secretary of State, had given the strongest responses, but as Canadian Ambassador Hume Wrong had left for Ottawa, he was meeting Makins by himself. President Eisenhower, said Bedell Smith, agreed that

Syngman Rhee should not have veto power over any armistice agreement, but as South Korean forces were the most numerous of those in the United Nations Command, the White House could hardly ignore his desires. That very morning, the President had met Congressional leaders at the White House where, after "a long and difficult meeting," they had agreed on the terms to be presented at Panmunjom. One feature of that accord was that a simple majority of the NNRC would be sufficient after all. The process for North Korean POWs would be identical to that for Chinese ones. After 90 days, POWs remaining in the custody of the NNRC would be released unless the North Koreans and Chinese wanted to refer the matter to the General Assembly. The United Kingdom and Canada, not to mention the Indian resolution of December 1952 at the United Nations, had carried the day!

In return for this concession, the White House had agreed with the Congressional leaders:

> [In the event the Panmunjom talks fail] the United States is resolved...to break off negotiations, to cease to recognize the demilitarized zone, to bomb Kaesong, to step up military and air operations, and to release the Chinese and Korean prisoners who do not wish to be repatriated.[125]

Significantly, there was no mention of nuclear weapons. To guarantee that the Chinese knew the consequences of rejecting the latest offer, U.S. officials warned them, via India, that non-acceptance would end the talks permanently.

Bedell Smith then appealed to Makins for British and Canadian support. Eisenhower, he said, "after great travail with the Congressional representatives...had been able to concede all the points of principle to which you attach importance. The administration had gone to [the] limit..." Makins agreed with this assessment and urged Churchill's government to support the White House this arrangement.[126] The British and Canadian governments did so,[127] and New Zealand Prime Minister Holland—in Washington en route to the Coronation of Queen Elizabeth II in London 2 June 1953—indicated that any proposal acceptable to both Washington and London would be acceptable to him.[128] Neither the Canadians nor the Australians liked the idea that North Korean/Chinese rejection would lead to the termination, rather than the suspension, of the Panmunjom talks, but as there was to such rejection, those considerations remained hypothetical.[129]

VIII The Prisoner-Of-War Issue (continued)

The next bone of contention concerned Syngman Rhee. The evening of 17-18 June 1953, at the very moment when the Panmunjom talks appeared on the brink of success, Rhee ordered the immediate and unconditional release of 25,131 North Korean POWs who did not want to return home. All but 971 (subsequently recaptured) quickly blended into the South Korean population.[130] Rhee's action delayed but did not prevent the armistice, largely because the Chinese and the North Koreans still wanted one and had already resigned themselves to the loss of those people. However, between 18 June and 27 July (the date of the signing of the Armistice Agreement), it was not always clear that Rhee had not totally sabotaged the Panmunjom talks. Aware that other U.S. allies might think that the U.S. had conspired with Rhee, President Eisenhower took steps publicly to distance the position of the U.S. government from that of South Korea.[131]

Not surprisingly, leaders of the Old Commonwealth countries had strong feelings on this matter. Their combat forces would continue to face the possibility of serious injury or imminent death. The Foreign Office, where the Marquis of Salisbury (the Secretary of State for Commonwealth Relations) remained the Acting Foreign Secretary, and Pearson in Ottawa saw no point in a special session of the General Assembly. A demand for one, they thought, would be a vote of non-confidence in Eisenhower's leadership, and the Soviets would certainly exploit the situation. "The United States must be given time to try to influence Rhee," they believed. Pearson privately suggested that in the event that talks between Rhee and U.S. officials failed, the U.S. could recommend that the General Assembly reconvene.[132] There were subsequent Anglo-Canadian discussions about a possible meeting of the General Assembly if the Panmunjom talks were to collapse or if there were an Armistice Agreement which Rhee refused to respect. Pearson also warned—publicly—that Canada had "no obligation to support or participate in any operation brought on by the Government of the Republic of South Korea [sic] which might prejudice an armistice agreement..."[133] Casey of Australia sent Rhee an angry letter of protest.[134] (In his capacity as President of the United Nations General Assembly, not in any Commonwealth role, Pearson also sent Rhee a letter of reprimand.[135]) However, as none of these scenarios materialized, any possible disagreement with Secretary of State Dulles or other members of the Eisenhower administration remained in the realm of the hypothetical.[136] The Commonwealth Prime Ministers, including those of India, Pakistan, and Ceylon, discussed Korea when they met in London 3 and 4 June after the Queen's Coronation on 2 June, but their discussions had little impact upon subsequent developments.[137]

On 9 June 1953, as the truce talks headed for a final showdown, the Eisenhower administration sought a demonstration of solidarity from its allies, whose support it sought for a warning to the North Koreans and Chinese. The statement said that the countries of the United Nations Command would "fully and faithfully...carry out the terms of the armistice," and threatened:

> The consequences of...a breach of the armistice would be so grave that, in all probability, it would not be possible to confine hostilities within the frontiers of Korea.[138]

Although the sixteen nations of the United Nations Command had agreed in mid-1952 to issue such a declaration within twenty-four hours of any armistice agreement, by mid-1953 the British, Canadian, and New Zealand governments had developed second thoughts. (Australian authorities thought it unwise to change the rules in the middle of the game.) The British Foreign Office asked the State Department for a delay. In the interval, it would consult the other Old Commonwealth governments. On 23 July, four days before the signing of the Armistice Agreement, the statement still had not been issued and the British government had decided unequivocally not to endorse it:

> Her Majesty's Government have [sic] refused to enter into any advance military commitments as to what action might have to be taken outside the frontiers of Korea in this hypothetical emergency.

As far as Churchill's government was concerned, the U.S. declaration had become "unnecessary and undesirable."[139] If the White House insisted, let it proceed without the threat. However, the statement was "bound," said one official at the Foreign Office, "quite needlessly, to antagonize Asian opinion generally."[140] For their part, the French wanted the warning to include French Indo-China (Vietnam, Laos, Cambodia), where they feared Chinese aggression once the Korean War came to an end. This time, the combined will of the United States and France proved more powerful than that of the United Kingdom, Canada, and New Zealand. There would be a threat, as well as an indirect reference to French Indo-China:

> We, the United Nations Members whose military forces are participating in the Korean action, support the decision of the Commander-in-Chief of the United Nations Command to conclude an armistice agreement. We hereby affirm our determination fully and faithfully to carry out the terms of that armistice. We expect that the other parties to the agreement will likewise scrupulously observe its terms...

We affirm, in the interests of world peace, that if there is a renewal of the armed attack, challenging again the principles of the United Nations, we should again be united and prompt to resist. The consequences of such a breach of the armistice would be so grave that, ain all probability, it would not be possible to confine hostilities within the frontiers of Korea.

Finally we are of the opinion that the armistice must not result in jeopardizing the restoration or the safeguarding of peace in any other part of Asia.[141]

As for the dissident POWs, the Panmunjom accord allowed ninety days during which their countries of origin might try to persuade them to change their minds and then 120 additional days of confinement. Few changed their minds, and by 20 January 1954, all were free to leave their camps in the Demilitarized Zone along the inter-Korean border, where they had lived since the Armistice Agreement, and go to South Korea or Taiwan. A grand total of 21 Americans, 1 Briton, and 327 South Koreans also refused repatriation.

IX The Significance of Commonwealth Diplomacy in Ending the Korean War

In brief, the Commonwealth leaders did facilitate the Panmunjom Armistice Agreement. India proposed an ultimately successful resolution at the United Nations, which the Old Commonwealth supported and persuaded successive United States governments to accept. Once Stalin died, the North Koreans and Chinese also accepted the Indian resolution as a basis for negotiations. Commonwealth leaders opposed the use of nuclear weapons in Korea and the expansion of the Korean War beyond the Korean peninsula, but their success is attributable in large measure to the fact that many U.S. authorities agreed with them.

Several factors other than solidarity within the Old Commonwealth made a difference. These included differences of opinion among American decision-makers, the opinions of other countries of the United Nations Command (particularly France), and, above all, the death of Joseph Stalin. Old Commonwealth governments did not always agree with each other, and the Canadians and South Africans did not always exploit their Commonwealth connections as fully as they might have. Arguably the United Nations was a more effective forum than the Old Commonwealth.

Notes

1. Peter Lowe, pp. 77-78.

2. Steven Hugh Lee, p. 162.

3. Letters in File: Churchill, Winston, Chronological [2 of 2: 1949-1953]. PSF: General File, 1945-1953, Box 99, HST.

4. Churchill to Truman, 12 Feb. 1951, ibid.

5. Farrar-Hockley, II, pp. 249-250.

6. Farrar-Hockley, II, pp. 343-344.

7. Farrar-Hockley, II, p. 241.

8. Farrar-Hockley, II, pp. 256-259.

9. Farrar-Hockley, II, p. 238.

10. Steven Hugh Lee, p. 154.

11. Rosemary Foot, A Substitute for Victory: The Politics of Peacemaking and the Korean Armistice Talks (Ithaca: Cornell University Press, 1990).

12. Foot, pp. ix-86, especially pp. xi, 5-7, 66.

13. Bruce Cumings, Korea's Place in the Sun: A Modern History (New York: W.W. Norton, 1997), pp. 40-41, 45; Andrew C. Nahm, Introduction to Korean History and Culture (Seoul: Hollym, 1993), pp. 43, 67-68, 97-99.

14. M.L. Dockrill, "The Foreign Office, Anglo-American Relations and the Korean Truce Negotiations, July 1951-July 1953," in Cotton and Neary, p. 101.

15. Foot, pp. 42-73.

16. Ron Robin, "Behavioral Codes and Truce Talks: Images of the Enemy and Expert Knowledge in the Korean Armistice Negotiations," Diplomatic History, XXV, 4 (Fall 2001), pp. 626-627.

17. Foot, p. ix.

18. Robin, p. 625.

19. Pierre Berton, Marching as to War: Canada's Turbulent Years, 1899-1953 (Toronto: Doubleday Canada, 2001), p. 562.

20. Berton, p. 549.

21. Anthony Eden, Full Circle: The Memoirs of Sir Anthony Eden (London: Cassell and Company, 1960), p. 16.

22. Eden, p. 28.

23. Peter Lowe, pp. 86-87.

24. Stairs, p. 139.

25. See the volumes in the DO 35 series at the PRO.

26. Pearson, Ottawa, to Wrong, Washington, 10 July 1953, DCER, 1953, pp. 120-121 (that letter includes correspondence between Nehru and Pearson); Pearson to Wrong, 14 July 1953, DCER, 1953, pp. 124-125; David M. Johnson (Canada's Permanent Representative to the United Nations) to Pearson, Ottawa, 25 July 1953 (two letters of the same date), DCER, 1953, pp. 134-136.

27. The relevant correspondence appears in *Documents on Canadian External Relations*, 1953, pp. 39-45.

28. Wilgress, Ottawa, to Pearson, Ottawa, 30 April 1953, *DCER*, 1953, pp. 50-51.

29. Robin, p. 646.

30. Dockrill, p. 110.

31. McGibbon, I, p. 272.

32. Eden, p. 15.

33. Caroline Moorehead, *Dunant's Dream: War, Switzerland and the History of the Red Cross* (New York: Carroll and Graf, 1998), pp. 569-579.

34. Dockrill, pp. 105-106.

35. Foot, p. 102.

36. Foot, pp. 93, 100, 133-134, 153, 168, 172, 209.

37. Foot, p. 100.

38. Extract from *Australian Newsletter*, No. 274, 15.5.52, included in DO 35/5813, PRO.

39. Australian External Affairs, Canberra, to Australian High Commission, UK, 16 June 1951, DO 35/5813, PRO.

40. The Australian proposal appears in DO 35/5813, PRO. The quotation comes from a letter from the Department of External Affairs, Canberra, to Crotonate [Menzies], Washington, 4 June 1952, a copy of which appears in DO 35/5813, PRO.

41. Department of External Affairs, Canberra, to Crotonate [Menzies], Australian Embassy, Washington, 4 June 1952, DO 35/5813, PRO.

42. "Memorandum—Korean Armistice Negotiations," attached to letter of Lloyd to Bishop, 22 June 1952, DO 35/5813, PRO.

43. Franks, Washington, to Foreign Office, London, 19 May 1952, DO 35/5824, PRO.

44. C.H. Johnson, Foreign Office, London, to Major-General W.H.A. (Alex) Bishop, Commonwealth Relations Office, 20 June 1952, DO 35/5813, PRO.

45. External Affairs, Wellington, to N.Z. High Commissioner [Corner], London, 6 June 1952, a copy of which Corner gave Bishop at the CRO and which is available in DO 35/5814, PRO.

46. Hamilton, South African High Commission, London, to Bishop, CRO, 11 June 1952, DO 35/5815, PRO.

47. Franks, Washington, to FO, London, 4 Sept. 1952; FO, London, to Franks, Washington, 5 Sept. 1952; DO 35/5828, PRO.

48. Franks, Washington, to Foreign Office, London, 16 Aug. 1952, DO 35/5828, PRO.

49. *Ibid.*

50. C.H. Johnson, London, to Franks, Washington, 5 Sept. 1952, DO 35/5828, PRO.

51. Johnson, London, to Franks, Washington, 5 Sept. 1952, DO 35/5828, PRO.

52. Franks, Washington, to Foreign Office, London, 20 Aug. 1952.

53. C.H. Johnston, Foreign Office, London, to Franks, Washington, 19 Aug. 1952; Commonwealth Relations Office to UK High Commissioners in Ottawa, Canberra, Wellington, and Pretoria, 22 Aug. 1952; DO 35/5828, PRO.

54. Franks, Washington, to Foreign Office, London, 22 Aug. 1952, DO 35/5828, PRO.

55. UK High Commissioner in Canada, Ottawa, to CRO, London, 9 Sept. 1952, DO 35/5828, PRO.

56. Brief for the British Secretary of State for Mr. Pearson's Visit, n.d., DO 35/5829, PRO.

57. Ibid.

58. Brief for the Minister of State for Mr. Pearson's visit, n.d., DO 35/5829, PRO.

59. A. Hamilton, South Africa House, London, to N. Pritchard, Commonwealth Relations Office, London, 28 Aug. 1952, DO 35/5828, PRO.

60. UK High Commissioner in South Africa to CRO, 29 Aug. 1952, DO 35/5828, PRO.

61. United Kingdom High Commissioner in New Zealand, Wellington, to CRO, London, 5 Sept. 1952; DO 35/5828, PRO.

62. British Embassy, Washington, to FO, London, 23 Sept. 1952, DO 35/5829, PRO.

63. A copy of this Resolution is available in DO 35/5829, PRO,

64. This is certainly Foot's opinion; p. 153.

65. Jebb, United Nations, to FO, London, 28 Sept. 1952, DO 35/5829, PRO.

66. Memo by Johnston, 27 Sept. 1950, DO 35/5829, PRO.

67. Bishop, CRO, London, to British High Commissioners in Ottawa, Canberra, Wellington, Pretoria, New Delhi, Karachi, and Colombo, 18 Sept. 1852, CO 35/5829, PRO.

68. FO, London, to British Embassy, Vienna, 22 Sept. 1952, DO 35/5829, PRO. See also FRUS, 1952-1954, various items, pp. 485-489.

69. Memorandum from Pearson to the Cabinet, Ottawa, 6 Oct. 1952, DCER, 1952, p. 169.

70. United Nations Yearbook, 1952, p. 195 (re A/C 1/730).

71. Expressed by Casey in the House of Representatives, 16 Sept. 1952; statement included in DO/35, 5829, PRO. Also expressed by New Zealand government; British High Commissioner in New Zealand, Wellington, 26 Sept. 1952, DO 35/5829, PRO.

72. British High Commissioner in South Africa to CRO, London, 18 Sept. 1952, DO 35/5829, PRO.

73. Noted in correspondence of C.H. Johnston, FO, London, to UK Embassy, Washington, 27 Sept. 1952.

74. Acheson, Present at the Creation, p. 696.

75. Acheson, Present at the Creation, p. 700. For further information on consultations among U.S. authorities, Indian diplomats, and representatives of the Commonwealth belligerents on the Indian plan regarding POWs, see File: Consideration of an Armistice Question in the UN, 1952 [2 of 2], in SMOF: Selected Records Relating to the Korean War, Department of State: Topical File Subseries, Box 12, HST.

76. Memorandum by the Secretary of State for Foreign Affairs, C.H. Johnston, 4 Dec. 1952, DO 35/5833.

77. Stueck, pp. 298-302.

78. Peter Lowe, pp. 83-85.

79. Dockrill, p. 111.

80. Bowles, New Delhi, to Acheson, Washington, 21 Nov. 1952; File: Consideration of an armistice question in the UN, 1952 [2 of 2, Nov-Dec. 1952], SMOF: Selected Records Relating to the Korean War: Department of State, Topical File Subseries, Box 12, HST.

81. Stueck, p. 232.

82. McGibbon, I, pp. 279-280.

83. McGibbon, I, p. 281.

84. A copy of the draft Indian Resolution (updated to 29 Aug. 1952) appears in the *United Nations Yearbook*, 1952, pp. 166-174.

85. After his return to Australia, Plimsoll discussed his Korean experiences with Ben Cockram, Deputy British High Commissioner in Australia. Cockram forwarded a summary of the conversation to Bishop, London, 8 Jan. 1953, a copy of which appears in DO 35/5821, PRO. See also Stephen E. Ambrose, *Eisenhower: The President* (New York: Simon and Schuster, 1984), pp. 30-31.

86. Xiaoming Zhang, "From an abortive air war to the China-Soviet Wartime Relationship" and the subsequent discussion period, meeting of the Society for the History of American Foreign Relations, Ryerson University, Toronto, 22 June 2000.

87. Vladislav Zubok and Constantine Pleshakov, *Inside the Kremlin's Cold War: From Stalin to Khrushchev* (Cambridge, Mass.: Harvard University Press, 1996), p. 71.

88. Zubok and Pleshakov, p. 155.

89. Wolff, p. 9, and related documents, pp. 41-45.

90. Stueck, p. 305.

91. Dimitri Volkogonov, *Stalin: Triumph and Tragedy* (edited by Harold Shukman, New York: Grove Weidenfeld, 1988).

92. Cited in Stueck, p. 307.

93. Stueck, pp. 326-330.

94. *CWIHP* Bulletin, Issue 12/13 (Fall/Winter 2001), p. 226.

95. Foot, pp. 159-189. See also Foot's article, "Nuclear Coercion and the Ending of the Korean Conflict," *International Security*, XIII, 3 (Winter 1988/89), pp. 92-112. Foot herself disagrees that nuclear weapons frightened the Chinese and North Koreans into making concessions, but she does outline the arguments, especially on pp. 176-183. Edward C. Keefer believes that the nuclear threat was a major reason for a willingness to compromise on the part of the North Koreans and Chinese, but he also notes Stalin's death; Edward C. Keefer, "President Dwight D. Eisenhower and the End of the Korean War," *Diplomatic History* X, 3 (Summer, 1986), pp. 267-289. Both Foot and Keefer note that Eisenhower and Dulles were to emphasize the importance of the nuclear threat. Roger Dingman thinks that contemporaries and historians have ex-

aggerated the nuclear threat; Roger Dingman, "Atomic Diplomacy During the Korean War," *International Security*, XIII, 3 (Winter 1988/89) (pp. 79-91). Writing in 1988, before Chinese documents became available, Daniel Callingaert said that he could not be certain whether the nuclear threat cowed the Chinese, but he thought that it probably did; Daniel Callingaert, "Nuclear Weapons and the Korean War," *Journal of Strategic Studies*, XI (June 1988), pp. 195-196.

96. Zubok and Pleshakov, p. 155.

97. Ambrose, pp. 51-52, 97-106.

98. Minutes of the 131st Meeting of the National Security Council (NSC), 11 Feb. 1953, Dwight David Eisenhower Papers as President, 1953-1961, Anne Whitman File, NSC Series, Box 4, DDE.

99. Minutes of the 144th Meeting of the NSC, ibid.

100. Minutes of the 145th meeting, 20 May 1953, ibid.

101. Keefer, p. 277.

102. Dingman, p. 83; Stueck too thinks that Allied opinion mattered; pp. 311, 321-322.

103. Dingman, p. 84.

104. Foot, *A Substitute*, p. 168. The quotation is a translation of Zhou's own words, cited by Foot.

105. Foot, A Substitute, pp. 164,171-172, 174.

106. Phil Williams, Donald M. Goldstein, and Henry L. Andrews Jr., *Society In Korea: War, Stalemate, and Negotiation* (Boulder: Westview Press, 1994), pp. 113-114. The quotation "caused friction within NATO" comes from Edward C. Keefer, "President Dwight D. Eisenhower and the End of the Korean War," *Diplomatic History*, X (Summer 1986), p. 270.

107. McGibbon, I, p. 322.

108. McGibbon, I, p. 323.

109. Special Estimate 41, "Probable Communist Reactions to Certain Possible UN/US Military Courses of Action with Regard to the Korean War," 8 April 1953, R.G. 263, Box 1, File 40, NARA.

110. Special Estimate 42, "Current Communist Tactics," 24 April 1953, R.G. 263, Box 1, File 43, NARA.

111. Ambrose, p. 106; Stanley Weintraub agrees that Eisenhower's prestige allowed him to accept terms which the Truman administration could not (pp. 355, 358).

112. Farrar-Hockley, II, pp. 388-389.

113. Pearson, Ottawa, to Wrong, Washington, 12 May 1953, *DCER*, 1953, p. 76.

114. O'Neill, p. 341.

115. O'Neill, pp. 341-342, 349-350.

116. Australian Ambassador, Washington, to Crotonate [Menzies], Canberra, 14 May 1953, DO 35/5836, PRO. Also (regarding Rhee's threats to continue the fight in defiance of any cease-fire), Makins, Washington, to Foreign Office, London, 19 May 1953, DO 35/5836, PRO.

117. Makins, Washington, to Foreign Office, London, 19 May 1953, DO 35/5836, PRO.

118. Second letter of Makins, Washington, to Foreign Office, London, 19 May 1953, DO 35/5836, PRO.

119. *United Nations Yearbook*, 1952, pp. 200-202. A copy appears in the Appendix.

120. Explained by the UK High Commissioner to Canada to the Commonwealth Relations Office, London, 21 May 1953, DO35/5836, PRO. See also Wrong, Washington, to Pearson, Ottawa, 12 May 1953, *DCER*, 1953, p. 78; Pearson to Wrong, 12 May 1928, *DCER*, 1953, pp. 78-79; Wrong to Pearson, 19 May 1953, *DCER*, 1953, pp. 87-88; Acting Secretary of State for External Affairs (Paul Martin), Ottawa, to Charge d'Affairs in the United States, 21 May 1953, *DCER*, 1953, pp. 89-90.

121. Department of External Affairs, Canberra, to Australian Embassy, Washington, 21 May 1953, DO 35/5836, PRO. Also, see O'Neill, p. 353.

122. *Ibid.*

123. Webb, Wellington, to Munro, New Zealand High Commissioner, London, 21 May 1953, DO 35/5836, PRO.

124. R.H. Belcher, Washington, to Bishop, CRO, 19 May 1953, DO 35/5836, PRO.

125. O'Neill, p. 351.

126. Makins, Washington, to Foreign Office, London, 23 May 1953, DO 35/5836, PRO.

127. CRO to UK High Commissioners in India, Canada, Australia, New Zealand, South Africa (repeated to Pakistan and Ceylon), 24 May 1953; UK High Commissioner in Canada to CRO, London, 24 May 1953, DO 35/5836, PRO. See also Wrong, Washington, to Pearson, Ottawa, 23 May 1953, *DCER*, 1953, pp. 95-96, and 30 May 1953, p. 102-104.

128. Belcher, Washington, to N. Pritchard, CRO, London, 21 May 1953, DO 35/5836, PRO.

129. Acting Secretary of State for External Affairs (Paul Martin), Ottawa, to Wrong, Washington, *DCER*, 1953, p. 98; O'Neill, p. 355.

130. Foot, *A Substitute*, p. 184.

131. 150th Meeting of the NSC, 18 June 1953, Dwight David Eisenhower Papers as President, Anne Whitman File, NSC Series, Box 4, DDE.

132. Foreign Office, London, to UK Embassy, Washington, 7 July 1953, DO 35/5840.

133. Pearson, Ottawa, to Wrong, Washington, 19 June 1953, *DCER*, 1953, p. 112. See also Pearson, *Mike*, II, p. 188.

134. O'Neill, p. 359.

135. Pearson, *Mike*, II, pp. 189-190.

136. Hume Wrong, Washington, to the High Commissioner for Canada, London, 8 July 1953; Jebb, United Nations, to Foreign Office, London, 10 July 1953, DO 35/5840, PRO.

137. O'Neill, pp. 342-344.

138. Sir Roger Makins, Embassy of the United Kingdom, Washington, to Foreign Office, 9 June 1953.

139. Brief for Lord Salisbury (Acting Foreign Secretary) for the Cabinet, 23 July 1953, DO 35/5825-5826, PRO. See also O'Neill, pp. 363-367.

140. Korea Joint Policy Statement. Letter by N. Pritchard, 23 July 1953, DO 35/5825/5826, PRO.

141. O'Neill, p. 367.

Korean Peninsula

Chapter Five

Post-War Problems and the Commonwealth's Response

I The Neutral Nations Supervisory Commission

The Korean Armistice Agreement signed 27 July 1953 established a Neutral Nations Supervisory Commission (NNSC) to assist with implementation of the accord. India participated as chair of the Neutral Nations Repatriation Commission (NNRC). Soldiers from two Communist countries, Poland and Czechoslovakia, served on the NNSC and NNRC, as did soldiers from two Western European nations, Sweden and Switzerland.

The POW issue, which had delayed the cease-fire, proved to be an ongoing source of controversy, indeed one which arguably jeopardized the cease-fire. While the Panmunjom Armistice Agreement allowed POWs to refuse repatriation, there was still room for argument about who actually wanted to refuse repatriation. For the United Nations Command, this was not a problem. Most of its soldiers wanted to return home, and if they did not, they had the democratic right to live somewhere else. The North Koreans and the Chinese had reluctantly agreed to the principle of voluntary repatriation, but they did not readily accept that tens of thousands of their soldiers had chosen to stay with the enemy. Under the circumstances, they wanted to verify the POWs' choice. Did they really intend to live in South Korea or on Taiwan? The Armistice Agreement permitted an interview or explanation, and the North Koreans and Chinese insisted on their rights. Many of the POWs thought that they had a right not to listen, and South Korean President Syngman Rhee agreed with them. Indian insistence that the North Korean and Chinese POWs who did not want to return home must listen to "explanations" from soldiers from their homeland as to why they should return became highly provocative.

The ensuing dispute actually endangered the safety of the Indian soldiers with the NNRC. Indian authorities wondered whether South Korean forces might question their neutrality and attack them. (The Indians had actually killed and wounded some of the POWs in their care whom they had found threatening.[1]) They also had doubts whether U.S. soldiers near the DMZ would protect them from the South Koreans. On a few occasions, Menon appealed to Commonwealth governments for support.[2]

At the request of U.S. and Indian authorities, Anthony Eden (not Commonwealth foreign ministers as a body) was willing to discuss "specific instances of alleged 'unneutral' behaviour on the part of the NNRC" with Indian authorities. In other words, Eden would serve as an intermediary between the complaining Americans and the Indians.[3] Moreover, at Nehru's request, St. Laurent agreed to speak on the Indians' behalf to U.S. authorities in Washington.[4] Australian officials saw fault on all sides. A despatch of 10 October 1953 complained that the U.S. was not consulting its allies of the UNC.[5] This comment arose specifically because of a letter which General Mark Clark, head of the UNC, had written to the Repatriation Commission. On 11 October, the head of the Australian delegation to UNCURK, Thomas Kingston Critchley, wired Canberra from Pusan:

> I believe the [Indian] Chairman of the Repatriation Commission may have been unduly influenced by the Czech and Polish members. The Indians have certainly given the impression of wanting to avoid offending the Communists.
>
> 2. Rhee has taken advantage of recent incidents to keep feeling high amongst the Koreans. In addition to editorials and public statements, slogans have appeared in Seoul reading: "Release non-repatriable prisoners," "Drive the Indian soldiers out of Korea" and "United Nations should punish barbarian Indian troops." Mass demonstrations have also started. A spokesman for the Indian Command has declared that it would be difficult for the Indian troops to stop a mass desertion of prisoners and that such a desertion was a possibility.[6]

More than the safety of the Indians was at stake, he thought. The entire armistice was in jeopardy.[7]

Nevertheless, the Old Commonwealth governments did not consult closely even on this issue. On 12 October, Australia's High Commissioner in New Delhi reported that his Canadian counterpart, Escott Reid, had "been a visitor to [India's Department of] External Affairs several times in the last two days. The nature of these Indo-Canadian exchanges is not known, but it is known that Nehru has exchanged personal messages with St. Laurent."[8] On 12 October, the Australian Department of External Affairs sent a summary of Critchley's message to the Australian High Commissioner in New Delhi, with copies to Australian High Commissioners in London and Wellington (but not Ottawa or Pretoria), as well as to Australian Ambassadors in Washington and Tokyo. The letter rejected a suggestion from Spender, still the Australian Ambassador in Washington, "that we [Australians] have friendly and exploratory discussions with India in New Delhi, expressing our...sympathy and support but suggesting wisdom of trying to avoid giving any ground to Rhee which he may use to...[subvert] the truce or...create a crisis." Canberra noted that "U.K. and Canada are already in touch with India, and we feel that a formal approach by Canberra should not be made." Yet, informally, Australia's High Commissioner in New Delhi might "happen" to discuss the NNRC with Nehru when making a visit for other reasons. Above all, Nehru should not have the impression "that we are ganging up on them [the Indians]." At the same time, the High Commissioner could tell Nehru that, in the opinion of the Australian government, "a formal demand by India for a public assurance from United States and United Nations Command...would not be justified unless it can be shown that nothing short of this will restrain Rhee from organising a wholesale outbreak of prisoners."[9]

Certainly, information reaching Canberra from British authorities as well as from Critchley in Pusan was not conducive to support of the Indians. On 20 October, Critchley said that the "Czechs and Poles have been the driving forces of the [NNR] Commission." Also, thought Critchley, "The Indians have been too naïve... and overconfident in their ability to deal with fellow Asians."[10] Critchley regarded General K.S. Thimayya, head of India's contingent to the NNRC, as a "figure-head," subordinate to his political superiors.[11] The British High Commissioner in Canberra wrote that Churchill's government thought that the POWs, not the "Explainers" (North Korean and Chinese soldiers), should have the benefit of the doubt in the conduct of discussions arranged to persuade the reluctant to return to North Korea or the People's Republic of China.[12] Canada's views were somewhat different, and the Australian High Commissioner in Ottawa learned about them only because of a leak in the Canadian Department of External Affairs, not because Canadian authorities had attempted to keep him informed. Rumour was that Nehru had told Escott Reid that if matters remained tense in the DMZ, India would take its problems to the United Nations General Assembly:

> Reid personally contended that, in such an event, U.N.C. would be in a stronger position before the Assembly if it had done everything possible to encourage the prisoners to appear [before the NNRC and the 'Explainers.'][13]

In brief, British and Australian authorities appear to have been more sympathetic to Washington's critical attitude toward Indian "neutrality" than to India. Canadian authorities were more sympathetic to the Indians but did not discuss the mater with the Australians. The governments of New Zealand and South Africa appear to have been all but irrelevant.

II   Dealing with the Prisoner-Of-War Issue

If the Commonwealth as a whole was ineffective in resolving U.S.-Indian differences, the British government was not. On 22 October 1953, the Commonwealth Relations Office (CRO) sent a statement on British policy to the United Kingdom High Commissioner in Canberra, with a copy to the Australian High Commissioner in London. The statement noted the threat to take the dispute to the United Nations General Assembly. It also noted the Indian fear "that if prisoners do not attend explanations, Communists may legitimately claim armistice agreement has been broken." According to the CRO statement, the UK sought to "encourage" the Indians and to favour, at least in principle, attendance by North Korean and Chinese POWs at the "explanation" sessions. Finally, Churchill's government had suggested to U.S. authorities "that they should try and persuade Rhee to desist from inciting North Korean prisoners not to attend." The following day (23 October), the Australian High Commissioner in London reported that Washington "*had* acted on this [last] suggestion" (emphasis: the author's).

While Australian diplomats from the United Nations to Toyko monitored events in the DMZ,[14] the British High Commissioner in Canberra advised the Menzies government:

> We are doing what we can to encourage the Indians in what is admittedly a difficult position. We have suggested to them that the [NNR] Commission should continue to arrange for the Chinese who have passed successfully through the explanations procedure to reassure the North Koreans about its impartiality, and make clear that prisoners who had attended explanations once would not be obliged to attend again. We have suggested to the United States Government that they should try to persuade Rhee to desist from inciting North Korean prisoners not to attend and to suggest to him that the advantage lay in giving orders to the North Koreans [i.e., the recalcitrant POWs] to go through the explanation process. In his statement in Parliament on the 20th October, Mr. Eden reaffirmed our

confidence in the manner in which General Thimayya and the Indian troops…are doing their job.[15]

Still, Churchill's government had less than complete confidence in what the Indians were doing. On 21 October, the British High Commission in New Delhi advised the Indians to be more subtle and gentle:

(a) We agree that every effort should be made to persuade prisoners to attend the explanations, but we also agree that force shall not be used since a serious incident might make it impossible for the Americans to restrain Rhee, and would have a deplorable effect here and in America.

(b) We are disturbed at the Government of India's apparent interpretation of the Armistice Agreement [a reference to the Indian fear that if POWs would not "attend the explanations, the Communists may legitimately claim that the Armistice Agreement has been broken"] and advise them [the Indians] to avoid committing themselves on these issues until we can give our considered view on the legal position.

(c) We hope that they will not put the issue to the United Nations without further consideration and consultation, as a debate would not help at this stage.[16]

The Indians rejected the British advice. On 27 October 1953, the Australian High Commission in Ottawa reported news that it had learned from the Canadian Department of External Affairs. Thimayya thought that conditions had reached an intolerable impasse. As the UNC would not refer the problem to the United Nations General Assembly, India would refer Thimayya's report to that body before the Soviets could do so.[17]

On 29 October, the Australian High Commission in London advised Canberra that even if the North Korean POWs were to attend the explanations, North Korean authorities in Pyongyang probably still would not trust the procedure. Also, contrary to what he had initially believed, Thimayya had concluded that in the end very few of the unwilling POWs would be returning to North Korea or the People's Republic of China.[18]

At almost the same time, Australian authorities received information that the problems in the DMZ might not be a serious as they had appeared. From Washington, the Australian Embassy reported that two senior generals of the United Nations Command, one American and one British, had spoken to Thimayya separately. The two agreed that he and his soldiers were trying to be fair, that all POWs would be free to go where they wanted 120 days after the signing of the Armistice Agreement and that the NNRC would dissolve thirty days later, on 21 February 1954.[19]

An Australian report from Pusan dated 30 October 1953 stated that "the Australian and Canadian representatives on UNMAC [United Nations Military Armistice Command] are helping to improve relations between the Americans and the Indians."[20] Also, the British government sent a morale booster to New Delhi. The United Kingdom, it said,

(a) sympathized with their [the Indian soldiers'] difficulties and shared their view that force should not be used to bring [North] Korean prisoners before their explainers;

(b) hoped that they would be able to persevere in their difficult task;

(c) agreed that at this stage every effort should be centred on persuading [North] Korean prisoners to follow the procedure laid down by the [NNR] Commission; and

(d) had suggested to Mr. Dulles that representations might be made to the South Korean Government to persuade prisoners to attend the explanations. Mr. Dulles had been interested in this suggestion and had promised to see what could be done.[21]

However, despite subsequent conversations between Indian officials–most notably Ambassador Menon at the United Nations and General Thimayya in Korea's DMZ–and their British Canadian, and Australian counterparts[22]—time was the real problem solver. (On occasion, Menon also met U.S., Soviet, and Latin American diplomats.)[23] On 23 February 1954, the mandate of the NNRC expired and the NNRC dissolved. All remaining North Korean and Chinese POWs were free to relocate in South Korea or Taiwan, whether or not they had attended an explanatory session. The Indian soldiers returned to India.

III   Some Successes of the Neutral Nations Supervisory Commission

Korea's NNSC and one of its offshoots, the Neutral Nations Inspection Team (NNIT), faced additional challenges: marking a demarcation line between North and South Korea, and monitoring the terms of the agreement to guarantee that neither side cheated. Surprisingly perhaps, given all that had happened and would happen, establishing a demarcation line along the inter-Korean boundary proved surprisingly simple and uncomplicated. Both parties agreed that the demarcation line should coincide with battlefield realities, and without much difficulty they managed to agree as to what those realities were. The Military Armistice Commissions of both sides helped clear land mines and other weapons from the demilitarized zone (DMZ), two miles either side of the demarcation line, and to establish transportation routes to Panmunjom and throughout the DMZ.[24] Supervision was the responsibility of the NNSC.

IV The Geneva Conference of 1954: Korean Portion

There is no need to elaborate upon the Korean portion of the Geneva Conference of April-July 1954. Diplomats from the 16 countries of the UNC, North and South Korea, the People's Republic of China, and the USSR met to discuss ways to transform the Panmunjom Armistice Agreement into a permanent peace treaty. Pearson thought that the U.S. position was inflexible, more appropriate for a party which had actually won a war.[25] Whether greater flexibility might have produced greater dividends must await further disclosures from Soviet and Chinese archives. The point is that the Commonwealth coalition was unravelling, and chances of modifying U.S. policies might have lessened.

There was an initial success. On 7 April 1954, the British, Canadian, Australian, and New Zealand (but not the South African) Ambassadors in Washington received invitations to the State Department to discuss the forthcoming Geneva Conference. Their hosts were Walter S. Robertson, Deputy Assistant Secretary of State for Foreign Affairs, and Alexis Johnson, who would lead the U.S. delegation to the Geneva Conference. Arnold Heeney, the Canadian Ambassador, reported:

> The Commonwealth representatives questioned the wisdom of stating as one of the general objectives the emergence from the conference with a moral and propaganda victory, on the grounds that this gave the impression that serious negotiations were not expected. Robertson agreed that this objective had been overstated and badly worded.[26]

However, Pearson in Ottawa and Norman Robertson, Canada's High Commissioner in London, did not fully trust Churchill's government. They suspected that the Americans, British, and French would establish a triumvirate which would make the important UNC decisions at the Geneva Conference. Opinions of the thirteen lesser allies would count for very little. British Foreign Secretary Anthony Eden did occasionally consult his Canadian, Australian, and New Zealand colleagues (apparently not the South Africans).[27] However, when the U.S. government felt strongly on an issue, Eden agreed with French Foreign Minister Georges Bidault that to object would be more trouble than it was worth, regardless of the feelings of the Canadians, Australians, and New Zealanders.[28] At any rate, the Geneva Conference resolved nothing on Korea. Whether it might have if a united Old Commonwealth had successfully lobbied the Eisenhower administration belongs in the realm of the counterfactual.

V Other Duties of the Neutral Nations Supervisory Commission

The Swiss and the Swedes regarded their assignment as short-term, one that would last until the Geneva Conference of 1954 met and transformed the armistice of 1953 into a permanent peace agreement. They never anticipated that the Poles and Czechoslovaks would remain at their command posts on the North Korean side of the demilitarized zone until the government of North Korea expelled them years after the Cold War had ended. Nor could they have suspected that when Prince Philip made a courtesy visit to Panmunjom in April 1999, he would speak to Swiss and Swedish officers, still living in camps on the South Korean side.

In order to fulfil these tasks, soldiers from the five nations of the NNSC maintained posts throughout Korea. The Custodial Forces of India (CFI), more anxious than the others to appear neutral, remained inside the demilitarized zone. Indeed, at times when it appeared that the Armistice Agreement would collapse and soldiers of the NNSC would have to flee for their lives, the United Nations Command plotted escape routes which would enable the Indians to spend a minimum of time inside South Korea proper. Troops of the other four nations would live and work in the DMZ, as well as around Sinuiju and Manpo (both on the Yalu River), Chongjin (a port in the northeast), Hungnam (a port), and Sinanju (a railway junction linking Pyonyang, Sinuiju, and Manpo) in North Korea; and Inchon, Pusan, Kunsan, Kangnung, and Taegu in South Korea.[29]

VI Difficulties of the Neutral Nations Supervisory Commission

Article 13 (d) of the AA stipulated that both sides might repair weaponry already in Korea as of 27 July 1953 but that neither side should introduce new equipment. To prevent cheating, Swedish and Swiss, Polish and Czechoslovakian soldiers of the Neutral Nations Inspection Team would establish observation posts at five designated locations in South Korea and five more in North Korea.

One problem, perhaps minor in retrospect but serious at the time, involved the flying of flags. On 4 May 1954 the Polish and Czechoslovakian flew their countries' flags at Kunsan, one of their billeting posts in South Korea. A confidential memorandum of 20 May 1954 from the headquarters of the Far East Command of the U.S. Army raised several objections. The Swedes and Swiss were not interested in flying their flags in North Korea. South Koreans might take offense. Communists might accept the flying of such flags as a sign of appeasement.[30] After voluminous correspondence on the matter, the United Nations Command decided that this was not a problem after all. There was no reaction among the people at Kunsan, and North Korea indicated that if the Swedes and Swiss wanted to fly their flags at billeting posts there, they could do so. Hence, the Poles and Czechoslovakians could continue to do what they were already doing.[31]

Preventing violations of Article 13 (d) was a more serious matter. South Korea sat on the southern extremity of a peninsula, without any land connection to friendly territory. Any weaponry must necessarily arrive there through a limited number of airports and seaports. (The volume and quality of the weaponry could affect the military balance of power should hostilities resume.) Moreover, whatever the authoritarian shortcomings of Syngman Rhee's government, South Korea was a more open, less secretive, society than North Korea. For these reasons, Polish and Czechoslovakian observers could monitor the shipment of weapons to South Korea without serious difficulty.

By contrast, North Korea shared a land frontier with China, separated by two rivers and a connecting height of land. Weapons could travel from the PRC into North Korea along a number of rail lines. Swedish and Swiss soldiers at their five North Korean observation posts found themselves on a very short leash, unable to see what was happening at other border crossings, and the Poles and Czechoslovakians were certainly not prepared to blow the whistle. Two Swiss generals complained to the United Nations Command 1 October 1953:

> The NNITs in the north see nothing, cannot do their work because areas authorized for NNITs in the Agreement do not include many of the roads, rail lines and bridges over which material can be and is probably being transported from China into Korea.

> At Manpo there are three bridges over the Yalu. There is heavy traffic over at least two of these bridges which are outside the NNIT inspection area. Rail traffic has increased from approximately two trains per day to one train per hour. Spot checks of a certain few cars have shown rice and lumber.

There were other serious grounds for suspicion. A 23 December 1953 report of the United Nations Military Armistice Commission cited problems at the border town of Manpo:

Although informed by the Chinese that there were two regularly scheduled trains, in actuality, more and more trains per day passed into North Korea. Each train was composed of 20 box or flat cars or of oil tank cars, all of which were loaded with a single commodity. There were no trains carrying mixed cargoes. At first there were four or five trains per day; for the last 15 days of the period, however, from 20 to 25 trains per day or approximately one train per hour, passed into North Korea from Manchuria. Commodities reported included wood in various finished and unfinished stages, sacks of millet, meal and cement, boxes containing bridge materials or concrete ingredients, and large boxes or crates whose contents were unknown. Some trains had two locomotives. Those trains...were composed of cars larger than any observed in Europe...[32]

Trains from North Korea into China were also a concern, as Manchuria offered a safehaven for unauthorized military equipment and personnel. Inspection of outbound trains was as difficult as that of trains *from* China. Few if any Swedish or Swiss soldiers could speak the Korean language and had to rely upon their hosts for interpreters. North Korean authorities did not hasten to provide them and often required that security guards, also slow in arrival, must accompany the Swedish and Swiss "for their own protection." There was then pressure to be hasty, to inspect only the occasional boxcar, so that the train could be on its way.[33] The United Nations Command seethed with frustration as Communist members of the NNIT could monitor what was happening in South Korea, while the Swedes and Swiss soldiers laboured in North Korea's restrictive environment.[34] At a State Department meeting of 14 April attended by the Swiss and Swedish ambassadors to the United States, two State Department officials expressed the conviction that Swedish and Swiss members of the NNSC and NNIT had deterred "greater violations and...the resumption of hostilities." The Swedish ambassador (Boheman) asked whether Swedish and Swiss achievements had not been more than offset "by the continued presence and intelligence activities of the Czechs and Poles in South Korea."[35]

For his part, President Syngman Rhee had no doubts. Twice he stated his intention "to restrict the activities of the Poles and Czechs and request the NNSC to terminate its activities in Korea."[36] Nor did U.S. authorities disagree. A United Nations report of 28 April 1954 stated: "We must...impress upon President Rhee at every opportunity that we are endeavouring to eliminate the NNITs from South Korea but that until this has been achieved, he must not take unilateral action which would bring about armed clashes between his people and our armed forces."[37] The work of the NNSC was thankless.

VII Divisions Within the Neutral Nations Supervisory Commission

The NNSC quickly disintegrated into two conflicting units—the Poles and the Czechoslovakians versus the Swedes and the Swiss. Indian officers provided the only glue, and they left Korea early in 1954.

As far as the United Nations Command (UNC) was concerned, the Poles and the Czechoslovakians were collaborators of the enemy. They would spy for the enemy in South Korea, and they would hear no evil, see no evil, or speak no evil in North Korea. The Indians' track record was mixed. The UNC accepted their good faith but thought, at least in the initial stages, that the Indians were somewhat naive as far as the PRC and the North Koreans were concerned. For example, the Indians supported the Swedes and Swiss, who agreed that the United Nations Command need not engage soldiers from China or North Korea to hasten construction of buildings for interrogation of dissident POWs. They also agreed with the Swedes and Swiss against the Poles and Czechoslovakians that the NNRC should not use force to oblige dissidents to hear North Korean or Chinese officials appointed to persuade them to return home.[38] On the other hand, the Indians signed a NNRC report of 28 December 1953 endorsed by the Poles and Czechoslovakians, while the Swedes and Swiss submitted a minority report. Yet, on 3 January 1954, the United Nations Command praised "the strong stand taken by the Indians, Swedes and Swiss in prohibiting the use of force against defenseless prisoners."[39]

An official "History of the UN Command Repatriation Group" written after the NNRC disbanded in 1954 reported:

> On 17 October [1953], UNC observers reported that civilian Indian chairman of the sub-committees conducting explanations tended to be sympathetic to the Communists. These sympathies appeared to lessen as time went on and the Indians became aware of Communist methods.

> On 22 October [1953] Major General Stephen N. Shoosmith (British Army), Deputy Chief of Staff, UNC, visited General Thimayya, and on 25 October Lieutenant General Harrison, Chief of Staff UNC, also visited the Indian General. Their opinion was that the Indian representatives and the CFI were attempting to do a fair and neutral job.

> The Polish and Czech delegations were always in support of the Communists, whereas the Swiss and Swedes "gave every indication that their views coincided with UNC views." The Indian position was not so clearly established…[40]

Perhaps symptomatic of Indian behaviour was the chaplaincy issue. Once the POWs moved into the DMZ, they could no longer attend religious services led by chaplains of armies under the United Nations Command. The UNC insisted that the POWs had the right to such services led by ordained Christian clergy. The Poles objected, and Wilfred Burchett, Korean correspondent for the French Communist newspaper *L'Humanité*, explained that UN chaplains were but "agents disguised as chaplains...to direct [influence] the PWs [sic]." The Indians then provided four Roman Catholic chaplains from their own army but left the Protestants to fend for themselves.[41]

U.S. military officers who led the United Nations Command in Korea had nothing but praise for assistance rendered by Swedish and Swiss soldiers. They praised the Swedes, Swiss, and Indians for "prohibiting the use of force against defenceless prisoners" who did not want to return to their homes in China or North Korea.[42] The Swedes and the Swiss operated as such genuine members of the Western community that on 22 May 1954, the senior United States officer of the United Nations Military Armistice Commission (MAC) even considered honouring the Swedes and Swiss with letters of commendation or recognition by the President of the United States—although it wondered whether this might prove embarrassing to the two neutrals. President Eisenhower, the memorandum indicated, had already thanked the Prime Minister Nehru for the efforts of the CFI, and "the Swiss and Swedes are far more entitled to recognition...than were the Indians."[43] The Swedes and Swiss communicated regularly with the United Nations Command and kept it well informed of developments. Swedish and Swiss soldiers shared the frustrations of the UNC, and their officers and diplomats spoke as though the NNSC were living on borrowed time, about to abort because of its futility or worse (the opportunities it provided the Poles and Czechoslovakians to monitor events in South Korea).[44] On 6 July 1954, when it appeared that the Swedes and Swiss might wash their hands of the whole affair and withdraw from the NNSC, a speechwriter prepared a statement for the Commander in Chief. It called upon him to "take advantage of this opportunity to support publicly the Swiss and Swedish representatives and nations as strongly as possible, and to place the blame on the Communists and their 'neutrals'."[45]

VIII Canada and the Neutral Nations Supervisory Commission

When negotiators met in Geneva almost one year after the Armistice Agreement—first in a fruitless attempt to arrange a permanent peace settlement in Korea and then to terminate the war between the French Army and the Viet Minh—the

Korean arrangement served as a precedent, positive and negative. Delegates in Geneva saw no need for another five-nation commission and decided that a three-nation ICC could manage as well. Again, an Indian officer could serve as chair of Vietnam's International Control Commission (ICC), as well as the ICC's for Vietnam's neighbours in what was then French Indochina, Laos and Cambodia. In Vietnam, Laos, and Cambodia, Polish officers would protect Communist interests, but this time Czechoslovakian soldiers would not. However, neither Swedes nor Swiss would be there for balance in Indochina. Belgium and Canada were the NATO members under consideration—countries with disciplined and well trained armies, soldiers who could speak French, soldiers from countries with no capacity or desire for imperialism—and the task went to Canada.[46] Canadian forces remained in southeast Asia until 1973.

John Holmes, a participant at the Geneva Conference of 1954, wrote that once the Korean portion of the Geneva talks ended, he thought that his role as leader of Canada's delegation had also ended, and he left for home. He has written:

> When I left, there was a good deal of arguing over the composition of the supervisory body to be set up [for Vietnam]...[British Foreign Secretary Anthony] Eden [along with Soviet Foreign Minister Vyacheslav Molotov, co-chair of the Geneva conference] had been unable to secure agreement to his proposal for a genuinely Asian commission, not only because the Americans didn't like it but because the Russians wanted some *bona fide* Communists involved. On the Western side there was absolute resistance to anything resembling the Commission set up in Korea...in which two genuine neutrals, Sweden and Switzerland, were confronted by two not at all genuine neutrals, Poland and Czechoslovakia, with total stalemate as a result. The Western negotiators eventually assumed that there would have to be at least one Communist member of the Commission and therefore there would have to be an equal number of committed Western countries. Before I left Geneva, the Western country most prominently mentioned was Belgium...but the Communists rejected this suggestion because they considered the Belgians French agents. Canada's name had sometimes been mentioned jokingly, but there seemed no reason to take it seriously. Canada had already acquired, over Korea and other issues, the reputation of being the most objective of the NATO countries and it is believed that Krishna Menon persuaded [Chinese foreign minister] Zhou En-lai that Canada would be the best Western candidate.[47]

Holmes attended the Geneva conference and heard the corridor discussions. Primary and secondary sources repeat what he has said. When Canada's Geneva-based Permanent Delegate to the European Office of the United Nations contacted External Affairs Minister Lester Pearson 19 July 1954, less than forty-eight hours before the signing of the Indochina agreement, he said, "The suggestion made by the Chinese delegate at yesterday's meeting that members of the Commission should be India, Canada and Poland came as a complete surprise."[48] When Canada's ambassador to the United States, Arnold Heeney, met State Department officials 23 July 1954, in the aftermath of the Geneva Conference, to discuss Canada's acceptance or otherwise of the "invitation" to participate in the ICCs, nobody in the room knew who had nominated Canada for the role. The guess was that India's Krishna Menon had initiated the suggestion.[49] Historians Donald Masters, J.L. Granatstein and David Bercuson repeat part of the Holmes account and challenge none of it.[50]

Without challenging the accuracy of the Holmes interpretation, there is reason to ask whether there was more to the selection of Canada than that. The records of the United Nations Military Armistice Commission indicate that the United States—leader of the United Nations Command in Korea—was totally satisfied with the Swiss and Swedish track record in Korea. Swiss soldiers could speak French, and, unlike Belgians or Canadians, they were a known quantity in such situations. Were the Western Allies simply playing tit-for-tat: "If a Soviet bloc country like Poland were to be there, should not a NATO country also be there?"

James Eayrs has described events in his capacity as a political scientist, rather than as a participant like Holmes. Eayrs made no reference to the Korean precedent at all. He said that Anthony Eden would have preferred an all-Asian ICC, which would have included India, Burma, and Ceylon. Neither the Soviets nor the Americans would agree. Molotov wanted Pakistan and Indonesia, Czechoslovakia and Poland. Both the U.S. and British governments objected to Indonesia, then led by Sukarno, as too friendly to the Soviet Union. Molotov then suggested Burma instead of Indonesia, but the French thought Burma equally untrustworthy and nominated Belgium. On 18 July, two days before the conference was to terminate in success or in failure, Chinese Foreign Minister Zhou Enlai suggested that Canada would be preferable to Belgium.[51] Eayrs' account of events is highly credible. However, Swiss documents are now available, and they indicate that the Swiss government had made clear that Switzerland would not be a candidate. India and Poland would serve in Vietnam, but Switzerland would not. Whatever the Great Powers might have wanted, the Geneva Conference simply had to find somebody else for the ICC role. Under the circumstances, the selection of Canada deserves another look.

IX Switzerland and the Neutral Nations Supervisory Commission

On 23 September 1957, the Swiss Foreign Office prepared a document on Swiss neutrality. It began: "For centuries, the basis of Swiss foreign policy has been constant neutrality." Thus, in connection with the NNSC, Swiss soldiers found themselves in "a somewhat embarrassing situation" (sie...in eine etwas peinliche Situation versetzt haben). When the U.S. government first approached Swiss authorities about a possible Swiss role on the NNSC, Bern replied that Swiss neutrality was permanent. Hence, the NNSC role would be possible only if Switzerland could remain impartial. As a member of the NNSC, Switzerland would not want to be the representative of either party, and Swiss authorities doubted whether the NNSC could function in a manner compatible with Swiss values. For purely humanitarian reasons, Foreign Minister A. Daeniker explained, Switzerland swallowed those doubts and agreed to participate.[52] In doing so, Swiss authorities certainly facilitated the cease-fire of 27 July 1953, but events on the ground confirmed that they had been right to be sceptical.

If Holmes *did* know about a 35-minute meeting of 12 June 1954 between Zhou Enlai and the Swiss foreign minister, he could not have known the contents of their discussion in the detail that is now available. The Swiss foreign minister, Max Petitpierre, told Zhou that, far from being willing to accept a role in Vietnam, Switzerland wanted to withdraw its forces from Korea. First, there were loopholes in the Korean Armistice Agreement of the previous year, and those loopholes frustrated the Swiss soldiers in Korea. Secondly, the NNSC compromised Swiss neutrality. Switzerland had expected the role of an impartial observer, but that role had evolved into one of representing the interests of one of the parties to the conflict. Thirdly, under law, Swiss draftees served only in Switzerland. Only volunteers could undertake international assignments, and there was a shortage of volunteers. Petitpierre asked Zhou whether there were plans for a body similar to the NNSC in Vietnam, and Zhou replied in the affirmative, without giving details. Zhou also expressed gratitude for Switzerland's contributions to date on the NNSC, which he said were vital and must continue, despite any difficulties.[53]

Historian Marius Schwarb agrees that the history of the NNSC throughout 1953-1954 had been a story of unrelieved confrontation between Sweden and Switzerland on the one hand, Poland, and Czechoslovakia on the other.[54] Schwarb also saw the NNSC as a precedent for the ICC.[55] As the Foreign Minister had told Zhou Enlai, there was no reason to think that the situation in Vietnam would be an improvement over that in Korea.[56]

X   Summary

Korea provided the diplomats at Geneva with a foretaste of what they might expect in Vietnam. The Soviet Union and China were still friendly to each other, and Western diplomats anticipated that Communist governments in any one place would behave much as did any other. Those at Geneva knew what to expect of the Indians, and they knew what to expect of the Poles. Correspondence at the National Archives and Records Center (College Park, Maryland) provides no hint of dissatisfaction on the part of the UNC with the Swedes or the Swiss, and as Swiss soldiers could speak French as well as Belgians or Canadians, they might well have served on Indochina's International Control Commissions.

The United States government did not veto Swiss (or Swedish) participation on the ICCs. First, U.S. authorities were more than satisfied with what Swiss and Swedish soldiers had been doing in Korea. Secondly, the United States government never signed the Geneva accord on Vietnam, which took effect despite U.S. objections. Secretary of State John Foster Dulles thought that the French were making too many concessions to Ho Chi Minh and his forces, and he refused to be a party to what he considered appeasement. Other Western countries, but not the United States, agreed to abide by the terms of the Geneva settlement. Thirdly, the U.S. government clearly did not nominate Canada to the International Control Commissions. Fourthly, the Swiss were not at all inclined to serve on the ICC after their experience on the NNSC. They had not wanted to serve on the NNSC, and they wanted off it as quickly as possible. One U.S. military report of 20 July 1954, written hours before the signing of the Vietnam agreement, said bluntly:

> [T]he Swiss and Swedes consider the NNSC a complete farce, consider that continued participation puts them in an increasingly ridiculous position, and contemplate withdrawal at some future date.[57]

XI   The Emasculation of the Neutral Nations Supervisory Commission: Canadian Thoughts

For months after the Geneva Conference, U.S. and South Korean authorities worried about sensitive information which Polish and Czechoslovakian members of the NNSC might be gathering in South Korea. Whatever it was, they feared, was considerably less than any intelligence which the Swedes and the Swiss were gathering in North Korea. Either the NNSC should be shut down—and the refusal of the Swedes and the Swiss to remain in Korea would resolve that problem—or the NNSC should be confined to the DMZ.

At this point, Canadian and U.S. interests differed. Now that Canada had become a members of the ICCs, it wanted to play a meaningful role, not to engage in a charade. Canadian forces should have the greatest possible freedom to travel through North Vietnam, and Korea was setting a precedent. If the UNC were to confine Polish and Czechoslovakian officials to the Korean DMZ near the 38th parallel and excluded them from the rest of South Korea, the government of North Vietnam might restrict Canada's forces to the DMZ near the 17th parallel.

For the moment, France appeared to support Canada. The withdrawal of the Swedes and Swiss, they feared, would give the Poles a pretext not to co-operate in Vietnam. Angry at events in Korea, the Indians might become overly sympathetic to the Communists in Vietnam. At the very least, thought Jules Leger, Canada's Under-Secretary of State for External Affairs, the Swedes and the Swiss must remain at their posts in Korea until the spring of 1955, by which time French forces in North Vietnam would have withdrawn to the port of Haiphong.[58]

Pearson was concerned. He feared that Dulles might seek approval from the Group of Fifteen (G-15)—those UN members whose forces had fought in the Korean War—for the Swedes and the Swiss to curtail their activities. Canada could not be a party to such a demand, he told A.D.P. (Arnold) Heeney, Canada's ambassador in Washington:

> Because of Canadian membership on the International Supervisory Commissions in Indochina, whose functions are somewhat similar to those of the NNSC, the Canadian Government could not be associated with any concerted approach to the Swiss and Swedish governments to get them to withdraw their representatives, nor could it be a party to any authorization to the UN Command to evict the Czech and Polish representatives from South Korea.[59]

Heeney forwarded Pearson's thoughts to the State Department the very next day, 20 October 1954. By coincidence, that was the day for the evacuation of French forces from Hanoi, although Heeney did not mention the fact. Everett Drumright, the Deputy Assistant Secretary of State for Far Eastern Affairs, "noted the views," said Heeney, but he did not find them persuasive. Tough action with the NNSC in Korea, said Drumright, might help the ICCs in Indochina. As long as the Poles and other Communists thought that they could violate "international commitments with impunity," they would do so. Immediate and firm action in Korea might chasten the Poles and make them more co-operative in Vietnam. Moreover, said Drumright, Polish and Czechoslovakian members of the NNSC were gaining access to classified information in South Korea to which North Korean spies could not gain access.[60]

In turn, Drumright's arguments failed to convince Pearson. He was not in a position, he said, to argue with the U.S./South Korean charge that the Poles and Czechoslovakians were better spies than North Koreans could be. However, he thought that the solution should be to curtail their espionage, not to terminate the NNSC. Nor did Pearson share the State Department's opinion that the NNSC was a hopeless cause. "Recently," he noted, it had managed to file a unanimous report with the Military Armistice Commission, which included representatives from China and North Korea as well as from the United States and South Korea.[61]

Official Washington ignored Pearson. On 18 November, representatives of the G-15 countries met in Washington and listened to Robert Murphy, Deputy Under Secretary of State for Political Affairs. Murphy suggested that if Swedish and Swiss members of the NNSC would withdraw to the Korean DMZ, the Poles and Czechoslovakians would have to leave South Korea. According to Heeney, who represented Canada at the meeting, "No representative offered direct opposition to the United States proposal." The British and French offered to carry Murphy's suggestion to the Swedish and Swiss governments. As for the others,

> the Greeks gave wholehearted support to the United States position. The Australian and New Zealand representatives were non-committal but certainly not opposed.

Canada, evidently, was a minority of one. Heeney agreed that the Czechoslovakians and the Poles "were violating the spirit of the terms of reference of the NNSC, [and] that the Swiss and Swedish members could not discharge their mandate in North Korea." At the same time, Heeney forwarded Pearson's opinion that it was useful to have inspection teams behind Communist lines "even if they were not completely effective."[62]

Pearson remained skeptical. Perhaps it might be possible to renegotiate the structure of the NNSC, but until that happened, it should try to perform as usual. Pearson disliked the idea that the UNC would be the side to render the NNSC "inoperative." What the impact would be on Indochina's ICCs remained to be seen. Because of Canada's unique position as both a member of the G-15 *and* a member of the ICCs, Canada could not join the other UN belligerents in asking the Swedes and the Swiss to curtail their activities. Pearson hoped that the Americans, British, French, Australians, and New Zealanders would understand.[63] Heeney replied that the State Department would probably understand Pearson's concerns even if it disagreed with him.[64]

On 2 December 1954, Pearson expressed dismay that the U.S., British, and French governments had approached and misled the Swedish and Swiss governments. Pearson had become aware of this because of cables from the Canadian embassy in Switzerland and the Canadian legation in Sweden. The Americans, British, and French had misrepresented the outcome of the 18 November G-15 meeting in Washington. The G-15, they indicated, had unanimously recommended a Swedish/Swiss withdrawal to the DMZ. The Big Three made no mention of Canadian reservations. Since Canada had agreed to be part of the ICCs, Canadian officials had frequently approached Swedish and Swiss officials for advice. In so doing, Canada had indicated that its leaders saw parallels between what the Swedes and the Swiss were doing in Korea and what Canadians were planning to do in Vietnam, Laos, and Cambodia. Under the circumstances, authorities in Stockholm and Bern wondered whether the Canadian government really did favour their withdrawal to the DMZ. Pearson decided to share his reservations with the Swedes and the Swiss.[65]

There were repercussions. William G. Jones, Acting Officer in Charge of Korean Affairs in the State Department's Office of Northeast Asian Affairs, expressed mild concern that Canada would share its reservations with Stockholm and Bern. As for Indochina, Jones thought, Pearson need not fear that what happened in Korea would have any impact. The Poles were so certain that their friends, the Viet Minh, could win a fair Vietnamese election that they would play by the rules in that country.[66] In Bern, Marcel Luy of the Federal Political Department expressed doubt that the Swiss government would oblige the G-15,[67] and Gunnar Jarring, the Swedish Foreign Minister, voiced similar sentiments. It was the responsibility of the United Nations General Assembly, not of the G-15, he thought, to change the NNSC's mandate—if it was to be changed.[68]

On 10 December, Luy advised the Canadian Embassy in Switzerland that the U.S. had approached the Swiss government a second time, on this occasion with three suggestions:

> withdraw to demilitarized zone, (b) reduce strength of their delegation, and (c) maintain liaison officers in South Korea while Poles and Czechs maintain liaison with North Korea.[69]

The Swiss government wondered whether Washington was acting unilaterally, and K.W.H. MacLellan, Second Secretary at Canada's embassy in Bern, shared Pearson's reservations with Luy. The Swiss government then decided not to answer the U.S.-UK-French proposal, not to withdraw the NNSC to the DMZ, but to suggest a "reduction of numerical strength of NNSC."[70]

On 23 December, Pearson reluctantly advised the Canadian legation in Stockholm that these suggestions probably would be tolerable. However, he warned:

> While we cannot prophesy what would be the effects on the armistice supervisory machinery in Indochina of the NNSC becoming even more ineffective, we think that the problems in both are sufficiently related that any significant development concerning the NNSC may have effects on the other.[71]

XII Canadian Isolation on the Issue of the Neutral Nations Supervisory Commission

It appears that Canada had no support from the other Old Commonwealth countries in connection with the NNSC. The United Kingdom in particular agreed with the Americans that the NNSC had become a liability and must be confined to the DMZ.

As far as the British were concerned, the realities of the moment had priority over hypothetical situations in Vietnam. The State Department maintained contact with the Old Commonwealth governments and with France on the NNSC problem to a greater extent than with any of the other sixteen countries which had sent combat forces to Korea. On 17 March 1956, there was a meeting about the NNSC with officials from the United Kingdom, Canada, Australia, and New Zealand (but not South Africa or France). The British delegate wrote, "The State Department emphasized that this information had not been given to any one other than the New Zealand, Canadian, Australian and United Kingdom representatives and...hoped it would not be passed on."[72]

On 29 April there was a similar meeting of officials from the same nations, plus France.[73] Churchill's government had every reason to regard itself as "inside the loop," fully consulted.

It also found the Eisenhower administration's position throughly credible, despite concerns (which it noted) expressed at those meetings by the Canadian representative. As far as the British government was concerned,

> The Neutral Nations Supervisory Commission has long since ceased to fulfil its functions under the armistice agreement because of Communist obstruction. We believe the proposal of the Governments of Sweden and Switzerland to withdraw all Neutral Nations Supervisory Commission personnel to the demilitarised zone are reasonable. They present a practi-

cal solution to this problem...[T]he activities of the Czechoslovakian and
Polish components of the Neutral Nations Supervisory Commission south
of the demilitarised zone are an inequitable burden on the United Nations
side.[74]

XIII   Aftermath

It would be difficult to compile evidence that the fate of the NNSC had any impact
upon the ICCs in Vietnam, Laos, or Cambodia. One many question the effectiveness of the ICC, but long after 1956 it continued to operate beyond Vietnam's
DMZ.[75] However, there were many ironies yet to come in the history of the NNSC.

From 1956 until the end of the Cold War, the NNSC offered a meeting place
where North Koreans and South Koreans could talk. On various occasions, representatives of the two Korean governments discussed formulae for Korean reunification and joint teams at international athletic events. It also operated what amount to
an inter-Korean postal service. If authorities in the north wanted to contact their
counterparts in the south, or vice versa, they sent their letters to the NNSC. The Red
Cross of North Korea and the Red Cross of South Korea also communicated via the
NNSC; for example, on 9 April 1980, the South Korean Red Cross contacted its
northern counterpart via the NNSC about South Korean fishermen and their boats
which had been missing since 21 January. Throughout April and May 1980, the
North Korean/Chinese contingent to the MAC accused the United Nations Command of shooting across the DMZ, and in May it protested the alleged shootings to
the NNSC. On 31 October 1981, there was shooting across the DMZ for one hour
and twenty-two minutes. Even the Polish and Czechoslovakian members of the
NNSC held the North Koreans responsible.

When President Ronald Reagan visited Korea in 1984, he asked the NNSC to
investigate the gradual remilitarization of the DMZ. Without fail, North Korea
would protest to the NNSC that the annual military exercises organized by the
United Nations Command for the armed forces of South Korea and the United
States, begun in 1976, were a violation of the Armistice Agreement. Except in 1986,
those exercises, codenamed "Team Spirit," took place regardless. In November 1986,
South Korean authorities asked for talks with North Koreans, again at the NNSC
conference room at Panmunjom, to discuss shared water resources. The Han River
estuary forms the Inter-Korean boundary northwest of Seoul; its tributaries collect
water from both sides of the DMZ.

Apart from facilitating communication between Pyongyang and Seoul, the NNSC proved itself useful. In September 1984, South Korea experienced serious flooding, and the North Korean Red Cross sent aid via the NNSC to the South Korean victims. Meetings at Panmunjom hosted by the NNSC facilitated visits of elderly family members to relatives on the other side of the DMZ and of cultural groups. Before North Korea and South Korea both joined the United Nations in 1991, their governments held discussions at Panmunjom, again in the NNSC conference room. In March 1993, the NNSC assisted with the repatriation of a former North Korean guerrilla in South Korea, Yi In-mo. Yi had spent forty-two years in South Korea, thirty-four of them in jail, but by 1993 he was old and feeble. His wife and daughter waited for him when he crossed the DML at Panmunjom.

As late as 30 December 1986, Kim Il Sung told the North Korean People's Assembly that his government wanted "to increase the authority of the NNSC and organize a neutral nations inspection force as a setup to watch the military actions of both sides in the DMZ along the military demarcation line in an effective way to promote the work of removing the military confrontation in a fair way and prevent military conflicts."[76] From 1987 to 1990, North Korea presented disarmament proposals which it wanted the NNSC to verify. In May 1992, officials of the Joint Nuclear Control Program from South Korea and North Korea met at the NNSC's Panmunjom conference room "to negotiate the regulations for South-North mutual inspection." These meetings continued for the remainder of the calendar year.

However, the Cold War had ended, and Communists ceased to govern first Poland and then Czechoslovakia in 1989. In April 1992, Czechoslovakian President Vaclav Havel visited South Korea. At the stroke of midnight 1992/3, Czechoslovakia disintegrated into the Czech Republic and Slovakia. The Czech and Slovak governments decided that henceforth Korea would be a Czech responsibility. To the dismay of the North Korean government, the Poles and Czechs joined the Swedes, Swiss, Russians, and Singaporeans in sending observers to Operation Team Spirit 1993. The North Korean government used the occasion to say that the Czechs had no right to remain in Korea. In 1953, North Korea had invited Czechoslovakia. Czechoslovakia no longer existed. The Czech Republic had no right to appoint itself to fill the void. The choice should belong to North Korea, which reportedly would find Cuba, Syria, or Iran more acceptable.

North Korea found itself totally alone. The Czechs claimed that they had the same right to inherit the NNSC role from Czechoslovakia as Russia had had to inherit the Soviet functions at the United Nations. At the very least, said the Havel government, Czechs should remain until somebody else was ready to replace them. North Korea ordered the Czechs to leave, and Prague protested that North Korean treatment of the Czech forces was "uncivilized and inhuman." In retaliation, the Czech government ordered thirteen North Koreans from the embassy in Prague to return home, but it did agree to withdraw its soldiers from Panmunjom by 10 April. South Korea found the Czechs' departure "regrettable" and said that it had "undermined the functions of the NNSC and intensified tensions in the Korean Peninsula."

Early in May 1994, North Korea renounced further participation in the Military Armistice Commission and persuaded the Chinese contingent to leave. Beijing agreed to go but said that it still recognized the authority of the MAC. Before the death of Kim Il Sung 8 July, the North Korean government ridiculed the NNSC and said that it preferred direct bilateral talks with the United States. It had its way. North Korea was well on its way to becoming a nuclear power. In the words of one commentator:

> In mid-1994, the United States nearly plunged into a conflict that the commander of the American forces in South Korea, General Gary Luck, estimated would have killed a million people, including as many as 100,000 American soldiers, and would have cost more than $100 billion (about double the total cost of the Persian Gulf War).[77]

That crisis of May-June 1994 was so serious that the Clinton administration despatched former President Jimmy Carter to the scene. He, rather than the NNSC, defused the issue.

In 1995, the North Korean government, by then led by the son of Kim Il Sung, Kim Jong Il, expelled the Poles. First Pyongyang argued that it had expected the Poles to leave when the Czechs left. When they did not, Pyongyang forced the issue, cutting the supply of gas, electricity, and water to the Poles, then threatening to arrest any who did not leave. The Poles retreated to Warsaw but claimed to be an ongoing part of the NNSC nonetheless. The Polish government claimed support from South Korea, the United States, and China, and it demanded that North Korea reduce its embassy staff in Warsaw by fifty per cent. Daily meetings of the NNSC ended, but Polish members of the NNSC returned to the section of Panmunjom *south* of the DML at intervals of three months for NNSC meetings. At the same time, North Korea prevented the Swedes and the Swiss from sending their troops north of the DML, even within the DMZ.

The United Nations Command rejected the idea that the NNSC was an anachronism, and the South Korean government criticized North Korean restraints on the

NNSC even within the DMZ. From Washington, the Clinton administration protested the expulsion of Poland from the NNSC, but Pyongyang responded that the Armistice Agreement was nothing more than "a mere scrap of Paper." After all, South Korea had refused to sign the Armistice Agreement in 1953, and the United States itself had violated Article 13 (d). To make matters worse, the UNC had chosen a South Korean to head its section of the MAC in 1991.

The NNSC continues to function, with Swedish and Swiss contingents on the south side of the DMZ. In 1999, the Swedish contingent, with moral support from the Poles and the Swiss, sponsored a concert by a Czech pianist at Panmunjom. The United States and North Korea held bilateral talks in Berlin, and Japan, the United States, South Korea, and North Korea had ongoing talks on North Korea's nuclear ambitions. However, the role of the NNSC was not what it had been. By 1995, North Korea's complaints about violations of Article 13 (d) were probably stale, but the UNC's decisions to "reinterpret" Article 13 (d) in 1955 and 1956 had given North Korea its opportunity.

XIV   Summary

On matters relating to the fate of the NNSC, the Old Commonwealth countries did not work as a unit. The United Kingdom agreed with the United States, and of the Five(the Old Commonwealth) as of the Sixteen (the countries with forces in the United Nations Command), Canada was a minority of one. The will of the U.S. became United Nations policy over Canadian objections, but in the end, the Canadian defeat did not matter. In Vietnam, the ICC remained free to travel to destinations in both North Vietnam and South Vietnam. Whether the world benefited from such travels is another matter.

From a Canadian standpoint, Canada's concerns were reasonable. Hindsight demonstrates that they were unnecessary. Without British support, Canadian chances of persuading U.S. authorities to change their minds were close to nil.

Notes

1. Australian Delegation to UNCURK, Pusan, to Department of External Affairs (DEA), Canberra, 8 Oct. 1953, Series A5954 (A5954/69), Item 1665/6, National Archives of Australia, Canberra. Cited hereafter as Series A5954.

2. Australian Mission to the UN to DEA, Canberra, 5 Oct. 1953, Series A5954.

3. Australian High Commissioner's Office, London, to DEA, Canberra, 8 Oct. 1953, Series A5954.

4. Australian High Commissioner in Ottawa to DEA, Canberra, 9 Oct. 1953, Series A5954.

5. A.S. Watt, Canberra, to Australian Embassy, Washington, 10 Oct. 1953, Series A5954.

6. Australian Delegation to UNCURK (Critchley), Pusan, to DEA, Canberra, 11 Oct. 1953, Series A5954.

7. *Ibid.*

8. Australian High Commissioner's Office, New Delhi, to DEA, Canberra, 11 Oct. 1953, Series A5954.

9. DEA, Canberra, to Australian High Commissioner in New Delhi, 12 Oct. 1953, Series A5954.

10. Critchley, Pusan, to DEA, Canberra, 20 Oct. 1953, Series A5954.

11. Another despatch from Critchley, Pusan, to DEA, Canberra, 20 Oct. 1953, Series A5954.

12. British High Commissioner, Canberra, to DEA, Canberra, 22 Oct. 1953, Series A5954.

13. Australian High Commissioner's Office, Ottawa, to DEA, Canberra, 21 Oct. 1953, Series A5954.

14. Australian Mission to the UN to DEA, 26 Oct. 1953; Australian Embassy, Tokyo, 26 Oct. 1953, Series A5954.

15. British High Commissioner in Canberra to DEA, 26 Oct. 1953, Series A5954.

16. S.J.G. Fingland, Office of the High Commissioner for the United Kingdom, Canberra, to DEA, Canberra, 26 Oct. 1953, Series A5954.

17. Office of the Australian High Commissioner, Ottawa, to DEA, Canberra, 28 Oct. 1953, Series A5954.

18. Australian High Commissioner's Office, London, to DEA, Canberra, 29 Oct. 1953, Series A5954.

19. Australian Embassy, Washington, to DEA, Canberra, 28 Oct. 1953, Series A5954.

20. Anonymous, Pusan, 30 Oct. 1953, to DEA, Canberra, Series A5954.

21. Office of the High Commissioner for the United Kingdom in Canberra to the DEA, Canberra, 3 Nov. 1953, Series A5954. The British High Commissioner forwarded to Australia's DEA part of a letter which the British Government had sent to the Government of India (cited in the text here).

22. Australian Mission to the UN to DEA, Canberra, 31 Oct. 1953, Series A5954.

23. Australian High Commissioner's Office, New Delhi, to DEA, Canberra, 8 Jan. 1954, Series A5954.

24. "United Nations Command Summary of the Implementation of the Armistice Agreement in Korea (Excluding Operations of the NNRC)," in file "NNIT Evaluation 1954," box 3, R.G. 333,

NARA. See also file "Staff Meeting of the Marking of the MDL [Military Demarcation Line]," box 2, R.G. 333, NARA.

25. Delegation to the Geneva Conference on Korea to Secretary of State for External Affairs (SSEA), Ottawa, 28 April 1954, *DCER*, 1954, p. 100.

26. Heeney, Washington, to Pearson, Ottawa, 8 April 1954, *DCER*, 1954, p. 38.

27. Pearson to Norman Robertson, 30 March 1954, *DCER*, 1954, pp. 29-30; Robertson to Pearson, 1 April, 1954, *DCER*, 1954, pp. 31-32; Pearson to A.D.P. Heeney, 5 April, 1954 *DCER*, 1954, pp. 36-37.

28. Delegation to the Geneva Conference on Korea to the SSEA, Ottawa, 4 June 1954, *DCER*, 1954, p. 107.

29. Undated statement; also Disposition Form "Subversion of NNIT Efforts," 26-28 Dec. 1953; in file: Miscellaneous 1953, box 2. R.G. 333, NARA.

30. Memorandum signed by J.O.C., Headquarters, Far East Command, J3 Division, 20 May 1954, file: NNSC Negotiations 1954, box 2, R.G. 333, NARA.

31. Disposition Form "Flying of National Colors (Poles and Czechs), 21 May 1954; Memorandum "Flying of National Colors (Poles and Czechs), 3 June 1954; undated June memorandum from CINCUNC Tokyo; file: NNSC Negotiations 1954, box 2, R.G. 333, NARA.

32. Undated document; also report of the NNNSC, Panmunjom, 18 Nov. 1953; also Disposition Form "Subversion in NNIT Efforts," 23 Dec. 1953; also Disposition Form "Subversion in NNIT Efforts," 26-28 Dec. 1953; in file Miscellaneous 1953, box 2, R.G. 333, NARA. The quotations come from the report of 26-28 Dec.

33. *Ibid.*

34. Disposition Form "Ineffectiveness of NNSC and NNITs," 15 Jan. 1954; Disposition Form "NNSC Operations in Korea," 2 March 1954; Confidential Memorandum, Headquarters, Far East Command, J3 Division, "Ineffectivness of NNSC and NNITs in North Korea," n.d., file: NNSC Negotiations 1954, box 2, R.G. 333, NARA.

35. Memo of Conversation, State Department, Washington, 14 April 1954, file: NNSC Negotiations 1954, box 2, R.G. 333, NARA.

36. Disposition Form "ROK Intentions to Restrict the NNSC," 29 June 1954, file: NNSC Negotiations 1954, box 2, R.G. 333, NARA.

37. Attachment to memorandum "The Commander in Chief: SUBJECT: Proposed Visit by General Wacker [chief Swiss commander on NNSC]," 28 April 1954, in file "NNIT Evaluation 1954," box 3, R.G. 333, NARA.

38. File "History of the UN Command Repatriation Group," box 2, R.G. 333, NARA.

39. "United Nations Command Report on Operation of Neutral Nations Repatriation Commission," file "NNIT Evaluation 1954," box 3, R.G. 333, NARA.

40. File "History of the UN Command Repatriation Group," box 2, R.G. 333, NARA.

41. File "History of the UN Command Repatriation Group," box 2. R.G. 333, NARA.

42. "United Nations Command Report on Operation of Neutral Nations Repatriation C4ommission" in file "NNIT Evaluation 1954," box 3, R.G. 333, NARA.

43. Disposition Form "Letters of Recognition for Swiss and Swedes," 22 May 1954, file: NNSC Negotiations 1954, box 2, R.G. 333, NARA.

44. Aide-memoirs of Swedish and Swiss ambassadors, submitted at the time of the 14 April 1954 meeting with State Department officials in Washington; also Disposition Form "NNSC," 17 June 1954; Confidential Memorandum, Far East Command, J3, Operations and Training Branch, 19 June 1954; file NNSC Negotiations 1954, box 2, R.G. 333, NARA.

45. Disposition Form "Proposed Statement by CinC in Connection with Swiss/Swedish Withdrawal from NNSC," 6 July 1954, file: NNSC Negotiations 1954, box 2, R.G. 333, NARA.

46. "Memorandum of Conversation by Paul J. Sturn of the Office of Philippine and Southeast Asian Affairs," Washington, 23 July 1954, FRUS, 1952-1954 (vol. XIII), pp. 1874-1876; cited hereafter as Sturn's Memorandum of Conversation. Here Deputy Under-Secretary Robert Murphy of the State Department made clear to A.D.P. Heeney, Canada's ambassador in Washington, that it was "in the free world's interest" that Canada should be part of the ICC.

47. John Holmes, "Geneva: 1954," International Journal, XXII (Summer, 1967), pp. 469-483; reprinted in J.L. Granatstein, Canadian Foreign Policy since 1945: Middle Power or Satellite? (Toronto: Copp Clark, 1969), pp. 69-75. The quotation is taken from p. 69.

48. Permanent Delegate, Geneva, to Secretary of State for External Affairs, Ottawa, 19 July 1954, DCER. 1954, p. 1675.

49. Sturn's Memorandum of Conversation, FRUS, 1952-1954, pp. 1874-1976.

50. Donald C. Masters, Canada in World Affairs, 1953-1955 (Toronto: Canadian Institute of International Affairs, 1965 [1959]), pp. 82-83; J.L. Granatstein and David Bercuson, War and Peacekeeping: From South Africa to the Gulf—Canada's Limited Wars (Toronto: Key Porter, 1991), p. 201.

51. James Eayrs, In Defence of Canada-Indochina: Roots of Complicity (Toronto: University of Toronto Press, 1983), pp. 48-49.

52. "Dokumentation zur neutralen Politik der Schweizerischen Eidgenossenschaft," 9 Sept. 1957, Fonds E 2800, 1967/59, vol. 60, Swiss Federal Archives, Bern.

53. "Entretien avec M. Zhou-Enlai, 12 June 1954, Fonds E 2800, 1967/59, vol. 20, Swiss Federal Archives, Bern. Cited hereafter as "Entretien."

54. Marius Schwarb, Die Mission der Schweiz in Korea: Ein Beitrag zur Geschichte der schweizerischen Aussenpolitik im kalten Krieg (Peter Lang: Bern, 1986), pp. 192-204.

55. Schwarb, p. 203.

56. "Entretien."

57. Major General Elmer J. Rogers, Jr., Tokyo, to Chiefs of Staff, Washington, 20 July 1954, in file NNSC Negotiations 1954, box 2, R.G. 333, NARA.

58. Jules Leger to Lester Pearson, 14 Oct. 1954, DCER, 1954, pp. 141-143.

59. Pearson, Ottawa, to Heeney, Washington, 19 Oct. 1954, DCER, 1954, pp. 143-144. The quotation comes form p. 144.

60. Heeney to Pearson, 20 Oct. 1954, DCER, 1954, pp. 145-146.

61. Pearson to Heeney, 28 Oct. 1954, DCER, 1954, pp. 147-148.

62. Heeney to Peason, 18 Nov. 1954, *DCER*, 1954, pp. 148-150.

63. Pearson to Heeney, 27 Nov. 1954, *DCER*, 1954, pp. 150-153.

64. Heeney to Pearson, 30 Nov. 1954, *DCER*, 1954, pp. 157-9.

65. Pearson to Heeney, 2 Dec. 1954, and Pearson to the Legation in Sweden, 2 Dec. 1954; *DCER*, 1954, pp. 155-157.

66. Heeney to Pearson, 3 Dec. 1954, *DCER*, 1954, pp. 157-159.

67. Embassy in Switzerland to Pearson, 6 Dec. 1954, *DCER*, 1954, p. 159.

68. Canadian Legation in Sweden to Pearson, 11 Dec. 1954, *DCER*, XX, p. 160.

69. Embassy in Switzerland to Pearson, 14 Dec. 1954, *DCER*, XX, pp. 160-161.

70. *Ibid.*

71. Pearson to the Minister in Sweden, 23 Dec. 1954, *DCER*, XX, pp. 161-162.

72. E. Youdo, UK Embassy, Washington, to Foreign Office, London, 17 March 1956, DO 35/5904, PRO.

73. Commonwealth Relations Office, London, to United Kingdom High Commissioners in Canada, Australia, New Zealand, and South Africa, 29 April 1956, DO 35/5904, PRO.

74. Commonwealth Relations Office, London, to United Kingdom High Commissioners in Canada, Australia, New Zealand, South Africa, 29 April 1956, DO 35/5904, PRO.

75. Walt W. Rostow, National Security Adviser to President Lyndon Johnson, referred to the ICC as "a farce"; see Edelgard Mahant and Graeme S. Mount, *Invisible and Inaudible in Washington: American Policies toward Canada* (Vancouver: UBC Press, 1999), p. 49.

76. All the information about the NNSC in this section comes from a Lexis-Nexis search on the NNSC. Lexis-Nexis was particularly helpful in transmitting North Korean policy statements broadcast on Radio Pyongyang and recorded by the BBC.

77. Bruce Cumings, "Toward a Comprehensive Settlement of the Korean Problem," *Current History* (XCVIII, 632 [December 1999]), p. 405.

Conclusions

The record shows that the Old Commonwealth countries did have some impact on the policies of the Truman and Eisenhower administrations and that some of the changes were significant. One reason why the changes were not as significant as they might have been was a lack of co-ordination among the Old Commonwealth governments. Initially, the Canadian government of Louis St. Laurent, which had overwhelming support from French-speaking Quebec, tried to de-emphasize the British connection. In the 1920s and 1930s, Canada had achieved autonomy, which the Liberal government did not want to surrender. Australia's Minister of External Affairs, Sir Percy Spender, was more anxious to obtain a security guarantee in the form of a military alliance with the United States than to maintain Commonwealth solidarity, and until early 1951 when he achieved his goal, he did not want to risk provoking Washington. Among the governments of the Old Commonwealth, the United Kingdom, Australia, and Canada had the greatest interest in the formation of policies surrounding the Korean War. New Zealand and South Africa followed but did not lead. Distance from the conflict was a factor in Wellington and Pretoria. The small size of the New Zealand and South African electorates was also relevant, and, given that Afrikaaners dominated the South African electorate, South African authorities had limited interest in a co-ordinated Commonwealth approach toward the rest of the world. Prime Minister Daniel Malan did not even bother to attend the conference of Commonwealth Prime Ministers in January 1951 but sent a subordinate, T.E. Donges. Despite the existence of a Commonwealth Relations Office, old habits die hard, and it is arguable that the British had more experience in leading than in consulting the Dominions.

The first crisis was over UNTCOK. Should there be elections if those elections could take place only in South Korea? This issue concerned Canada and Australia, members of UNTCOK, not the rest if the Old Commonwealth. (It also involved India, another member of UNTCOK.) There appears to have been no co-ordination at all between Ottawa and Canberra on this issue, despite the merits of their opposition to such elections, and Ottawa's opposition was stronger than Canberra's. Neither Patterson, Canada's representative on UNTCOK, nor Evatt, Australia's Minister of External Affairs, had much credibility with U.S. authorities, and the Truman administration carried the day. UNTCOK would conduct elections on Washington's terms, despite strong opposition from Ottawa and limited opposition from Canberra. While there is no guarantee that a victory for the Canadian-Australian perspective would have averted the Korean War, the U.S. victory set the stage for it.

There was no disagreement within the Old Commonwealth on the desirability of resisting North Korean aggression. On that point, the five governments stood unequivocally with the Truman administration. However, Bevin wisely persuaded U.S. authorities to soften their rhetoric in Washington and at the United Nations. The degree of Soviet involvement, Bevin noted, was not altogether clear, and he was right. After the Cold War, documentary evidence from Moscow confirmed that the attack was a North Korean initiative, not a Soviet one. Bevin did not want to force the Soviet Union into a corner from which constructive diplomacy would be impossible. The five Old Commonwealth governments persuaded Washington to modify UN resolutions in such a way as to limit the problem to the Korean Peninsula and to exclude the question of Taiwan, and to fudge the South Korean government's claim to be the one and only legitimate Korean government. Whether any of this mattered is unclear, but it may have. The United Nations did not specifically hold the Soviet Union responsible for the outbreak of the war, and once Stalin died, the Soviet Union was able to play a useful role in ending the hostilities. The early resolutions also enabled the United Nations to settle for something less than the unconditional surrender of North Korea. The Truman administration and the Joint Chiefs of Staff agreed with the Old Commonwealth governments that it would be dangerous to extend the war into the territory of the People's Republic of China, but given the pressure from General MacArthur to do that, the White House, the State Department, and the Joint Chiefs must have welcomed the counter-pressure. Had all the pressure come from MacArthur's direction, capitulation to that pressure might have been more tempting than any alternative.

Although the National Security Council was receiving advice that an invasion of North Korea might be illegal and of dubious value, the only Old Commonwealth government to question MacArthur's October invasion of North Korea was that of Canada. Among his Old Commonwealth peers, Pearson appears to have been a minority of one in taking Panikkar's warnings seriously and wanting to declare a cease-fire once all living North Korean soldiers had returned north of the 38th parallel. Hindsight shows that he was right, but by himself he made little impact. His suggestion of the Nampo-Wonsan line would not have prevented the Chinese intervention; by that point, Mao's government had decided to send the Chinese People's Volunteers into Korea. Stueck suggests that a unilateral United Nations Command cease-fire at the more northerly line recommended by Bevin might have limited the scale of the Chinese intervention and postponed decisive action until the spring of 1951. Meanwhile, all parties would have had a few months for negotiations, but that is sheer speculation. At any rate, Dean Acheson consistently rejected British suggestions that the People's Republic of China take the China seat at the United Nations, where it could negotiate. Canadian officials would not help the British to promote this cause, and the United Kingdom was the only Old Commonwealth government to have diplomatic relations with the People's Republic of China during, or for many years following, the Korean War. Some UN allies, not necessarily members of the Commonwealth, may have prevented the bombing of Chinese air bases in Manchuria and, by extension, a further escalation of the conflict.

When the tide of battle turned again in late November 1950 and the United Nations Command had to flee south, President Truman spoke publicly about the possible use of nuclear weapons in Korea. Clement Attlee spoke for a wide cross-section of British opinion in suggesting to President Truman that a total United Nations defeat was preferable to the use of such weapons. Canadian and Australian authorities agreed. However, a significant number of U.S. officials agreed with them, and President Truman appears not to have meant what he said at his press conference. As on the issue of carrying the war onto Chinese territory, the Old Commonwealth may have strengthened the resolve of the Truman administration to stay the course, do what it was planning to do anyway, and not capitulate to pressure from the right-wing. Similarly, the Old Commonwealth governments applauded MacArthur's dismissal, but Truman, Acheson, Marshall, and the Joint Chiefs of Staff agreed with them. Nevertheless, it is possible that Commonwealth sentiment had some impact in strengthening the resolve of MacArthur's civilian superiors, despite MacArthur's widespread popularity and apparent political strength.

Early in 1951, the Old Commonwealth governments did soften the resolution which condemned the People's Republic of China as an aggressor. While most agreed that any such resolution might serve no useful purpose and perhaps might do more harm than good, Canadian Prime Minister Louis St. Laurent found it too logical to oppose. All the Old Commonwealth governments, however, saw merit in modifying the resolution in such a way as to permit ongoing diplomatic ties between London and Beijing and ongoing economic ties between Mao's China and Hong Kong. Modification of the earlier resolution enabled Hong Kong to survive economically, and it softened any temptation on the part of the People's Liberation Army to attack that colonial enclave. Hong Kong would survive as a British possession for an additional 47 years, by which time the People's Republic of China had abandoned many of its revolutionary, communist practices and would allow Hong Kongers to live much as they always had. Hong Kongers could continue to have families of more than one child, travel to the West, and protest Beijing's policies as could very few other Chinese on territory of the People's Republic of China. Hong Kong could continue as one of the world's financial centres. On this occasion, the Old Commonwealth governments did more than simply reinforce a position already held by the Truman White House. They persuaded the Truman White House to do what it had not wanted to do. Such success was possible because the Old Commonwealth governments agreed with one another and because U.S. officials respected their peers among the Commonwealth allies in a way that they had not respected Evatt or Patterson.

Another such success followed in 1952 when the Old Commonwealth governments persuaded the Truman administration to accept, albeit reluctantly, the Indian formula for a truce. In the short run, that did not matter. Stalin and his allies rejected it. Yet, the Indian formula became the basis of cease-fire talks in 1953 after Stalin died, despite the Eisenhower administration's initial thoughts on widening the war. Without pressure from the Old Commonwealth governments, Eisenhower and Dulles might well have sought a more substantial military victory rather than the less costly diplomatic compromise. Syngman Rhee and certain prominent Republicans certainly wanted them to do so. At the same time, Soviet and Chinese attitudes following the death of Stalin might have been more persuasive than any policies or actions of Commonwealth leaders in persuading President Eisenhower and his associates neither to expand the conflict nor to use nuclear weapons.

Any Commonwealth coalition disappeared in the aftermath of the Korean War. When the neutrality of the Indian forces on the Neutral Nations Repatriation Commission became questionable in the eyes of U.S. and South Korean authorities, St. Laurent's government in Ottawa was more sympathetic to the Indians than were the governments led by Winston Churchill at Westminster and Sir Robert Menzies in Canberra. On this score, the St. Laurent cabinet appears not to have communicated effectively, if at all, with its Australian counterparts. The role of governments in New Zealand and South Africa was without consequence. Time rather than diplomacy resolved the Indian problem. On the eve of the Geneva Conference, Lester Pearson and his principal advisors did not completely trust the British Foreign Office. Whether a more cohesive Commonwealth might have managed to salvage at least something from the failed Geneva conference is not clear. Two years later, the Eisenhower administration won a total victory regarding the expulsion of Polish and Czechoslovak soldiers from South Korea in 1956, despite Canadian objections. Once again, as in October 1950 when MacArthur was crossing the 38th parallel, Canada was a minority of one. The other Old Commonwealth governments agreed with Washington. Hindsight indicates that there was no price to pay. Vietnam's International Control Commission failed to prevent a wider war, but Ho Chi Minh's government in Hanoi did not curtail the travels of Canadians in North Vietnam because Polish and Czechoslovak soldiers could no longer go to South Korea.

To summarize, during the Korean War it was possible for leaders and diplomats of the Old Commonwealth countries to make a difference. All five countries had combat forces in the war zone, and their forces were making a significant contribution to the cause led by the United States. On most occasions, all five countries had leaders respected and trusted by their U.S. counterparts. The Truman and Eisenhower administrations hoped for the ongoing presence of Commonwealth forces in Korea once there was an armistice. Old Commonwealth opinion had the greatest impact on those occasions when there were differences of opinion within Washington itself and when all Old Commonwealth governments agreed with one another. On occasion, a united Old Commonwealth could actually persuade the White House to travel in a different direction. There does not appear to be a single instance when one or two Old Commonwealth governments on their own could influence U.S. decisions or policies. A country the size of Canada—or any of the other Old Commonwealth countries—may well conclude that multilateral diplomacy can be more rewarding than bilateral diplomacy with the United States, at least in certain circumstances.

Bibliography

Archival Sources

Dwight David Eisenhower Presidential Archives, Abilene, Kansas
    Papers as President, Anne Whitman File
    John Foster Dulles Papers

Harry S. Truman Presidential Archives, Independence, Missouri
    Department of State: Topical File
    General File
    President's Secretary's File (PSF)
    Staff Members' Official Files (SMOF):
        Selected Records relating to the Korean War
    Student Research File
    Subject File
    Topical File Subseries

National Archives of Australia (Canberra).
        Series A 621
        Series A 816/1
        Series A 5954
        Series A 11099/1

National Archives of Switzerland (Bern). Fonds E 2800, 1967/59, vol. 60.

National Archives of the United States (College Park).
    R.G. 263 (National Intelligence Estimates)
    R.G. 333 (Neutral Nations Supervisory Commission)

Public Record Office (Kew Gardens). CAB 1/1988.
        DO 35/5813-5904.
        PREM 8/1156; PREM 8/1171.

United Church of Canada (Toronto). Files of the Board of Overseas Missions relating to Korea.

United Nations (New York). Series-0684-001.

Newspapers

Globe and Mail, 1950-1956, 2001-

Korea Herald, 2001-

New York Times, 1950-1956, 2001-

Printed Primary Sources

Commission of Inquiry into the Australian Secret Intelligence Service. *Report on the Australian Secret Intelligence Service*. Canberra: Australia Government Publishing Service, 1995.

Government of Australia. *Documents on Australian Foreign Relations*, 1945-1949.

Government of Canada. *Documents on Canadian External Relations*, 1947-1956.

Government of the United Kingdom. *Documents on British Policy Overseas*, Series II, vol. IV (Korea: 1950-1951). London: Her Majesty's Stationery Office, 1991.

May, Ernest R., and Philip D. Zelikow (eds). *The Kennedy Tapes: Inside the White Hoouse during the Cuban Missile Crisis*. Cambridge, Mass.: Harvard University Press, 1997.

United Nations. *Yearbooks*, 1945-1956.

United States, Department of State. *Foreign Relations of the United States*, 1947-1956.

United States, *Public Papers of the Presidents*, 1950-1953.

Woodrow Wilson International Center for Scholars. *Cold War International History Project*, vols. V-XI.

Memoirs

Acheson, Dean. *Present at the Creation: My Years in the State Department*. New York: W.W. Norton, 1969.

Eden, Anthony. *Full Circle: The Memoirs of Sir Anthony Eden*. London: Cassell, 1960.

Pearson, Lester B. *Mike: The Memoirs of the Rt. Hon. Lester B. Pearson*. Toronto: University of Toronto Press, 1972, vol. II.

Peng Dehuai. *Memoirs of a Chinese General*. Beijing: Foreign Language Press, 1984.

Rusk, Dean. *As I Saw It*. New York: W.W. Norton, 1990.

Trudeau, Pierre Elliott. *Memoirs*. Toronto: McClelland and Stewart, 1993.

Truman, Harry S. *Years of Trial and Hope: Memoirs*. New York: Signet, 1956.

Secondary Sources

Alexander, Bevin. *Korea: The First War We Lost*. New York: Hippercrene, 1993.

Ambrose, Stephen. *Eisenhower, the President*. New York: Simon and Schuster, 1984.

Andrews, Allen. *Brave Soldiers, Proud Regiments: Canada's Military Heritage*. Vancouver: Ronsdale Press, 1997.

Armstrong, Charles K. *The North Korean Revolution*. Cornell: Cornell University Press, 2003.

Bell, Coral. *Dependent Ally: A Study in Australian Foreign Policy*. St. Leonards, New South Wales: Allen and Unwin, 1984.

Bercuson, David. *Blood on the Hills: The Canadian Army in the Korean War*. Toronto: University of Toronto Press, 1999.

Bercuson, David. *True Patriot: The Life of Brooke Claxton, 1898-1960*. Toronto: University of Toronto Press, 1993.

Berton, Pierre. *Marching as to War: Canada's Turbulent Years, 1899-1953*. Toronto: Doubleday Canada, 2001.

Bothwell, Robert, and J.L. Granatstein. *Pirouette: Pierre Trudeau and Canadian Foreign Policy*. Toronto, University of Toronto Press, 1990.

Breuer, William B . *Shadow Warriors: The Covert War in Korea*. New York: Wiley, 1996.

Bullock, Alan. *Ernest Bevin: Foreign Secretary, 1945-1951*. New York: W.W. Norton, 1983.

Calingaert, Daniel. "Nuclear Weapons and the Korean War," *The Journal of Strategic Studies*, XI (June 1988), pp. 177-202.

Catchpole, Brian. *The Korean War*. New York: Carroll and Graf, 2001.

Chen Jiang. *China's Road to the Korean War: The Making of the Sino-American Confrontation*. New York: Columbia University Press, 1994.

Clearwater, John. *U.S. Nuclear Weapons in Canada*. Toronto: Dundurn, 1999.

Cohen, Andrew. *While Canada Slept: How We Lost Our Place in the World*. Toronto: McClelland and Stewart, 2003.

Cottrell, Alvin J., and James E. Dougherty. "The Lessons of Korea: War and the Power of Man," *Orbis*, II (Spring, 1958), pp. 39-65; reprinted in Sidney Fine (ed.), *Recent America: Conflicting Interpretations of the Great Issues*. New York: Macmillan, n.d.

Crozier, Brian. *The Rise and Fall of the Soviet Empire*. Roseville, California: Forum 2000.

Cumings, Bruce (editor). *Child of Conflict: The Korean-American Relationship, 1945-1953*. Seattle and London: University of Washington Press, 1983.

Cumings, Bruce. *Korea's Place in the Sun: A Modern History*. New York: W.W. Norton, 1997.

Cumings, Bruce, "Toward a Comprehensive Settlement of the Koran Problem," *Current History*, XCVIII, 632 (December 1999), pp. 403-408.

Cumpston, I.M. *History of Australian Foreign Policy, 1901-1991*. Canberra: I.M. Cumpston, vol. I. 1991.

Dingman, Roger. "Atomic Diplomacy during the Korean War," *International Security*, XIII, 3 (Winter 1988/89), pp. 50-91.

Dockrill, M.L. "The Foreign Office, Anglo-American Relations and the Korean Truce Negotiations, July 1951-July 1953," in James Cotton and Ian Neary (eds.), *The Korean War in History* (Atlantic Hills, N.J.: Humanities Press International), 1989.

Donaghy, Greg (ed.) *Canada and the Early Cold War, 1943-1957.* Ottawa: Canadian Government Publishing,1998.

Donaghy, Greg (ed.) *Canadian Diplomcy and the Korean War.* Ottawa: Department of Foreign Affairs and International Trade, 2001.

Eayrs, James. *In Defence of Canada–Indochina: Roots of Complicity.* Toronto: University of Toronto Press, 1983.

English, John. *The Worldly Years: The Life of Lester Pearson, 1949-1972.* Toronto: Knopf of Canada, 1992.

Farrar-Hockley, Anthony. *A Distant Obligation.* London: HMSO, 1990.

Farrar-Hockley, Anthony. *An Honourable Discharge.* London: HMSO, 1995.

Foot, Rosemary. "Nuclear Coercion and the Ending of the Korean Conflict," *International Security,* XIII, 3 (Winter 1988-89), pp. 9-112.

Foot, Rosemary. *A Substitute for Victory: The Politics of Peacemaking at the Korean Armistice Talks.* Ithaca: Cornell University Press, 1990.

Foot, Rosemary. *The Wrong War: American Policy and the Dimensions of the Korean War.* Ithaca: Cornell University Press, 1985.

Foster, Simon. *Hit the Beach: The Drama of Amphibious Warfare.* London: Cassell, 1999 [1995].

Gammer, Nicholas. *From Peacekeeping to Peacemaking: Canada's Response to the Yugoslav Crisis.* Montreal and Kingston: McGill-Queen's University Press, 2001.

Gaston, Peter. *Thirty-Eighth Parallel: The British in Korea.* Glasgow: A.D. Hamilton, 1976.

Ghent, Jocelyn Maynard. "Canada, the United States, and the Cuban Missile Crisis," *Pacific Historical Review,* XLVIII, 2 (May 1979), pp. 159-194.

Goulden, Joseph C. *Korea: The Untold Story of the War.* New York: Quadrangle, 1982.

Granatstein, J.L., and David Bercuson. *War and Peacekeeping: From South Africa to the Gulf–Canada's Limited Wars.* Toronto: Key Porter, 1991.

Grey, Jeffrey. *The Commonwealth Armies and the Korean War: An Alliance Study.* Manchester: Manchester University Press, 1988.

Hastings, Max. *The Korean War.* New York: Simon and Schuster, 1988 [1987].

Holmes, John. "Geneva 1954," *International Journal,* XXII (Summer, 1967), pp. 469-483.

Homes, John. *Life with Uncle: The Canadian-American Relationship.* Toronto: University of Toronto Press, 1981.

Hopkins, Michael. "The Price of Cold War Partnership: Sir Oliver Franks and the British Commitment in the Korean War," *Cold War History,* I, 2 (Jan. 2001).

Keating, Tom. *Canada and World Order: The Tradition in Canadian Foreign Policy*. Toronto: McClelland and Stewart, 1993.

Kaufman, Burton I. *The Korean War: Challenges in Crisis, Credibility, and Command*. New York: Knopf, 1986.

Keefer, Edward C. "President Dwight D. Eisenhower and the End of the Korean War, " *Diplomatic History*, X, 3 (Summer, 1986), pp. 267-289.

Korean Institute of Military History. *The Korean War*. Lincoln and London: University of Nebraska Press, 2001.

Latourette, Kenneth Scott. *A History of the Expansion of Christianity*. New York: Harper and Brothers, 1944, vol. VI.

Lee, David, and Christopher Waters (ed.). *Evatt to Evans: The Labor Tradition in Australian Foreign Policy*. St. Leonards, New South Wales: Allen and Unwin, 1997.

Lee, Steven Hugh. *Outposts of Empire: Korea, Vietnam, and the Origins of the Cold War in Asia, 1949-1954*. Montreal and Kingston: McGill-Queen's University Press, 1995.

Lone, Stewart. *Korea since 1850*. Melbourne: Longman Cheshire, 1993.

Lowe, David. *Menzies and the Great World Struggle: Australia's Cold War, 1948-1954*. Sydney: University of New South Wales Press, 1999.

Lowe, Peter. *The Korean War*. New York: St. Martin's Press, 2000.

MacMillan, Margaret, and Francine McKenzie (editors). *Parties Long Estranged: Canada and Australia in the Twentieth Century*. Vancouver: UBC Press, 2003.

Mahant, Edelgard E., and Graeme S. Mount. *Invisible and Inaudible in Washington*. Vancouver: UBC Press, 1999.

Manchester, William. *American Caesar: Douglas MacArthur, 1880-1964*. Boston: Little, Brown, and Company, 1978.

Martin, A.W. *Robert Menzies: A Life, 1944-1978*. Melbourne: Melbourne University Press, 1999, vol. II.

Masters, D.C. *Canada in World Affairs, 1953-1955*. Toronto: Canadian Institute of International Affairs, 1959.

Matray, James Irving. *The Reluctant Crusade: American Foreign Policy in Korea, 1941-1950*. Honolulu: University of Hawaii Press, 1985.

McCormack, Gavan. *Cold War History: An Australian Perspective on the Korean War*. Sydney: Hale and Ironmonger, 1982.

McCullough, David. *Truman*. New York: Simon and Schuster, 1992.

McGibbon, Ian. *New Zealand and the Korean War*. Wellington: Oxford University Press, 1992.

McLin, Jon B. *Canada's Changing Defense Policy, 1957-1973: The Problems of a Middle Power in Alliance*. Baltimore: Johns Hopkins University Press, 1967.

Milliken, Jennifer. *The Social Construction of the Korean War: Conflict and Its Possibilities.* Manchester: University of Manchester Press, 2001.

Milner, Marc. *Canada's Navy: The First Century.* Toronto: University of Toronto Press, 1999.

Moorehead, Caroline. *Dunant's Dream: War, Switzerland and the History of the Red Cross.* New York: Carroll and Graf, 1998.

Nahm, Andrew. *An Introduction to Korean History and Culture.* Seoul: Hollym, 1993.

New Zealand, Government of. *Ice and Fire: New Zealand and the Korean War.* Wellington: Government of New Zealand, c. 2003.

O'Neill, Robert. *Australia in the Korean War: Strategy and Diplomacy.* Canberra: The Australian War Memorial and the Australian Government Publishing Service, 1981.

Prince, Robert S. "The Limits of Constraint: Canadian-American Relations and the Korean War, 1950-51," *Journal of Canadian Studies*, XXVII, 4 (Winter 1992-1993), pp. 129-152.

Redford, Robert. *Canada and Three Crises.* Toronto: Canadian Institute of International Affairs, 1968.

Robin, Ron. "Behavioral Codes and Truce Talks: Images of the Enemy and Expert Knowledge in the Korean Armistice Negotiations," *Diplomatic History*, XXV, 4 (Fall 2001).

Roe, Patrick C. *The Dragon Strikes–China and the Korean War: June-December 1950.* , California: Presidio Press, 2000.

Sandler, Stanley. *The Korean War: No Victors, No Vanquished.* Lexington: University Press of Kentucky, 1999.

Sands, Christopher. "How Canada Policy is Made in the United States," in Maureen Appel Molot and Fen Osler Hampson, *Vanishing Borders.* Don Mills: Oxford University Press, 2000, pp. 47-72.

Sheng, Michael. "The Psychology of the Korean War: The Role of Ideology and Perception in China's Entry into the War," paper presented to the Annual Meeting of The Society for Historians of American Foreign Relations, Toronto, June 2000.

Sinclair, Keith. *A History of New Zealand.* Aukland, Penguin, 1984 [1959].

Siracusa, Joseph M., and Yeong-Han Cheong. *America's Australia: Australia's America.* Claremont, California: Regina, 1997.

Stacey, C.P. *Canada and the Age of Conflict.* Toronto: Macmillan, 1977 (2 vols.)

Stairs, Denis. *The Diplomacy of Constraint: Canada, the Korean War, and the United States.* Toronto: University of Toronto Press, 1974.

Stueck, William. *The Korean War: An International History.* Princeton: Princeton University Press, 1995.

Stueck, William. *Rethinking the Korean War: A New Diplomatic and Strategic History.* Princeton: Princeton University Press, 2002.

Terry, Allison. *The Battle for Pusan: A Korean War Memoir.* Novato, California: Presidio, 2000.

Thomson, Dale. *Louis St. Laurent, Canadian.* Toronto: Macmillan, 1967.

Trainor, General (Ret.) Bernard. "Memories and Significance of the Korean War," luncheon speech to the conference of the Society for Historians of American Foreign Relations, Toronto, June 2000.

Volkogonov, Dimitri. *Stalin: Triumph and Tragedy* (edited by Harold Shukman). New York: Grove Weidenfeld, 1988.

Watson, Brent Byron. *Far Eastern Tour: The Canadian Infantry in Korea, 1950-1953.* Montreal and Kingston: McGill-Queen's University Press, 2002.

Weathersby, Kathryn. "Soviet Aims in Korea and the Origins of the Korean War, 1945-1950: New Evidence from Russian Archives," *Cold War International History Project Working Paper #8* (Nov. 1993).

Weintraub, Stanley. *MacArthur's War: Korea and the Undonig of an American hero.* New York: Simon and Schuster, 2000.

Williams, Phil, Donald M. Goldstein, and Henry L. Andrews, Jr. *Society in Korea: War, Stalemate, and Negotiation.* Boulder, Colorado: Westview Press, 1994.

Woodward, Bob. *Bush at War.* New York: Simon and Schuster, 2002.

Woo-Kuen, Han. *The History of Korea.* Translated by Lee Kyung-shik, Seoul: Eul Yoo, 1987.

Yufan, Hao, and Zhai Zhihai. "China's Decision to Enter the Korean War: History Revisited," in Kim Chull Baum and James I. Matray (eds.), *Korea and the Cold War: Division, Destruction, and Disarmament.* Claremont, California: Regina, 1993.

Zhang, Shu Guang. *Mao's Military Romanticism: China and the Korean War, 1950-1953.* Lawrence: University Press of Kansas, 1995.

Zhang, Xiaoming, "From an abortive air war to the China-Soviet Wartime Relationship", paper presented to the Annual Meeting of the Society for Historians of American Foreign Relations, Toronto, June 2000.

Zhihua, Shen. "Sino-Soviet Relations and the Origins of the Koran War: Stalin's Strategic Goals in the Far East," *Journal of Cold War Studies,* II (Spring 2000), pp. 44-68.

Zubok, Vladislav, and Constantine Pleshakov, *Inside the Kremlin's Cold War: From Stalin to Khrushchev.* Cambridge, Mass.: Harvard University Press, 1996.

Index

NOTE: Such words as Asia, Canada, Cold War, Commonwealth, Europe, Korea, Korean War, North Korea, South Korea and United States appear so frequently that they are not listed in the index. The names of U.S. presidents apply to the individuals, not to their administrations. References to capital cities apply to the cities themselves, not to alternatives to their countries.

also by Graeme S. Mount

CHILE AND THE NAZIS: *From Hitler to Pinochet*

One of the first authors to provide evidence of the events and circumstances surrounding Chile's reluctance to sever diplomatic
ties with Nazi Germany allowing it to maximize its opportunities
there, influencing Chilean politicians, military operations, and
the popular media.

> Mount sees forces at work that other historians of the region
> have preferred not to notice. —*The Guardian Weekly*

> Mount's cool, clear prose avoids the expressions of outrage
> that blunt so many books about the right in Chile. His reve-
> lations are enough. —*The Guardian Daily*

> A good and worthwhile book, which gives a very complete and well-documented
> diplomatic history of Chile during WWII. —*Outlook*

> A most impressive book...about a hitherto little-known, but fascinating aspect of
> twentieth-century history. —*Stan Hordes, University of New Mexico*

204 pages, photographs
Paperback ISBN: 1-55164-192-5 $19.99 ♦ Hardcover ISBN: 1-55164-193-3 $48.99

of related interest

PURE SOLDIERS or SINISTER LEGION: *The Ukrainian 14th Waffen-SS Division*
Sol Littman

Traces the 14th Waffen-SS Division's fortunes from its formation
in April 1943, to its surrender to the British in May 1946, their
subsequent stay as prisoners-of-war in Italy, and their eventual transfer as agricultural workers in Britain. In 1950 they began
their immigration to Canada and the United States. Along the
way they were recruited by the British as anti-Soviet spies and by
the CIA as political assassins. In spelling out the Division's history,
the author attempts to shed light on its true nature.

> There have been few detailed studies of Nazi war criminals
> who came to Canada after WWII. Littman's book...makes a
> welcome, if chilling, addition. —*Francis Henry, Emeritus, York
> University, Toronto*

> A well-researched, carefully documented forcefully presented exposé. —*Dov Bert
> Levy, former consultant to the U.S. Justice Department*

SOL LITTMAN is the recently retired Canadian Director of the Simon Wiesenthal Center,
author of *War Criminal on Trial*, and founding editor of the *Canadian Jewish News*.

264 pages, 6x9, photographs, bibliography, index
Paperback ISBN: 1-55164-218-2 $26.99 ♦ Hardcover ISBN: 1-55164-219-0 $55.99